POLITICS, PROFESSIONALISM, AND URBAN SERVICES

Politics, Professionalism, and Urban Services
The Police

Peter F. Nardulli
University of Illinois

Jeffrey M. Stonecash
Syracuse University

 Oelgeschlager, Gunn & Hain, Publishers, Inc.
Cambridge, Massachusetts

International Standard Book Number: 0-89946-076-3

Library of Congress Catalog Card Number: 80-27169

Printed in West Germany

Library of Congress Cataloging in Publication Data

Nardulli, Peter F
  Politics, professionalism, and urban services, the police.

  Includes index.
  1. Champaign, Ill.—Police. 2. Police—United States—Case studies. I. Stonecash,
Jeffrey M., joint author. II. Title.
HV8148.C272N37   363.2'09773'66   80-27169
ISBN 0-89946-076-3

To Ann and Susan,
with love

Contents

Contents

ix / Contents

List of Figures

List of Tables

Preface

This is both a general book on urban politics and a book on the specifics of police operations in a medium-sized American city. As a general book about urban politics, it questions some basic facets of the prevailing paradigm in studies of urban service delivery as well as some of the conclusions of works coming from that tradition. More specifically, this book largely rejects the aggregated approach used in earlier studies and the contention that politics does not matter. Instead, this book sketches a different approach and suggests that the relationship between sociopolitical considerations and the delivery of urban services is more complex than earlier researchers believed. To understand that relationship clearly, it is necessary to delineate clearly the *sources* of sociopolitical influences as well as the *content* of these influences. In addition the *linkages* between these sources and the service-delivery process must be well understood. Once these matters have been addressed, we can begin to make and test meaningful empirical statements about the relationship between politics and service delivery.

Despite the concern with sociopolitical factors in this book, the role of professional-rational considerations in the service-delivery process is not ignored—on the contrary. One of the main empirical thrusts of this book has been to identify and measure various types of need-related and/or professional-rational factors. These aré important, we feel, because one could not obtain an accurate picture of the service-delivery process without their inclusion. This dimension is especially important because, as will be seen in various parts of the data analysis, the sociopolitical and professional-rational determinants of service disbursements or demands are often interrelated. Both must be integrated into a single analysis in order to obtain a valid understanding of the service process.

As a book about policing and police services, this work addresses both the demand for police services and police response in one medium-sized American city—Champaign, Illinois. As a prelude to addressing the demand for police services, some background information is provided on the neighborhoods within Champaign and on the Champaign police. Then demand levels (total number of calls for police services) across individual blocks in Champaign are assessed in several different ways. The general conclusion that emerges from the data analysis is that although need-related factors are the primary determinants of call levels, sociopolitical characteristics are also important. Moreover, the importance of these characteristics varies by type of call.

The problems involved in analyzing police responses to service requests required a selective approach. Only certain dimensions of the notion of police response (speed, effort, outcome) were examined in three substantive areas of police activity (assault, common-crime, and accident cases). The primary questions asked in each of these analyses were: how are cases handled? and what accounts for differences in the way cases are handled? In answering these questions, the unit of analysis shifts to individual cases; and information from a number of different sources was integrated into a single data file. The empirical analysis revealed that the types of factors affecting police response (resource availability, professional-rational, sociopolitical) varied across the three dimensions of response analyzed as well as across the three types of cases. For the most part, however, factors that could be categorized as professional-rational were most influential. But in certain areas—case outcomes, in particular—sociopolitical considerations tended to play a more important role. Moreover, the analyses suggested that future research efforts should pay more attention to the views of individual service deliverers—patrol officers in this case—as sources of sociopolitical influences.

Acknowledgments

This book, like all long-term research projects, was made possible only with the help and cooperation of a large number of people. Neil Weisman, former director of the Champaign-Urbana High Crime Program, made available to us all the data on calls for police service during 1976. William Dye, Champaign chief of police, was extremely cooperative and granted us access to the case files maintained by the department. Lt. Tom Whipple gave us hours of his time and taught us more about policing than any book we have encountered. Capt. John Jones and Gary Spear were also very helpful at various points in this research. We are also greatly indebted to the police officers who allowed us to look over their shoulders during the observational phase of this study.

This book would not have been possible without the financial support of the Research Board of the University of Illinois and the Institute of Government and Public Affairs. They provided research assistants, release time, and computer funds, which were essential in conducting the project. We are especially grateful to Samuel K. Gove, the director of the Institute of Government, for his strong and active support. In addition, the Criminal Justice Commission for East Central Illinois and the Illinois Law Enforcement Commission provided supplemental funds required for the final stages of the analysis.

Robert Illyes performed very ably as a computer programmer and wrote the programs to match addresses and census blocks and to integrate the various data sets. Jodi Landsman, Colleen Walsh, Colleen McSweeney, James Mrowicki, and Sharon Ganellen spent endless hours in the police department collecting file data on individual cases. John Carroll, Keith Emmons, Tammy Turner, and Cathy Johnson were invaluable assistants during the data-analysis phases. Anna Merritt did her normally excellent job in editing the draft manuscript; and Florence Edmison, Lorena McClain, Velma Sykes, and Jean Baker contributed to the typing effort.

I: INTRODUCTORY MATTERS

Chapter 1

Introduction

The last decade has seen a good deal of community-level political research directed at urban-service-delivery systems. As Douglas Yates has stated:

> Now that the "urban crisis" has been discovered, debated, and in some quarters dismissed, government officials and academic analysts alike have increasingly come to focus on "service delivery" as the central issue and problem of urban policy making. [Yates 1974, p. 214]

Such a focus is long overdue. For one thing, although service-delivery questions may not have the glamor of community-power issues or the urban crisis, they touch on vital aspects of everyday urban living. Robert Lineberry put it well when he wrote:

> Public services are the grist of urban politics. It is remarkable, therefore, how little attention has been paid to their delivery and allocation until very recently. . . .
> Public services—from crime prevention to street cleaning to schools— are the principal responsibility of urban governments. They consume collectively more tax dollars than any public function except national defense and are more likely than other governmental outputs to represent, quite literally, life and death matters. [Lineberry 1977, pp. 12, 13]

The increased focus on urban-service-delivery systems is also welcome because it permits urban researchers to define and address important questions in a more sophisticated manner than has been possible in other areas of concern to them. This creates the potential not only for direct policy benefits but also for the development and empirical investigation of insights that could enhance our understanding of politics—at the urban level and beyond. Many earlier themes in urban political studies either had little policy significance or defied systematic empirical analysis; some suffered from both deficiences. The study of urban services provides a focus of real practical significance. At the same time, many issues in this area are manageable in terms of contemporary social science methodology.

The importance of this last point should not be minimized. Urban services are real. In many cases they are observable, recorded, or consumed. Thus, their disbursement can be empirically assessed by social scientists. Moreover, similar types of services are delivered by individuals working in bureaucracies across communities that differ markedly in economic, social, and political composition. This permits the development of research strategies that can examine some basic principles of political and bureaucratic behavior. It allows us to examine "who gets what" at a very immediate level and to assess the impact of different types of bureaucratic structures on the quality and quantity of agency outputs. It permits an analysis of the impact that views held by line personnel have on day-to-day operations in a bureaucratic setting. It makes possible an assessment of the effects of community preferences and political structure on the type and flow of urban services.

Despite the opportunities provided by this urban-services focus, much work needs to be done before its potential—both policy-relevant and intellectual—can be realized. As in the early stages of any intellectual tradition or approach, the theoretical and empirical work on urban service delivery has been rough and in need of refinement. A paradigm has been developed in this area that was extremely useful in directing early research. However, it has also had a constraining effect on new lines of thought. It has focused too much on overall patterns of service disbursements across artificial aggregates of individuals (census tracts, for example) and not enough on the dynamics of individual service decisions made by real service deliverers to real consumers. It has been overly concerned with simplistically defined notions of discrimination and inequality and has tended to equate these concepts with "politics." Not enough thinking has gone into the nature of basic structural determinants of service disbursements. Researchers have been content with references to vague terms such as "bureaucratic decision rules" and have not been sufficiently concerned with clearly defining or addressing the content of decisional criteria.

Although this may sound like a harsh indictment of prior service-delivery studies, it is not intended as such. It is merely a recognition that the prevailing paradigm in this area needs rethinking, reworking, and retooling. This book will address some of the problems raised. We will also try to examine the plausibility of some of our ideas by relating them to one type of service agency (a police department) in one medium-sized jurisdiction (Champaign, Illinois). Although this is a fairly intensive study, the limitations involved in such a modest effort will prevent us from conclusively resolving any issues. We do hope, however, that some of the questions we raise and some of the findings we present will lead future researchers to rethink the traditional approach to the study of urban services.

Before our ideas and findings can be presented, something must be said about the police as a subject of inquiry and about the scope of this study.

POLICE DEPARTMENTS AND
SERVICE DELIVERY

The choice of police services as the focus of this inquiry was not based on any scientific criteria; we do not claim that police departments are representative of other types of service agencies (in fact, quite the contrary is probably true). The police were chosen simply because our earlier professional contacts with the department involved had given us access to an enormous amount of "calls for service" data. These data would have cost tens of thousands of dollars to collect—not to mention the difficulty of securing the cooperation of a good-sized police department in doing so. Moreover, access to much more data was guaranteed. Together, these bodies of data permitted us to approach the problem of police-service delivery from a unique vantage point. The temptation was simply too great to resist.

This much having been confessed, it should be noted that the selection of the police was not such a bad choice. Police departments are fascinating and important entities that have attracted the interest of schoolchildren, scholars, and reformers for a long time. The nature of the police role has put police at the center of some of the great controversies of the last three decades—the civil rights movement of the 1950s and 1960s, and the crime surge and the antiwar movement of the 1960s and 1970s. Moreover, during this time police expenditures have increased dramatically. Next to education costs, police expenditures are normally the largest budget item for municipalities (Judd 1979, p. 205)—and for good reason. Police departments are multifaceted, around-the-clock agencies that perform a wide range of services. They investigate crimes, direct traffic, mediate family disputes, patrol dangerous beats, and respond to almost any type of call anywhere within their jurisdiction at any time.

For all these reasons—nature of their role, resource requirements, scope of duties—the police are an important object of study. But each of these goes to the point of studying the police *as a service-delivery unit.* There is another set of reasons for doing so. It concerns studying the police *from a service-delivery perspective.* With the exception of a handful of recent studies (Mladenka 1978; Lineberry 1977, pp. 138-142; Bloch 1974), the urban-services police operations have not been studied as have the operations of urban agencies concerned with such things as housing, environmental inspection, and sanitation. This is significant because viewing police operations from an urban-services perspective could contribute to recent trends in police studies and introduce new and important questions.

Although there is a wide variety of "police studies" ranging from historical to ethnographic to economic, much of the literature has been administrative in nature. This concern with administration has an historical origin. By the turn of the nineteenth century most large police departments had been taken over by the political machines that dominated every facet of urban political life. Police departments were used as sources of patronage, wages were low, graft and incompetence were widespread (Fogelson 1977). Prohibition only exacerbated the problem. This raised the ire of those involved in the progressive movement, who for over fifty years had tried to reform urban police departments. They advocated the use of minimal education requirements, entrance examinations, psychological screening, civil service protections, and so on. They also wanted to insulate the departments from political influences.

The preoccupation of this body of thought with the input side of the system reflected the progressives' belief that politics was the root of most urban-governmental problems. These reformers and their intellectual heirs wanted to know how to obtain "good" recruits—and insulate them from "bad" political influences. More recently there has been a good deal of interest in the police conversion process: how best to use available resources, and what difference resource levels and arrangements make. Thus, recent studies have focused on the impact of manpower levels (Kelling et al. 1974), the deployment of one-officer versus two-officer patrol cars (Boydstud, Sherry, and Moelten 1977), the effectiveness of "aggressive" patrolling (Wilson and Boland 1978), the importance of response time (Clawson and Chang 1977), the effectiveness of detective squads (Greenwood and Petersilia 1975) and the impact of team policing (Schwartz and Clarren 1977).

By explicitly recognizing police departments as service agencies and applying an urban-services perspective to police operations, it is possible to systemize and broaden the conversion-process focus. Comparison with other urban services, and the extension of concepts developed in the study of other areas, will inevitably produce insights into how police departments operate and how they can maximize the use of their resources. In addition, once police departments are recognized as service-delivery agencies that provide a wide range of services, perhaps scholars will become more interested in the non-crime-related facets of their activity, areas that consume most police resources. This may then lead to a more comprehensive understanding of the totality of police operations.

Another benefit of approaching police operations from an urban-services perspective is that it introduces a more traditional political concern to the study of policing: Who gets what and how? In other words, it focuses attention on who benefits from the disbursement of police resources and on how they are disbursed. This perspective could well shed light on some of the enduring controversies surrounding police relations with all types of minority communities. A concern with allocational questions also focuses attention on the implications of various systemic modifications—made in the name of efficiency, crime deterrence, economy, and whatever—on different segments of a community.

Despite the importance of allocative questions in the area of policing, earlier researchers have not systematically addressed them for two reasons. The first concerns the availability of useful data. In the past police departments have been neither avid nor systematic record keepers. Moreover, the data they kept were not easily accessible to outsiders. Both situations are changing. Professionalization and the availability of advanced computer technology has enhanced the desire and ability of many police departments to keep track systematically of what they do and for (or to) whom they do it. Moreover, police professionalization and the comparative calm of the 1970s have led to more open departments. They are more confident about themselves as bureaucracies and more comfortable with the communities they serve. Thus the police are much more apt to be receptive to outside researchers and evaluators.

The second reason that allocative questions have not been systematically pursued in the area of police services is their inherent complexity. Police services are multifaceted, mobile, and often citizen initiated. It is much easier to examine and assess the frequency and type of garbage pickup, or the location and quality of fire departments and libraries, than to measure and assess the operations of a police department. One reason for this difficulty has been the preoccupation on the part of some service scholars with the notion of equality. Such a focus may make sense when dealing with garbage pickups, stop signs, or potholes. It is relatively easy to measure their distribution and most would agree that this distribution should be roughly equal across comparable neighborhoods.

The situation is somewhat different in dealing with a police department. Examining average response times, or patrol officers or cars per thousand residents across different types of neighborhoods, might not provide a meaningful measure of service. Moreover, although patrol officers per thousand residents might be a meaningful indicator of one facet of police services (a general deterrence dimension, perhaps), the number of responses to specific requests in a neighborhood would be a necessary indicator of other facets of police services. This, of course, causes additional problems. For example, how does one compare a neighborhood that records a high level of complaints to the police about teenage drag racers, to another that has a high frequency of calls about illegally parked cars, to another that has a high incidence of calls to resolve marital or neighborhood squabbles?

The possible existence of spillover effects compounds the comparability problems. Residents in one area who are vigilant in helping the police curtail drag racing may save the life of a child in an adjacent neighborhood. Downtown merchants who have illegally parked cars removed may be helping consumers who live throughout the city. On the other hand, a neighborhood's demands for extra patrols to curb vandals or burglars may lead the thieves to frequent other areas of the city. Another problem concerns the assessment of any inequities that might be uncovered. This would be particularly acute in the area of citizen-initiated services. What would it mean if one area had a higher level of assault or burglary calls? How would one go about equalizing such levels? Would one want to?

POLICE SERVICES AND THE
SCOPE OF THIS STUDY

Although the allocational issues involved in the study of police services are complex, their importance makes them worth the effort. Moreover, it is possible to reduce complex research problems to manageable proportions. A first step is to focus on one research setting, as has been done here. A second is to reduce the substantive scope of the inquiry, as has also been done. In the present case, this means examining only certain aspects of a multifaceted police organization.

From a functional perspective, police departments comprise a number of different units. The five most common are the investigative (or detective) squad, traffic control, a juvenile unit, administrative (or support) services, and the patrol division. Detectives are usually responsible for all follow-up investigations and play a major role in the crime-related tasks performed by police departments. Where specialized traffic-control units exist, they are usually concerned with traffic-law enforcement and the handling and investigation of major traffic accidents. Juvenile units, of course, deal with youthful offenders and are apt to engage in programs and activities very different from those of other units. Administrative units provide valuable support services such as research and development, record keeping, purchasing, and jail maintenance.

As vital as these various units and activities are to the functioning of police in urban society, the patrol division constitutes the core of all municipal police forces. The patrol division not only is the most visible unit but also handles the bulk of "police work"; its activities will be the central focus of the empirical portion of this study. Moreover, we will be concerned primarily with the citizen-initiated aspects of patrol activities —what might be termed citizen-assistance services. These services include collecting and recording information on crimes, settling disputes of various sorts, clearing accidents, helping to put invalids in bed, chasing loose animals, and supervising the towing of cars parked on private property.

Restricting the empirical aspects of this work to citizen-assistance services is not as limiting as it may seem at first glance. The activities subsumed under this category not only are very diverse but also include much of what patrol officers do. Those tasks that are not included— patrolling, handling routine traffic violations, and so on—are very different. They are proactive and are much more susceptible to hierarchical control than citizen-assistance activities. Their inclusion would have required the development of a somewhat different conceptual framework and a wholly different research strategy. They were simply beyond the scope and resources of this study.

PLAN OF THE BOOK

To study the citizen-assistance services delivered by urban police departments requires an analysis of both the demand for those services (because they are citizen initiated) and the police response to those demands (because they ultimately control what happens). Consequently, the empirical portion of this work is separated into demand and response sections. Before these analyses can be presented, however, some groundwork needs to be laid. First, Chapter 2 sets forth our views on some basic issues in the literature on the delivery of urban services. It is both a critique of the existing approach and a general outline for future research that reexamines the role of bureaucratic and political influences on the service-delivery process.

Chapters 3 and 4 outline the setting of this study. First there is an overview of the political and social dimensions of Champaign, with special emphasis on those political characteristics discussed in Chapter 2. This is followed by an outline of Champaign's neighborhoods and their distinguishing features. Chapter 4 describes the basic organization of the Champaign Police Department. In addition, it provides a brief organizational history of the department's development into a professional force. Finally, relations between the department and Champaign's various subcommittees are reviewed.

Chapters 5 and 6 report the demand analysis. Chapter 5 is primarily concerned with developing a theoretical framework for understanding the demand for police services. It also outlines the empirical approach to be used in assessing the demand model and describes the available data. Chapter 6 gives the results of the quantitative analysis. It presents both an aggregated and a disaggregated analysis and is primarily concerned with the relative impact of locational, or need-related, and sociopolitical factors.

The next section, Chapters 7 through 10, is concerned with police response. Chapter 7 outlines the problems involved in understanding this notion and the approach to be used in studying it. It describes the data bases to be used and how they were constructed. The next three chapters are concerned with three dimensions of the notion of police response in three different areas. The factors affecting speed, effort, and outcome in the handling of assault, common crime, and traffic-accident cases are examined. The concern here is largely with the impact of resource constraints, professional-rational considerations, and sociopolitical factors on the different response indicators.

Chapter 11 is an attempt to summarize our findings and their implications.

REFERENCES

Bloch, Peter B. 1974. *Equality of Distribution of Police Services: A Case Study of Washington, D.C.* Washington, D.C.: Urban Institute.

Boydstud, John E.; Sherry, Michael E.; and Moelten, Nicholas P. 1977. *Patrol Staffing in San Diego.* Washington, D.C.: Police Foundation.

Clawson, Calvin, and Chang, Samson K. 1977. "The Relationship of Response Delays and Arrest Rates." *Journal of Police Science and Administration* 5:53.

Fogelson, Robert. 1977. *Big City Police.* Cambridge, Mass.: Harvard University Press.

Greenwood, Peter W., and Petersilia, Joan. 1975. *The Criminal Investigation Process,* vol. I: *Summary and Policy Implications.* Santa Monica, Calif.: Rand Corporation.

Judd, Dennis. 1979. *The Politics of American Cities: Private Power and Public Policy.* Boston, Mass.: Little, Brown.

Kelling, George L.; Pate, Tony; Dieckman, Duane; and Brown, Charles E. 1974.

The Kansas City Preventive Patrol Experiment. Washington, D.C.: Police Foundation.
Lineberry, Robert L. 1977. *Equality and Public Policy: The Distribution of Municipal Public Services.* Beverly Hills, Calif.: Sage.
Mladenka, Kenneth R. 1978. "The Distribution of Urban Police Services." *Journal of Politics* 40:112.
Schwartz, Alfred, and Clarren, Summer N. 1977. *The Cincinnati Team Policing Experiment.* Washington, D.C.: Police Foundation.
Wilson, James Q., and Boland, Barbara. 1978. "The Effect of Police on Crime." *Law and Society Review* 12:367.
Yates, Douglas. 1974. "Service Delivery and the Urban Political Order." In *Improving the Quality of Urban Management,* edited by Willis D. Hawley and David Rogers. Beverly Hills, Calif.: Sage.

Chapter 2

Urban Service Delivery, Bureaucracies, and Politics: A Reassessment

Although the question, "Who gets what?" has intrigued political scientists for over thirty years, it had not been systematically addressed at the urban level until very recently. Urbanists have traditionally been more concerned with the distribution of power (who governs?) than with the distribution of governmental outputs. Spurred on by the early work of some economists (Shoup 1968; Hirsch 1968); by legal issues such as equal protection of the law and the distribution of urban services (see *Hawkins* v. *Town of Shaw*, 437 F.2d 1286 5th cir. 1971); and by the nagging question of whether variations in power structures make any difference in the performance of bureaucratic routines, political scientists have increasingly turned their attention to allocative questions at the local level. Moreover, despite the fact that the empirical analysis of urban services is hardly a decade old, a consensus has emerged on which factors most affect the service-delivery process. In a manner reminiscent of the comparative-state-politics literature of the late 1960s and early 1970s, many urban-services scholars contend that "politics" is not very important in understanding the service-delivery process. Rather, it is internal bureaucratic factors, most notably decision rules, that determine how services are distributed.

The purpose of the chapter is not to argue that these conclusions are totally unfounded and that only through an understanding of politics can we comprehend urban service delivery. Indeed, politics probably does play only a marginal role in the delivery of certain types of urban services. The failure of early researchers to recognize this limited role may have led them to have unrealistic expectations about the impact of political factors. The failure of politics to affect service levels in the expected manner in a number of early empirical studies undoubtedly led researchers to discard it as an influential factor and to look elsewhere for an understanding of the service process. These unrealistic expectations were not the only factor accounting for the haste with which early service-delivery researchers disavowed the importance of sociopolitical influences and embraced bureaucratic decision rules as an alternative paradigm. Other problems were their narrow conception of politics and the overly simplistic, almost naive, way in which they assessed the impact of sociopolitical factors on indicators of service delivery. These factors may well have contributed to the meager and often confusing results of their empirical analyses.

A final factor contributing to this consensus is the almost mystical significance attributed to the concept of bureaucratic decision rules. Unlike sociopolitical influences, the impact of decision rules has never been subjected to empirical examination. Indeed, the concept of decision rules usually emerged as a residual explanation to account for empirical patterns that seemed to be inconsistent with other explanations. Since the studies were usually designed to examine the impact of sociopolitical factors, they were ill suited to test or even to elaborate on the nature of service-agency decision rules. In fact, very little is known about the content of bureaucratic decision rules either within an agency or across agencies. Nor is much known about the limits of these decision rules across agencies.

To clarify these comments and to develop their implications this chapter will examine the concept of bureaucratic decision rules and the role of sociopolitical influences in the service-delivery process. Particular attention will be paid to the content and sources of various influences and the linkages between them and service-agency operations. Such a distinction is crucial for thinking clearly about the service-delivery process and will help clarify many of the ambiguities present in earlier analyses. Before we turn to these issues, it will be useful briefly to review and critique their treatment in earlier studies of service distribution.

SOURCES, CONTENT, LINKAGES: A REVIEW

A review of earlier studies of service delivery reveals that although the notions of sources, content, and linkage are mentioned in the literature, their treatment has been inadequate. For example, the literature has been preoccupied with two largely undifferentiated *sources* of influence: politics and bureaucratic influences. Presumably, sociopolitical influences are those that emanate from the wishes, views, or interests of persons or entities outside of a service agency. Moreover, the *content* of these sociopolitical influences is normally presumed, at least implicitly, to be in favor of the middle or upper classes. Stated differently, it is presumed that all relevant groupings want more of whatever service is examined; because middle or upper class groups have more power, they are expected to obtain more services. This is why most distributional studies have been structured so that service levels in underclass neighborhoods could be compared with those in other areas.

Bureaucratic influences have been defined as those that derive from within the bureaucracy, particularly its hierarchy. These influences manifest themselves in the form of bureaucratic procedures, norms, and policies that influence service practices directly or influence the decision rules that in turn affect service delivery. The *content* of these bureaucratic influences is normally seen as flowing from such things as professional standards, need calculations, and user demands. Therefore, these are largely seen as semiprofessional or rational influences. That is, although no one sees bureaucratic procedures and norms as being the most efficient or rational means of organizing the service process, most concede that these procedures are at least loosely related to the formal ends of the service agency.

At least two observations should be made regarding the treatment of the linkage between sources of influence and service-agency operations in the recent literature. First, virtually nothing has been written about the linkage between bureaucratic influences and agency operations. Although these linkages are presumed to be strong, thus accounting for the dominance of bureaucratic influences on service delivery, no one has really examined the linkages themselves or the implications of the presumption that they are strong. This is important because service deliverers are not automatons who blindly respond to hierarchical stimuli. Second, in contrast to the treatment of bureaucratic linkages, a good deal has been written about the linkage between politics and the service process. The thrust of these discussions is that the linkage is very weak.

A number of reasons have been suggested to explain the weak linkage between politics and service-delivery agencies. Some have to do with the nature of political "actors" and institutions, whereas others point to the character of urban bureaucracies. The political process is characterized by low levels of constituent activity on distributional questions along with low levels of information and visibility on these issues. Urban neighborhoods rarely function as organized political activists and put little coherent pressure on politicians or bureaucrats about distributional questions (Nivola 1978, p. 60; Jones 1977, p. 300). At the same time, elected political officials have little information on bureaucratic practices and on their distributional implications (Mladenka and Hill 1978, p. 131). These factors, together with the potential dangers of becoming involved in distributional questions, result in their low salience. (Antunes and Mladenka 1976, p. 163). Another line of argument suggests that the development of urban bureaucracies has resulted in a greater emphasis on professional management skills and expertise (Lowi 1964; Schiesl 1977). As a result of this change, urban bureaucracies have become increasingly autonomous (Lowi 1967; Yates 1977, pp. 18-41; Antunes and Mladenka 1976, p. 153; Mladenka 1977, p. 280; Prottas 1978, p. 288), and the primary source of service-distribution patterns is the independent, internal practices or "decision rules" of bureaucracies (Nivola 1978, p. 60; Mladenka and Hill 1978, p. 131; Jones 1977, p. 301; Antunes and Plumlee 1977, p. 320; Antunes and Mladenka 1976, p. 163; Levy, Meltsner, and Wildavsky 1974).

There are a number of problems with the treatment of each of these three basic concepts. The major problem with the treatment of *sources* of influence concerns the tendency of researchers to view the service bureaucracy as a monolithic whole, dominated by its hierarchy. Although hierarchies are important components of a bureaucracy and are often very influential in determining agency operations and outcomes, other organizational subcomponents can play an equally important role. For example, in certain types of service agencies organizational work groups and individual service deliverers can greatly influence both operations and outcomes. This is an important point because it is unlikely that the content of the influences emanating from these subcomponents would be similar to those emanating from the hierarchy. Further, in agencies in which these subcomponents affect outputs, a wholly different research strategy may be required to understand their impact—a point that will be developed later.

This discussion suggests some of the problems with previous treatments of the *content* of influences on the service-delivery process. To the extent that organizational subcomponents such as work groups and service deliverers influence outputs, it is impossible to argue that the content of bureaucratic influences is largely professional-rationalistic. Such things as vested interests, group norms, and individual beliefs and attitudes become relevant in attempting to understand the content of bureaucratic influences. Moreover, it should be stressed that such influences may be exerted even when hierarchies are the dominant source of influence within a service agency. Organizational leaders are individuals who have their own set of beliefs and values. Moreover, as leaders they are concerned not only with the technical facets of formal goal attainment but also with internal cohesion and organizational survival. This may require the introduction of explicitly political criteria in some organizational calculations or operations.

In addition to the problems posed by earlier analyses of the content of bureaucratic influences, there are also problems with analyses of the content of external sources of influence. As mentioned earlier, most analyses have presumed that all groups within a community desire—indeed, demand—more of whatever services are offered. The problem with this, and with the implications drawn from empirical studies suggesting that better neighborhoods do not always get more, is that they ignore the distinction between public and private regardingness. (Banfield and Wilson 1971). That is, it is possible that not everyone demands more of everything. The content of views emanating from certain groups in certain cities might constitute support for the allocation of services or resources on the basis of need, demand, or some other professional-rationalistic criterion. This has heretofore unrecognized implications for both the structure of service-delivery analyses and the interpretation of the empirical findings.

Nothing needs to be said here concerning the treatment of bureaucratic linkages because they have not been dealt with in the literature. As for political linkages, although researchers have noted the general weakness of these linkages, they have failed to recognize variations in them. That is, in some cities and with regard to some service agencies the linkages may be stronger than in others. More research needs to be done on the factors affecting these linkages; at the same time, the impact of these factors should be examined empirically.

BUREAUCRATIC INFLUENCES: THE MEANING AND ROLE OF DECISION RULES

When early distributional studies of urban services were unable to show that politics was a major source of influence, it was only natural that researchers looked toward the bureaucracies that delivered them as alternate sources. After all, services do not deliver themselves, and the bureaucracies that do deliver them were purposively organized entities designed to achieve certain ends in an efficient manner. Their modus operandi may not have always been the most efficient or rational, but it has stood the test of time. These established procedures normally had the support of the line personnel responsible for implementing them; indeed, these personnel often had a role in shaping them. These practices or norms also usually enjoyed the support of the bureaucracy's hierarchy, as long as they were not flagrantly inefficient and were not causing a stir among the citizenry or the political establishment.

Despite the centrality of standard operating procedures in most organizational operations, the notion of bureaucratic decision rules—a social science construct designed to capture these influences—has not contributed as much to our understanding of urban service delivery as it might have. In the rush to embrace bureaucratic decision rules to fill the void created by the impotency of "political" variables, this concept has been left both underdeveloped and overemphasized. Researchers expended little energy developing the structure of these decision rules or the nature of the criteria embodied in them. An implicit assumption was that although the deployment of decision rules did not optimize the use of available resources, the criteria embodied in them were derived from professional standards, demand- or need-based calculations, or some other essentially neutral source. In addition, service-delivery scholars did not consider that the relevance of decision rules, as a source of influence on the service-delivery process, may vary with the nature of the service task. A consideration of each of these issues will clarify the concept of decision rules and their role in the study of urban service delivery.

The Nature of Decision Rules

Bureaucratic decision rules can be conceived of as weighted sets of criteria used in the performance of routine organizational tasks or decisions. Theoretically they can involve anywhere from one criterion to a large number. The upper limit of the number of criteria in an effective decision rule would vary across tasks and would be bounded by the service deliverer's ability to integrate and synthesize information. Single-criterion decision rules probably exist only with regard to very simple service tasks. Consider the filling of potholes along a designated street. The operative decision rule here may simply be to fill up the largest holes first; the number actually filled may be determined by resource constraints (manpower, available asphalt). But the decision rule pertinent to which streets to work on might be considerably more complex. Relevant factors might include traffic flows, street quality, and the relationship of a street to the overall community traffic plan. In addition, however, the level of complaints from citizens might play a role as well as the street's proximity to such things as city hall, downtown, the mayor's home, or a major shopping center. Here again, however, although these considerations may affect priorities, available resource will determine overall service levels.

Thus, the statement that bureaucratic decision rules largely determine patterns of service delivery tells us very little. At least as important as the identification of decision rules as a source of influence on service distribution is the indentification of the nature of the criteria embodied in these decision rules. Table 2-1, showing hypothetical representations of several decision rules, illustrates this point as well as some general types of criteria that might be embodied in relevant decision rules. The weight attached to each reflects its relative importance in the decision.

A number of things should be stressed about the types of criteria depicted in Table 2-1. First, they represent only a first attempt at categorizing the types of criteria that may be embodied in service decision rules. Other categories undoubtedly exist, and refinements could be made in the existing ones. A second point is that different characteristics of the bureaucracy and the nature of the task to which the decision rule pertains are apt to affect the significance of these different types of criteria across service areas. Such factors would include the effectiveness of the organizational control system, the type of task (ministerial-discretionary), the structure of the interactions among line personnel, and the nature of the political linkages between the political system and the service bureaucracy.

Consider first the effectiveness of the organizational control system. Where it is effective (information flows are good, evaluative criteria exist, effective sanctions are available), the impact of nonhierarchical factors such as work groups and individual criteria will be reduced. The impact of professional-rational factors—where they exist—will be enhanced. Closely related to this factor is the nature of the task governed by the decision rule. Where the task is largely ministerial (picking up garbage, installing street signs, filling potholes) and professional-rational standards exist, their impact is apt to be enhanced. However, in highly discretionary tasks (ticketing or arrest encounters, housing inspections), the attitudes and preferences of the service deliverer are apt to take on greater significance. This is especially true where professional-rational criteria are nonexistent and/or where organizational control mechanisms are ineffective. With regard to the structure of work-group interactions, it is thought that the impact of work-group criteria will be enhanced in situations where coworkers engage in constant interaction over a long period of time. Where tasks are performed in solitude, the impact of individual factors will be relatively more influential than work-group criteria. Finally, the impact of environmental criteria may vary with the strength and directness of the linkages between the political system and the service agency. More will be said on this later.

In the previous discussion we were concerned only with factors affecting the relative significance of different types of criteria, not with their

Table 2-1. Representations of Three Hypothetical Decision Rules

---

Decision Rule 1

4 * PROFCRIT1 + 3 * PROFCRIT2 + 2 * ENVCRIT1 + 1 * WRKGRPCRIT1

Decision Rule 2

3 * PROFCRIT1 + 4 * WRKGRPCRIT1 + 2 INDCRIT1

Decision Rule 3

3 * ENVCRIT1 + 4 * WRKGRPCRIT1 + 3 * WRKGRPCRIT2 + 5 * INDCRIT1 + 4 * INDCRIT2

where PROFCRIT = Professional-rational criteria. These are defined here as fairly neutral criteria derived from professional standards, rationalistic calculations, or need or demand levels. They are related to the formal purposes of the service organization in the sense that they can be used to implement those goals in a fairly efficient, politically acceptable manner. Moreover, they normally have the support of important members of the bureaucracy's hierarchy who presumably employ organizational incentives and sanctions to insure that these criteria are used.

ENVCRIT = Environmental criteria. These are defined here as criteria embodying the values, preferences, interests, and needs of important groups or elements in the environment of the bureaucracy, as perceived by members of the hierarchy or communicated to them. Their relevance reflects the belief that no organization can exist independent of, or in isolation from, its environment. The environment provides resources, consumer satisfaction, and political backing. These environmental considerations are conveyed—through formal and informal channels of communication—from hierarchical personnel to those responsible for service delivery or for the supervision thereof. The explicitness of the conveyance may vary across different situations.

WRKGRPCRIT = Work-group criteria. These are defined here as criteria derived from the norms, traditions, and interests that arise from the interactions among service deliverers as a group. They are enforced through such mechanisms as peer pressure, and are important because there are often ambiguities or gaps in the enforcement of hierarchically imposed procedures. The void created by these gaps is largely filled by the work group, which relies on conventional wisdoms and group values or beliefs. There is little reason to believe that these gaps will always be filled in a manner consistent with the formal ends or purposes of the organization.

INDCRIT = Individual criteria. These are defined here as the individual values, attitudes, and preferences of service deliverers. They are relevant because people are not automatons.

---

content. This is a crucial point. The content of professional-rational criteria is dependent on such things as the state of knowledge or technology within a given area. It follows that this content would change with developments in knowledge or technology; their relative influence would depend only on organizational control mechanisms. The same point may be made with regard to individual preferences and attitudes. Where individual preferences can play a role, the content of the criteria will depend on the preferences of the individual service deliverers; the significance of these preferences will depend on other factors. In highly discretionary arrests encounters, for example, a racially prejudiced officer may be more likely to arrest blacks, whereas an unprejudiced officer may be less apt to do so. The racial views of street cleaners may be of less consequence. A final illustration concerns environmental criteria. The political linkage between a community and a service bureaucracy may be similar in two communities, but the content of the criteria may vary significantly. A traditional political system with a large working-class component may influence service distribution in one way, whereas a moralistic political system with a large middle-class component may influence distributions in another.

The Role of Decision Rules

Clearly, decision rules are apt to be complex phenomena, influenced in different ways by several factors. It should be clear that the significance of decision rules, as a source of influence on the service-delivery process, varies across service types. Their significance depends in part on the kind of task involved in the delivery of the service. Where tasks are routine, it becomes possible for organizations, individuals, or work groups to develop and test explicit criteria and to devise ways of implementing them. There are, however, infrequent and nonroutine types of tasks and decisions that affect the service-delivery process, where the notion of decision rules may not be especially helpful in understanding the process. This category would include such things as the placement of libraries, fire stations, and swimming pools; the designation of bus routes; and the allocation of police patrols.

Another factor that affects the relevance of decision rules is the structure of service disbursement. Where the bureaucracy controls the disbursement of services (garbage collection, pothole repairs, street-sign allocations), then bureaucratic decision rules are apt to be very useful in understanding the distributional process. However, where the consumer initiates the service disbursement (police and fire service calls, some environmental inspections), the concept of bureaucratic decision rules is less significant. They may have only indirect effects. A decision rule may, for example, dictate that there be no response to certain types of calls. However, for a complete understanding of the service-delivery process in areas where services are citizen initiated, one must look beyond the internal structure of the bureaucracy. Other models must be developed incorporating other considerations (need, citizen inclination to demand services, citizen sophistication).

POLITICAL INFLUENCES RECONSIDERED

Just as the importance of decision rules as a source of influence on the delivery of urban services varies across different types of services, so too does the importance of sociopolitical factors. In addition, the manner in which these influences affect service patterns varies with the type of service. Compare, for example, the probable impact of sociopolitical considerations on a one-time decision on whether to build (or where to locate) a capital-intensive service facility (library, senior citizen home, swimming pool) with its likely impact on citizen-initiated services such as environmental inspections, police service calls, or building inspections. In the former instance the decision is apt to be made by a political leader, by a commission, or by referendum. Sociopolitical considerations are reflected in the visible activity of various political groups such as local parties, neighborhood organizations, and ethnic groups. As for the latter type of service, however, the service-related decisions are made by the consumer. To the extent that sociopolitical considerations affect these decisions, they are apt to be related to such things as the social and governmental sophistication of the consumer. That is, controlling for need considerations, the better educated, more politically active citizens are more apt to demand various types of available urban services.

Because the role of sociopolitical factors is apt to differ across service types, this analysis will be restricted to one general category of services —those in which disbursement is routine and is controlled by the service bureaucracy. Included here would be such things as refuse removal, the handling of (not the demand for) routine police or environmental calls, and street paving. We will focus here on this category of services because it is precisely with regard to such services that the role of sociopolitical factors has been most hotly disputed. It was noted earlier that it is in these routine, bureaucratically controlled service activities that the role of decision rules is apt to be the greatest. This has led some who tend to view decision rules and sociopolitical factors as competing explanations to argue that "politics" plays no role in the delivery of such services. Thus a reassessment of the role of politics in this specific area should yield the most dividends.

If the role of sociopolitical considerations in this area is viewed in light of the typology of decisional criteria presented in Table 2-1, then a basis for conducting a reassessment of sociopolitical factors emerges. Sociopolitical influences can enter into service decisions through the implementation of criteria derived from individual values, attitudes, and predispositions of individual service deliverers; from the norms, traditions, and values of organizational work groups; and from the hierarchically imposed political judgments of organizational leaders. Although the main concern here is with the last-mentioned source of influence, each will be discussed with regard to the content and strength of its influence.

Sociopolitical Influence and Individual Service Deliverers

Studies of urban service delivery have largely ignored individual service deliverers as a source of sociopolitical influences on service decisions. These works have implicitly viewed service deliverers as automatons whose actions blindly reflect the views of the dominant political coalition or of the service bureaucracy's hierarchy. This rather mechanical conception of people might be a useful heuristic device in areas where service deliverers perform largely ministerial tasks. However, the tasks involved in delivering other types of services—police responses to calls for assistance, building and environmental inspections—contain a large discretionary component. The significant amount of discretion that some service deliverers enjoy gives them the opportunity—one might say the power—to act on their individual predispositions (attitudes, values, beliefs).

This power is enhanced if the service deliverer has control over the flow of information to the organizational hierarchy. This is an important asset since such information is essential for evaluating the performance of service deliverers and for exerting hierarchical control over them through the manipulation of sanctions. Another characteristic of some discretionary tasks that enhances the power of service deliverers is that their performance is often difficult to evaluate, regardless of the nature of information flows. One reason that some tasks involve a large discretionary component is that they involve unique situational considerations, the integration of which is difficult to prescribe in organizational handbooks. Multiple or ambiguous goals are often involved, and the weighting of different factors must be left to the professional judgment of the service deliverer. This ambiguity or multiplicity of goals enables these individuals to act on individual predispositions yet still legitimize their behavior in organizational terms.

For all these reasons the impact of service deliverers' sociopolitical predispositions must be considered when analyzing the delivery of highly discretionary services. In such an analysis two points should be kept in mind. The first concerns the content of individual predispositions, which is determined by background, socialization, and experiences, among other things. Because these are apt to differ, the predispositions of service deliverers within a given service agency are likewise apt to differ. Consider, as an illustration, racial views in a metropolitan police department. Most modern departments have contingents of "old timers," new recruits (often college educated), "locals," "professionals," blacks and whites. Even considering the socializing effects of the police academy or of shared work experiences, the racial views of these officers are likely to differ substantially. Some may be blatant racists, some may adhere to compensatory views, and others may be totally ambivalent.

What needs to be stressed here is that in order to analyze the real effect of racial predispositions on discretionary police tasks, one needs to know the views of individual officers (for empirical evidence in a different area, see Gibson 1978a, 1978b). This is essential because if race influences service decisions largely through the actions of individual officers, yet its impact is assessed only at an aggregated level, its real role may be obscured. Thus, where officers are fairly evenly distributed across the three racial categories previously noted (racist, ambivalent, compensatory), an empirical analysis of the impact of race that did not take these variations into account would be likely to conclude that race did not matter. Race might be a highly salient criterion to two sets of officers, but the influences of their opposite views would act to negate each other if viewed in the aggregate.

The second point to be noted here concerns the linkage between an individual's predispositions and his or her behavior in an institutional setting. In highly discretionary areas, where predispositions are expected to be most influential, it is likely that various well-established role orientations exist and provide guidance for the performance of organizational tasks. Where these tasks involve decision making, role orientations may be said to influence the type of decisional criteria utilized. This has implications for the role of sociopolitical considerations in service decisions.

Consider again the police example used earlier. Assume for the sake of simplicity that two role orientations exist for patrol officers. One is a professional role model that stresses the use and value of universalistic, rationalistic criteria; the other is a traditional role model that stresses the use and value of conventional wisdoms, street-acquired knowledge or stereotypes, and the like. Where an officer adheres to a professional role orientation, his personal predispositions are likely to play a less important role in his behavior than if he were to adhere to a more traditional role orientation. In the former case, sociopolitical considerations are not considered to be legitimate decisional criteria, whereas in the latter they are. Thus, although an officer's prior experiences may have led him to be a racist, his adherence to a professional role orientation may moderate the effect of his racial prejudices on his official actions. The same would also hold true for an officer having compensatory views. The impact of both sets of views would be greater where the officer adhered to a more traditional role orientation, in which such views were considered to have a legitimate role.

Sociopolitical Influence and Bureaucratic Work Groups

To say that suborganizational work groups—varying in nature from informal task pairings to labor unions—can act as a conduit for sociopolitical influences on the service-delivery process is to recognize these groups as distinct political entities. As such these groups have interests that differ from those of the organization as a formal entity and from the aggregation of the sociopolitical views of their members as individuals. Although a careful delineation of the content of these interests would contribute much to our understanding of the service-delivery process, it is largely beyond the scope of this work. Suffice it to say that these interests largely concern such things as work rules and conditions.

Student-teacher ratios, the amount of preparation time for teachers, the use of one- or two-officer squad cars, the use of two- or three-person garbage-truck crews, salary levels, and pension plans are just a few of the issues that can unite service deliverers as a group against the organization's hierarchy and the community as a whole. These issues are important for present purposes because they can affect who gets what. When service workers as a group prevail they get "more," usually at the expense of other groups. A worker victory usually restricts the power of the organizational hierarchy to determine the fate and/or course of the organization. In addition it usually reduces the total number of service units per tax dollar, thereby increasing service costs to the community.

The views and interests of service workers, at one aggregated level or another, influences the service-delivery process because of the ability of these groups to impede that process. Strikes, "blue flues," and work slowdowns are becoming commonplace in modern urban communities. The impact of these interests, however, is apt to vary across agencies and communities. The more vital the service (transportation workers, police, fire, refuse removal versus library workers, teachers), the greater the impact of workers' groups. Better organized groups are expected to be more influential than poorly organized groups. The receptivity of the community to worker grievances may also be an important factor here. A "labor" town, for example, might be more supportive of worker demands than a bedroom community of white-collar workers. Finally, the ability of the workers to cloak their demands in terms of improved service quality or professional standards is also apt to have an effect on the influence of their interests or views.

Sociopolitical Influence and Bureaucratic Hierarchies

Because members of bureaucratic hierarchies cannot personally monitor the actions of their employees, they establish rules, procedures, and policies to guide them. These are among the potentially most persuasive control mechanisms available to organizational managers. When applied, these bureaucratic guides are likely to influence or at least to constrain the behavior of line personnel. These rules and procedures are based largely on professional-rational considerations—need calculations, professional standards, efficiency, demand conditions, and prior experience. These considerations are relevant because of the training and socialization of managers and community expectations. Although this might seem commonplace, it should be stressed that, at least with respect to public bureaucracies, this has not always been the case. The reliance on professional-rational criteria reflects the widespread acceptance of the basic tenets of the municipal-reform movement in which "good-government" advocates fought the omnipresence of political influence in local governments and stressed the values of efficiency, professionalism, and bureaucratic independence.

Despite the pervasiveness of the reform ideology today, the rules and procedures of service agencies are still expected to have some socio-political content. One source of that content is the sociopolitical predisposition of hierarchical officials. Like service deliverers, these individuals are not automatons; their personal views are apt to color their actions, if only marginally. A second source of sociopolitical content in hierarchically imposed rules and procedures has to do with the multiple roles performed by most managers. In addition to their internal policy-making responsibility, numerous officials must deal on a continuing basis with important groups in the agency's environment. In exchange for the acceptable delivery of the desired type and quality of a particular urban service, agency officials attempt to secure financial and political support from the mayor or city manager, the council, the business community, the media, political-action groups, and the community at large.

It should be stressed that the support of these entities is needed not only to secure the resources to operate at a minimal level but also to expand the agency's scope of operations and to innovate. Expansion and innovation often require increased manpower levels and capital expenditures on plant and technology, for which strong community support is essential. This point is stressed because such expansions and innovations may be vital to a bureaucratic leader's position within his agency and for his career. Except in unique circumstances, few bureaucratic leaders would consider maintaining the status quo as an accomplishment. Innovators and leaders are the individuals for whom opportunity knocks.

To obtain the community support needed to achieve the prestige, accomplishment, and leadership qualities that accrue to the successful, bureaucratic officials must ensure that agencies operate in a manner consistent with the expectations of the entire community as well as of a variety of community subgroups. It should be stressed that this does not necessarily mean that specific policies or procedures are routinely adopted in response to group or citizen demands. Although that undoubtedly happens on occasion, most consumers do not have the specific technical information or expertise to formulate such demands. Moreover, it may violate a basic tenet of the post-municipal-reform ideology: bureaucratic independence. Political influence on bureaucratic policies is more likely to include such techniques as consensus building by the agency head, testing the water, and formal and informal contacts with relevant community groups. The aim of these efforts, of course, is to determine whether specific proposals fall within the often ambiguous zone of indifference that surrounds most agency operations.

The previous discussion describes the role of sociopolitical influence emanating from an agency's political environment in hierarchically imposed policies and procedures. There has been a good deal of controversy on this point. Much of the discussion, however, has been muddied by the failure to distinguish between the *content* of environmental influences and the *linkages* between this environment and the service bureaucracy. In addition, the theoretical expectations that would emerge from different combinations of each have not always been clearly stated. The following discussion will attempt to clarify these distinctions and to shed some new light on the matter.

Content

Like individuals, communities in the aggregate may vary in their attitudes, values, and beliefs. Although this may again seem commonplace, it is a point that has been overlooked in most studies of urban service distribution. An implicit assumption in most such studies is that enfranchised classes or groups always want more of whatever is being provided; when crude empirical examinations did not support this, researchers were quick to conclude that "politics doesn't matter."

The intensity and distribution of preferences and expectations within a community may vary across jurisdictions in a variety of ways. Views on public and private regardingness may be the most interesting. This factor has significant implications for the content of political influence in the more influential groups in some communities and, hence, for expectations concerning the nature of service distributions. Where private regarding-ness prevails in a largely middle-class community, one would expect, at least with regard to some services, empirical support for the underclass hypothesis. Where public regardingness prevails in such a community, one would not be justified in expecting empirical support for the underclass hypothesis. Failure to find such support would say nothing about the role of political influences in service delivery, since the content of these influences in such a case may well be that service agencies should perform wholly on the basis of professional-rational criteria, regardless of distributional consequences. This may result in an equal distribution of services or, where need is a relevant criterion, in a distribution favoring the underclasses. Whatever the case, one would not be justified in saying that "politics doesn't matter."

Linkages

Just as various factors affect the translation of individual predisposition into actions, numerous factors also affect the translation of various configurations of community preferences and expectations into bureau-cratic procedures and policies. Moreover, a discussion of these factors is crucial to an understanding of the role played by external sociopolitical influences in the service-delivery process. Four are of particular importance here: bureaucratic norms concerning the legitimacy of socio-political inputs; the ability of the local political system to produce a broadly based consensus concerning agency operations; the strength of structural linkages between the agency and the rest of the local political system; and the extent of structural biases in the local political process. Each of these factors will affect the transmission and reception of socio-political influences emanating from a service bureaucracy's environment, independent of the content of those influences.

Bureaucratic norms or views of the relevance and legitimacy of socio-political inputs concerning the bureaucracy's internal procedures and policies are important because these views affect bureaucratic responsiveness. As noted earlier, all organizations—and public bureau-cracies in particular—must be sensitive to the demands and needs of relevant entities in their environment. Although not all agencies are expected to be equally responsive, the situation is complicated because the factors affecting responsiveness are not altogether clear. Since professionalization may be such a factor, a discussion of it will suffice for illustrative purposes. The greater the degree to which scientific or universal standards or guidelines are available to—and are used by—an agency, the less responsive that agency is expected to be to sociopolitical inputs. In agencies that are not highly professionalized, bureaucratic officials may view these inputs as useful pieces of information for task performance. Moreover, where widely accepted procedures are not available, it may be more difficult for bureaucrats to justify the rejection of such inputs. Where professionalization is high, however, sociopolitical inputs may be viewed as irrelevant interferences impeding the efficient performance of agency tasks. In addition, agencies may be able to justify the rejection of these inputs on the basis of professional standards or proved principles of operations. Thus, an inverse relationship between agency responsiveness and professionalization is expected.

A local political system must continuously try to produce coherent, consensual preferences relevant to agency operations if it wishes to limit the size of the zone of indifference around agency operations (Lipsky 1976, p. 200). It is much easier for a bureaucracy to avoid sociopolitical inputs when no clear preferences are articulated and no competing alternatives are advocated by different groups. The likelihood that the political system will produce a consensus is apt to be affected by two characteristics: the extent of diversity within the political unit, and the ability of the political process to aggregate preferences. The greater the within-city diversity, the less likely a consensus is to emerge. With regard to the political process, it is likely that more hierarchical, integrated political processes—as in a machine arrangement—will be able to produce an agreement on desired policies (Greenstone and Peterson 1968, p. 272). Reformed nonhierarchical, pluralistic political systems have much more difficulty producing a consensus (Rogers 1971).

The nature of the formal or structural linkages between an agency and its environment will also affect the impact of sociopolitical influences on official policies and procedures. There are, for example, specific institutional practices that may increase or decrease the independence of bureaucratic officials. These include the extent of formal control by politicians over appointments and dismissals, and the extent of merit selection and civil service tenure. If the mayor or city council have appointment and removal powers, and if they do not have to make appointments from merit lists, then they have more control over the bureaucracy than if appointments must be made from lists of professionals and powers of removal are limited. The extent to which an agency is required to hold public hearings before initiating certain policies is also relevant here. Another aspect of linkage strength is the extent to which other political units have the resources to monitor agency operations. Although this is not a major concern for mayors and managers, who often have their own assistants, it is one for city councils and interest groups. If council members work full time, and have full-time staff assistants, then they have a greater potential to engage in bureaucratic supervision. Likewise, if interest groups can afford investigative staffs, they too can engage in monitoring activity. This is expected to increase sociopolitical influence on bureaucratic procedures and policies.

A fourth factor affecting the translation of sociopolitical influences into bureaucratic policies is the structure of the political process. Many of the proposals advocated by municipal reformers have worked to increase the role and influence of the middle class in community affairs. Nonpartisan elections, for example, have been found to reduce the turnout rate in municipal elections of lower-class voters, who rely more on party labels as voting guides than do middle-class voters (Salisbury and Black 1963, p. 590). In addition, nonpartisan elections have often weakened party organizations, which were useful in increasing the participation rate of lower-class people in municipal affairs (Greenstein 1976, p. 276). At-large elections have also worked against the representation of underclass interests in the political process (Hawley 1973, pp. 31-33; Eulau, Zisk, and Prewitt 1966, p. 215; Karnig 1976, p. 226). These effects are noteworthy because where the interests, values, and preferences of the middle class are distinct from those of the underclasses, the structure of the political process will help determine whose views will be reflected in a political decision. Holding other factors constant, the more reformed a local political system the more likely it is that the preferences of the middle class will be reflected in the policies of service bureaucracies.

* * *

This chapter outlines some of the primary factors that need to be addressed in a study of urban service delivery. Clearly, they are numerous and often quite complex. Moreover, many of them interact with one another in ways that affect their ultimate impact on service distributions. Examples of this interaction are found in Nardulli and Stonecash (1980) and Nardulli and Stonecash (forthcoming). Any systematic attempt to include all such considerations in a single research effort would require resources far beyond those available here. Nonetheless, we will be able to explore most of them in a preliminary fashion and some in greater detail. We begin with a discussion of the environment in which the police department operates, the links between the department and that evironment, and the general nature of the department.

REFERENCES

Antunes, George E., and Mladenka, Kenneth. 1976. "The Politics of Local Service Distribution." In The New Urban Politics, edited by Louis Masotti and Robert L. Lineberry. Cambridge, Mass.: Ballinger.

Antunes, George E., and Plumlee, John P. 1977. "The Distribution of an Urban Public Service: Ethnicity, Socioeconomic Status, and Bureaucracy as Determinants of the Quality of Neighborhood Streets." *Urban Affairs Quarterly* 12:313–332.

Banfield, Edward C., and Wilson, James Q. 1971. "Political Ethos Revisited." *American Political Science Review* 63:1048–1062.

Eulau, Heinz; Zisk, Betty H.; and Prewitt, Kenneth. 1966. "Latent Partisanship in Nonpartisan Elections: Effects of Political Milieu and Mobilization." In *The Electoral Process,* edited by M. Kent Jennings and L. Harmun Ziegler. Englewood Cliffs, N.J.: Prentice-Hall.

Gibson, James L. 1978a. "Race as a Determinant of Criminal Sentences: A Methodological Critique and a Case Study." *Law and Society Review* 12:455–477.

Gibson, James L. 1978b. "Judges' Role Orientations, Attitudes, and Decisions: An Interactive Model." *American Political Science Review* 72:911–924.

Greenstein, Fred. 1976. "The Changing Pattern of Urban Party Politics." In *The City Boss in America,* edited by Alexander. New York: Oxford University Press.

Greenstone, J. David, and Peterson, Paul E. 1968. "Reformers, Machines and the War on Poverty." In *City Politics and Public Policy,* edited by James Q. Wilson. New York: John Wiley.

Hawley, Willis. 1973. *Nonpartisan Elections and the Case for Party Politics.* New York: John Wiley.

Hirsch, Werner. 1968. "The Supply of Urban Public Services." In *Issues in Urban Economics,* edited by Harvey S. Perloff and Lowden Wingo, pp. 477–525. Baltimore, Md.: Johns Hopkins University Press.

Jones, Bryan D. 1977. "Distributional Considerations in Models of Government Service Provision." *Urban Affairs Quarterly* 12:291–312.

Karnig, Albert K. 1976. "Black Representation on City Councils: The Impact of District Elections and Socioeconomic Affairs." *Urban Affairs Quarterly* 12:223–242.

Levy, Frank; Meltsner, Arnold J.; and Wildavsky, Aaron. 1974. *Urban Outcomes: Schools, Streets and Libraries.* Berkeley: University of California Press.

Lipsky, Michael. 1976. "Toward a Theory of Street Level Bureaucracy." In *Theoretical Perspectives in Urban Politics,* Willis D. Hawley et al., pp. 196–213. Englewood Cliffs, N.J.: Prentice Hall.

Lowi, Theodore. 1964. *At the Pleasure of the Mayor.* New York: Free Press.

Lowi, Theodore. 1967. "Machine Politics—Old and New." *The Public Interest* 9:83–92.

Mladenka, Kenneth R. 1977. "Citizen Demand and Bureaucratic Response: Direct Dialing Democracy in a Major American City." *Urban Affairs Quarterly* 12:273–290.

Mladenka, Kenneth R. and Hill, Kim Quaile. 1978. "The Distribution of Urban Police Services." *Journal of Politics* 40 (February): 112–133.

Nardulli, Peter F., Stonecash, Jeffrey M. 1980. "The Analysis of Urban Service Distribution: A Theoretical Framework and Critique." Paper presented at the American Political Science Association Convention, Washington, D.C.
———— Forthcoming. "Analyzing Urban Service Distributions: Towards A Theoretical Framework." In *Analyzing Inequality in Urban Services,* edited by Richard C. Rich. Lexington, Mass.: Lexington Books, D.C. Heath and Company.
Nivola, Pietro S. 1978. "Distributing a Municipal Service: A Case Study of Housing Inspection." *Journal of Politics* 40:59–81.
Prottas, Jeffrey M. 1978. "The Power of the Street Level Bureaucrat in Public Service Bureaucracies." *Urban Affairs Quarterly* 13:285–312.
Salisbury, Robert H., and Black, Gordon. 1963. "Class and Party in Partisan and Nonpartisan Elections." *American Political Science Review* 67 (September).
Schiesl, Martin J. 1977. *The Politics of Efficiency: Municipal Administration and Reform in America: 1800–1920.* Berkeley: University of California Press.
Shoup, Carl. 1968. "Standards for Distributing a Free Government Service: Crime Prevention." *Public Finance* 19.
Yates, Douglas. 1977. *The Ungovernable City.* Cambridge, Mass.: MIT Press.

II: THE SETTING

Chapter 3

Political and Social Dimensions
of Champaign

Most public services are, in one way or another, affected by the operations of a public bureaucracy. If these bureaucracies were wholly independent entities, isolated from their environment, one would not need to look beyond their internal processes to understand how they affect allocational patterns. But no public bureaucracy enjoys such independence. A bureaucracy must reflect, as well as react to, various elements in its environment. Ignoring external considerations could easily lead to resource curtailments, loss of vital public cooperation, or public embarrassments. Police departments are no exception to these general strictures. Indeed, there is reason to believe that the police bureaucracy is particularly vulnerable to contextual influences. Much of its service activity is initiated by citizens and is divisible, that is, it can be varied from case to case. For these reasons something must be said about the context within which police services in Champaign are delivered.

This chapter will deal with two facets of the city of Champaign. The first section is concerned with several important characteristics of its political system, including a discussion of some general types of political preferences, of the linkages between the city and its public bureaucracies, and of certain structural biases that seem to exist in the system. The second main section outlines the sociospatial dimensions of the city. The aim here is to provide a familiarity with the internal neighborhood structure of Champaign—who lives where. This will prove helpful in interpreting the observed demand and allocative patterns.

THE POLITICAL SYSTEM

Political Preferences

The political climate or culture of a city is a complicated, multi-faceted phenomenon that could constitute a book in itself. Fortunately, two general studies of the political culture of Champaign are available (Elazar 1970; Rothman 1979). Each suggests that Champaign favors limited government and is unreceptive to redistributive government policies. In the view of both Elazar and Rothman, people in the cities like Champaign have a highly individualistic view of government—that is, a general belief that government should provide minimally necessary, collective services, and that individuals should take care of their own fates as much as possible.

A recent incident involving the city administration's attempt to upgrade street lighting on a major thoroughfare illustrates this view. The project, initiated by the city, was to replace a set of old streetlights with new sodium vapor lights. The initial investment in preparing the site was approximately $100,000. The project was to be funded by a combination of local funds, state funds, and a special assessment on the houses along the street. At first, the project was not well publicized; but as area residents became aware of it, they formed an investigative group to oppose it. Eventually the project was cancelled on the grounds that it was unnecessary and too expensive.

The most significant aspect of an individualistic political culture is that "government need not have any direct concern with questions of the 'good society'" (Elazar 1972, p. 94). This means that such cultures do not place a strong emphasis on questions of equity and the use of government to ameliorate or compensate for social inequalities. Rothman found this reflected in the attitudes of Champaign residents toward issues such as public housing and racial integration in the 1950s, 1960s, and early 1970s (Rothman 1979, ch. 6, 7). This individualism means that the potential exists for inequalities to develop without widespread concern or controversy.

Another characteristic of the individualistic political culture involves public attitudes toward bureaucracies and such bureaucratic traits as merit selection and autonomy. According to Elazar, individualistic political cultures tend to be ambivalent toward bureaucracies, desiring that they be businesslike but also open to political influence and responsive to individualistic needs or demands (Elazar 1972, p. 96). This again creates a strong potential and tolerance for differential distribution patterns. It also suggests that in such a system individuals might not be discouraged from actively seeking to influence bureaucratic behavior in order to secure special treatment.

Political Linkages

Several characteristics of Champaign's "reformed" political system lead one to think that public bureaucracies within the city are more independent than those in less reformed cities. First, elections are non-partisan and until 1973 all elections were at large. In 1974 the electoral system was changed so that five council members are elected from districts and four elected at large. Even with the 1974 modification this system dilutes the impact of geographically based interests, especially those of the underclasses. Moreover, council members and the mayor all serve part time; the city is run on a day-to-day basis by the city manager. The presence of a professional manager moves the public bureaucracies one step further from political pressures. Together with the fact that they are not under constant scrutiny since the public officials serve only part time, this simply enhances their latitude.

The relative independence of public bureaucracies in a city like Champaign does not mean that they need not be concerned with their environment. As indicated earlier, no organization can afford such indifference. Moreover, discussions with various officials involved in Champaign's city government suggest that there is a strong sensitivity to the climate of public opinion, and that the city's bureaucracies are affected by these attitudes. The following example illustrates this kind of relationship for the police department.

In 1979 significant increases in the level of calls for services led the police hierarchy to make some modifications in manpower allocations. All available police personnel were put "on the street," including those who had been assigned to desk duty for years. In addition, the department made major modifications in the structure of beats that resulted in major changes in manpower allocations across different parts of the city. The planned reallocation was developed wholly within the department and was scheduled to go into operation on a set date. No extensive advance publicity was intended, although it was planned that the change would be announced first to the city council and then to the public through a standard news release from the police department. Prior to the scheduled announcement, however, a reporter for a local newspaper learned of the planned policy change and wrote a story about it. The night before the story was to appear, the city manager's office received information concerning the pending story and decided that a concurrent announcement from the city administration on the policy change was necessary.

The principal concern of the police department and city manager was that the newspaper story might give "informed political interests" the impression either that current manpower allocation had been poorly planned or that the new allocation plan was intended to benefit some interests at the expense of others. Police and administration officials felt it important to demonstrate that the new allocation was a professional response to changes in demand for police services. Therefore, the city manager, his assistant, and the police chief met at city hall until well past midnight to draft an official position concerning the reallocation proposal. The intent was to avoid, or at least minimize, adverse reaction among perceived political power bases.

This incident illustrates several important points. One is that even while a department may be pursuing professional policies, and justifying its behavior on the basis of professional norms, it may feel that it should not antagonize established political interests within the city. This sensitivity to the political environment suggests a linkage of the bureaucracy to political considerations. Yet the incident also suggests that this link is not so strong that the organization is afraid to make changes, because the new policy was in fact implemented. What it does suggest is a concern with both rationalistic and political considerations.

Structural Biases

As discussed in Chapter 2, there is considerable evidence that certain political structures are not neutral in their representation of political preferences. Moreover, several characteristics of Champaign suggest that there is a bias in the political process such that the constraints within which public bureaucracies work are different from what they might be under other circumstances. This bias appears to exist in Champaign's voting system and in the structure of local interest groups; moreover, it has a distinct middle-class flavor.

Formal Representation. The electoral system in Champaign is nonpartisan and was of an at-large nature during most of the time prior to this study. Turnout for elections has generally been low. As discussed in Chapter 2, such characteristics tend to result in the relative overrepresentation of middle- and upper-class populations. In addition, the city has a large number of students and recently graduated former students who generally show little interest in voting and exert correspondingly little influence through elections. The consequence of all this is that most of the elected officials are likely to come from the middle class and to be concerned with middle-class interests. As Rothman notes:

> During the 1960's an overwhelming proportion of Champaign council members lived in one middle to upper class residential area in Southwest Champaign. [Rothman 1979, p. 184]

Although the switch to some district-based elections changed this some-what, the at-large council members still come disproportionately from Southwest Champaign.

Informal Representation. Champaign is not dominated by extensive, overt interest-group conflict. This is not because of a lack of political conflict over issues but because there has not been the development of interest groups that might oppose traditional groups such as the Chamber of Commerce. The black population of the city, which makes up about 11 percent of the total population, has no tradition of high political involvement (Rothman 1979, p. 185). As black organizations have developed, their efficacy has been hindered by divisions over policies(Rothman 1979, p. 219). Since the population of Champaign has traditionally been mobile, heterogeneous, and fragmented, few neighborhood groups have developed. This situation leaves the more traditional interest groups of urban politics (businessmen, realtors, and others) unopposed and able to exercise considerable influence. The net effect is probably that the middle- and upper-class populations enjoy a dominant position in the political process and strongly influence the nature of the constraints placed on the political system.

The review suggests that the middle and upper classes have some degree of overrepresentation, or relatively more influence that warranted by their proportion in the population. This middle- and upper-class population appears to have an individualistic notion of politics, which is likely to lead to support for private regarding attitudes. At the same time, a relatively high proportion of Champaign residents work at the University of Illinois; these individuals, because of their professional status or associations, are likely to be supportive of professional-rational criteria of behavior. Thus, it appears that the political climate of Champaign is that of an "individualistic" political culture tempered by the professional ties of many of its citizens. To the extent that the bureaucracy is sensitive to this climate, the bureaucracy should find support both for professional-rational behavior and for private regarding distributions or responses, although the exact mix of these two remains difficult to discern.

SOCIOSPATIAL DIMENSIONS

Champaign, like many cities, is geographically segmented in ways that may have important implications for the distribution of public goods and services. An understanding of its subcommunities is vital to an understanding of the city, as well as of its police resource-delivery mechanism. One simple way to obtain a rough "feel" for this community substructure is to examine its census tracts and the demographic traits of their residents. A map of Champaign's fourteen census tracts is found in Figure 3-1; Table 3-1 provides some general information on each tract.

A number of observations can be made with regard to the map and Table 3-1. The first is that tract 2, Northeast Champaign, is the black community. Almost 95 percent of its residents are black; the next highest percentage among the thirteen tracts is 15 percent. The data in Table 3-1 also make clear that tracts 4, 14, and to a lesser extent 3 are student districts. They all border the University of Illinois and have an exceptionally high proportion of residents living in group quarters. The residents of these tracts are also very mobile, as indicated by the data in columns 5 and 6. Finally, the reason for the very low population figure in tract 1 is that this tract is largely consumed by the downtown business district.

Table 3-2 yields some additional insights into the remaining tracts. First, it is clear that tracts 11 and 13, known as Southwest Champaign, house Champaign's upper crust as well as a goodly proportion of its middle class. These tracts have the highest median income, the greatest proportion of families with incomes exceeding $25,000, and the highest levels of educational achievement. Residents of these tracts also tend to be employed in the more prestigious occupational categories. An exam-

Table 3-1. Demographic Characteristics by Tract

Tract	Total Population	Percentage Black	Percentage Living in Group Quarters	Percentage Living in Same Residence in 1965	Percentage Living Outside Champaign SMSA in 1965
1	670	8.1	0	0.29	0.33
2	2,740	94.3	0.15	0.60	0.08
3	4,010	7.2	0.16	0.13	0.63
4	6,818	2.3	0.78	0.06	0.69
5	4,448	5.2	0.01	0.51	0.25
6	4,123	6.2	0.01	0.42	0.28
7	3,794	15.1	0	0.46	0.18
9[a]	4,349	8.4	0	0.49	0.18
10	4,633	2.0	0.01	0.55	0.19
11	5,193	.4	0	0.53	0.26
12	7,800	4.2	0.01	0.32	0.34
13	3,896	1.5	0	0.37	0.39
14	3,442	7.1	0.96	0.04	0.70
Champaign	55,916	12.5	0.16	0.37	0.35

[a]Tract 8 lies outside the city limits.

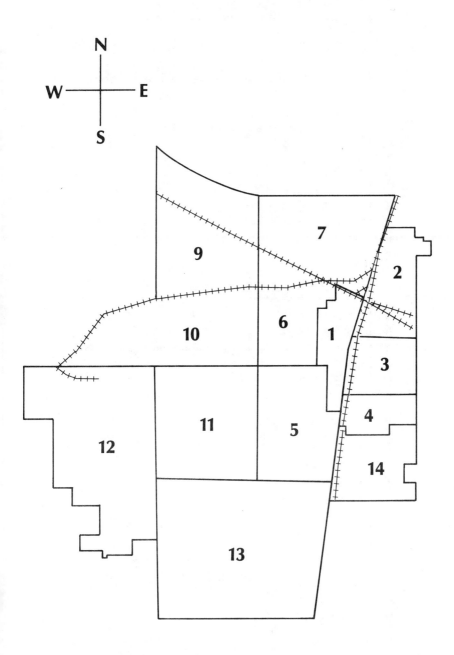

Figure 3–1. Champaign Census Tracts

Table 3–2. Income, Education, and Occupation Status of Champaign Census Tracts

Tract	Median Family Income	Percentage With Family Income Over $25,000	Percentage With Family Income Under $3,000	Percentage Who Did Not Complete Elementary School or Have Only Elementary Diploma	At Least Some High School Including Degree	At Least Some College Including Degree	Professional-Managerial	Clerical-Blue Collar	Service
1	9,750	0.08	0.07	0.26	0.40	0.24	0.28	0.39	0.34
2	5,932	0	0.25	0.48	0.44	0.08	0.09	0.49	0.42
3	5,760	0.02	0.19	0.20	0.29	0.51	0.42	0.35	0.21
4	5,604	0.02	0.27	0.05	0.21	0.75	0.36	0.41	0.23
5	12,124	0.12	0.08	0.11	0.41	0.48	0.44	0.45	0.09
6	10,687	0.09	0.06	0.19	0.42	0.40	0.35	0.53	0.13
7	8,642	0	0.08	0.32	0.56	0.14	0.17	0.64	0.19
9	10,306	0.01	0.05	0.15	0.63	0.22	0.17	0.65	0.15
10	11,777	0.07	0.04	0.13	0.49	0.38	0.31	0.56	0.10
11	14,828	0.20	0.04	0.05	0.34	0.60	0.53	0.41	0.06
12	12,119	0.02	0.04	0.07	0.46	0.48	0.43	0.48	0.10
13	15,571	0.21	0.03	0.01	0.29	0.69	0.55	0.41	0.05
14	—	0	1.00	0	0	1.00	0.22	0.40	0.38
	10,258	0.07	0.17	0.15	0.39	0.46	0.33	0.48	0.19

ination of the racial, educational, and occupational makeup of tracts 7 and 9 reveal that they are largely white, working-class areas. In tract 7, for example, 88 percent of the residents over 25 did not go beyond high school; 64 percent are employed in clerical–blue-collar jobs. In tract 9, 78 percent did not go beyond high school, and 65 percent are employed in clerical–blue-collar occupations.

The remaining tracts (5, 6, 10, and 12) cannot be so neatly categorized. Although there are distinct communities within each tract, at the tract level they can only be described as mixed. There are "faculty ghettos" in parts of tracts 5 and 6, but there are also smatterings of working-class neighborhoods. Tracts 10 and 12 have historically been populated by white middle- and working-class families in single-family residences. However, more and more apartments have been constructed in this area, which, unlike tracts 7 and 9, is not bounded by industry. Also, with the price of housing skyrocketing in the Champaign-Urbana area, more young faculty members as well as older graduate students have moved into the outlying areas constituting tracts 10 and 12.

NEIGHBORHOODS WITHIN THE CITY: A MORE IN-DEPTH VIEW

The census information given here, firsthand observations, and discussions with informed individuals suggest that there are several distinct sociogeographical subunits within Champaign that have some relevance for present purposes. They include Southwest Champaign, the Northend, the student district, the largely white working-class neighborhood in the northwest sector, and the mixed district; they are depicted in Figure 3–2. A sixth would be the Commercial-Industrial areas, which, although they are not contiguous, will be treated as a distinct unit. Each of these merits further discussion.

Southwest Champaign. The area designated as Southwest Champaign is the area's main country-club district and, in fact, surrounds the Champaign Country Club. It is a largely white corridor of new, expensive single-family dwellings (see Table 3–3) and is quite suburban in physical appearance. Although not everyone living in Southwest Champaign is wealthy, most would admit to being comfortable. This area houses many of the doctors, lawyers, higher-ranking university personnel, and other professionals in the community. Some indirect support for the argument that Southwest Champaign houses a healthy portion of the community elite can be found in the fact that this area scores the highest on each of the various elite scales reported in Table 3–3. Each figure in these

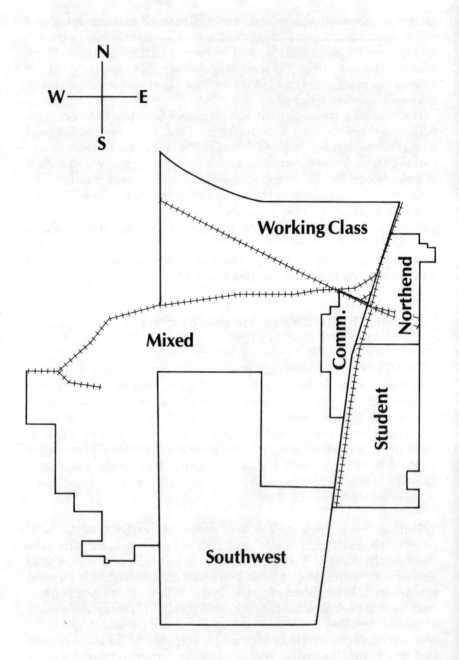

Figure 3–2. Champaign Neighborhoods

Table 3-3. Demographic Information on Residential Areas in Champaign

Area	Percentage Black	Percentage Home-owners	Average Home Value in 1969	Commercial Elite Scale	City Political Elite Scale[a]	Civic Elite Scale
Southwest Champaign	0.3	86	$31,445	1.26	0.27	0.99
Student district	7	23	8,944	0.35	0.05	0.14
Working-class sector	12	66	14,618	0.39	0.05	0
Mixed area	5	68	21,991	0.75	0.12	0.30
The Northend	93	50	13,024	0.20	0.09	0.13

Note: The figures are based on block-level data; hence, they represent averages of block data.
[a]These scores reflect the number of elites, loosely defined, in three different areas who reside on a given block. The commercial scale reflects the ownership of local businesses, the political elite scale reflects nonelected managerial positions in city government, and the civic elite scale reflects involvement in a number of different community activities. The derivation of each of these measures is explained in Chapter 5.

columns can be interpreted as the average number of each type of elite residing in each block within each subcommunity.

From the inside of a police car, Southwest Champaign appears somewhat remote. A police officer seldom encounters citizens on the street in this area, either by day or by night. In the winter, residents leave for work, school, or social affairs from their attached garages. When they return at night, they remain indoors, each family around its own fireplace. In the summer, residents are normally in their air-conditioned homes or on their enclosed backyard patios.

This lifestyle—although admittedly exaggerated here—makes for a limited street presence, which in turn leads to limited police-citizen contact and thus to limited familiarity. In areas like Southwest Champaign the police simply do not encounter citizens very often except when the latter call the police for some type of assistance. Even these encounters are relatively limited; residents of such middle-class areas seldom have occasion to call the police. Marital and neighborhood squabbles tend to be less frequent or at least not viewed by the participants as requiring police intervention. The low-density, residential nature of the area makes traffic, parking, and public-order problems minimal. The occasional burglary, vandalism, or traffic or juvenile problem presents the most likely opportunity for police-citizen contact.

The Northend. This subcommunity is, and historically has been, Champaign's black ghetto—literally, the "other side of the tracks." As Table 3-3 demonstrates, it is as far from Southwest Champaign demographically as it is geographically. The average value of homes in the Northend is barely 40 percent of the average in Southwest Champaign. The rate of home ownership is not even 60 percent of that in the southwest sector, although the Northend is largely a community of single-family dwellings. Only relatively recently have any significant public housing projects emerged. In short, this data and firsthand observations reinforce the view of the Northend as a relatively deprived lower-working-class community that emerged from the census data presented in Table 3-2.

The Northend looks as different from Southwest Champaign in a squad car as it does on paper. In the summer certain areas look much like low-income rural communities in the South. People are out in the streets, front porches, and front yards; few houses appear to have central air conditioning or sheltered patios. This presence, combined with the greater stability of the population (see Table 3-1) has led to greater familiarity between residents and the police, which is further enhanced by the greater incidence of police-citizen encounters in the Northend than in other areas of Champaign. The density of the population, the lower-class and lower-working-class lifestyles and behavior patterns, and the pressures emanating from financial stress and social frustration all lead to more frequent encounters between police and residents, especially juveniles and their parents.

The Student District. The main campus of the University of Illinois is located in Champaign-Urbana. With 34,000 students, it is one of the largest centers of higher education in the country. These students come from different parts of the state, the nation, and the world; they form a heterogeneous, mobile population, which changes cyclically. This mobility, together with the size of the student population, prevents the police from becoming familiar with the student community, although there is at least as much "street presence" as in the Northend. Unlike Southwest Champaign, the student district does not present the police with a homogeneous middle-class lifestyle. Students keep irregular hours, some drink to excess, others use and deal in drugs. Their newly acquired independence from daily parental authority can also lead to special kinds of problems.

Other characteristics of the students and the student district merit comment. The informal student lifestyle and the fact that they frequently go home on weekends and holidays make students easy targets for vandalism, burglary, and theft. The population density of the student district (most live in converted single-family dwellings, dormitories, or fraternity and sorority houses) and the persistent parking shortage also cause police problems. In addition, the district is centered around a commercial district called Campustown. Campustown contains bars, restaurants, drugstores, retail outlets, movie theaters, and other small shops. It is the center of night life and weekend activities for many students. Campustown also attracts many high school students and air force personnel from nearby Chanute Air Force Base in Rantoul. At night, and especially on weekends, the streets of Campustown are filled with cars endlessly circling the main drag; the sidewalks are teeming with people who frequently overflow onto the street. This continuing inter-action of different types of people, often in varying stages of inebriation, in a small congested area, presents the police with problems they do not encounter in other areas of Champaign. Moreover, the problems are aggravated by a continual flow of special events (athletic events, concerts, conventions) inherent in any major university setting.

The Working-Class and Mixed Districts. The neighborhoods desig-nated as working-class and mixed have much in common in comparison with the other types of neighborhoods. They house somewhat over half (52 percent) of Champaign's population and form a J-shaped sector, which separates the other distinct areas. The working-class neighborhood is largely white, lower-middle-class, and blue-collar in composition. It is also beginning to experience an increase in upwardly mobile working-class blacks, migrating across the tracks from the Northend. The mixed district is composed mainly of upwardly mobile, middle-class white families with a healthy mix of lower-middle- and working-class families. Otherwise, these two areas are somewhat similar in general appearance, although the mixed district clearly has a disproportionate number of nice homes and neighborhoods. Moreover, both areas, unlike Southwest Champaign and most of the Northend, border on the downtown area and have significant commercial and light-industrial areas within them and on their borders.

The diversity in these two districts is reflected in the types of police involvement required in the two beats which largely cover these areas. There are traffic and parking problems that result from the relative congestion of the commercial areas, although not to the extent found in Campustown. There are also assaults and public-order problems, but again not to the extent found in Campustown or the Northend. Common crime (vandalism, theft, burglary) is only a moderate problem when compared with the student district; serious crime is even more rare.

The Commercial-Industrial Area. Finally, the commercial and indus-trial sectors should be mentioned. Although these areas are not contig-uous, they will be treated in this analysis largely as a distinct entity. It is important to note that economically they have played a less dominant role than might have been expected in a relatively isolated area like Champaign-Urbana. As noted earlier, the major employer in the area is the University of Illinois.

Among the several distinct business areas is the downtown area. Downtown Champaign, like many other central business districts, is dying. Despite efforts at revitalization through the construction of a mall, the area is still losing business; the mall has done little other than add to the parking problems. Most of the business has been drawn away from downtown by two major shopping centers, a new one on the north end of the city and an older one to the west. In fact, the newer center dealt the final blow to downtown and had a severe impact on the older shopping center as well. It did not, however, have much impact on Campustown, which is the major remaining commercial center in Champaign.

Although Champaign has recently tried to develop an industrial community on its northern border, it has had only limited success. There are only two plants employing more than 1,000 people and only two more that employ between 350 and 500. Beyond this, there is a smattering of smaller, locally owned firms. The limited extent of this industrial community makes it, in the aggregate, a relatively minor consumer of police services.

* * *

Having briefly sketched the overall political tenor of the environment within the Champaign Police Department works, as well as the social substructure of the community, we turn now to a brief description of the police department, its reputation, and its relations with the community.

REFERENCES

Elazar, Daniel. 1970. *Cities of the Prairie: The Metropolitan Frontier and American Cities.* New York: Basic Books.
———. 1972. *American Federalism: A View From the States.* New York: Crowell.
Rothman, Rozanne. 1979. "The Great Society at the Grass Roots: Local Adaptation to Federal Initiatives of the 1960s—Champaign-Urbana." Unpublished manuscript.

Chapter 4

Champaign's Finest

The description and analysis of allocational issues requires some understanding of various organizational characteristics. The basic organizational structure is of major importance because it shows how the agency handles the tasks it must perform and how it allocates manpower. This can help put given segments of an analysis into some contextual perspective. It also provides a basis for comparing the agency being studied with other similar agencies, which in turn might be valuable in interpreting a given set of results. An agency's organizational-political history is also important. It can yield important insights into the organization's links with its political environment and can put those linkages into historical perspective. Another area that needs to be covered is the agency's image in a community and the history of its relations with different groups in that community. This is particularly important in the case of an agency like the police, which offers services that are largely citizen initiated and which deals with people on a continuing basis. A clear picture of these relationships will help in understanding demand levels as well as response patterns.

ORGANIZATIONAL STRUCTURE

The Champaign Police Department is located near the edge of downtown Champaign in the northeast quadrant of the city. It has been housed since 1935 on the lower floors of the City Building. The size of the force has more than quintupled since 1935, and the present facilities are quite cramped. In 1976 this facility housed roughly 92 people; Figure 4-1 depicts its organizational arrangement. As this diagram indicates, there are really three organizational units below the level of the chief: the criminal-investigation division, the staff-services division, and the uniformed division. The criminal-investigation division handles all follow-ups on crime reports and handles referred juvenile cases. The staff-services division handles procurement, budgetary matters, criminal-records maintenance, the detention facility, crime reports, and so on. The uniformed division, which is of most concern in this study, includes most line personnel, who answer calls, respond to alarms, provide general patrol, initiate automobile and pedestrian stops, and so forth.

The patrol division is formally divided into two units, a traffic unit and a patrol unit. In 1976 the traffic unit was a state-funded Selective Traffic Enforcement Patrol (STEP) unit, composed of one sergeant, four patrolmen, and four squad cars. STEP officers receive special training for handling accidents, radar, traffic control, and the like. They normally work only the day shift and only at six intersections with high accident rates. Although traffic-law enforcement is not the exclusive province of STEP units (regular patrol officers are responsible for this function in non-STEP areas), these officers will only respond to nontraffic calls in emergency situations when regular units are unavailable. Members of the patrol division, in contrast to STEP officers, are generalists who work around the clock, throughout the city. They are divided into three shifts. One lasts from 7:00 A.M. to 3:00 P.M. and has fifteen officers; another from 3:00 P.M. to 11:00 P.M. with eighteen officers; a third from 11:00 P.M. to 7:00 A.M. with seventeen officers. Each of these is under the direct command of a shift lieutenant and two sergeants. An additional overlap shift lasts from 7:00 P.M. to 3:00 A.M.; it has three officers and was implemented to cover the exceptionally high call levels during the nighttime hours.

Each officer in the uniformed division is assigned to one of six beats; these coincidentally, correspond roughly to the six neighborhoods identified in Chapter 3. The beats are depicted in Figure 4-2. Table 4-1 reports some data on manpower allocations across the six beats.[1] A cursory examination of that table indicates some marked disparities in patrol allocations across the various categories. Beat 2, which corresponds to the Northend, is the most heavily patrolled sector of the city, followed closely by Beat 3, the student district. This is mainly the result of the relatively heavy reliance on two-officer squads in these areas. More will be said later about these disparities and their implications.

Although the material presented here gives some idea of the general nature of the Champaign police department, it sheds little light on its

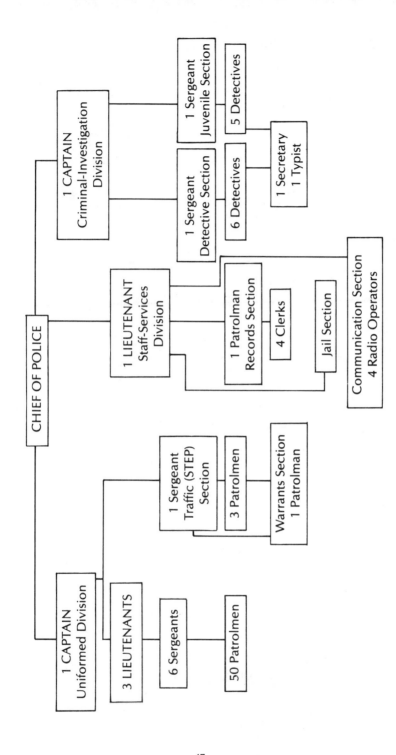

Figure 4–1.   Organizational Structure of the Champaign Police Department, 1976

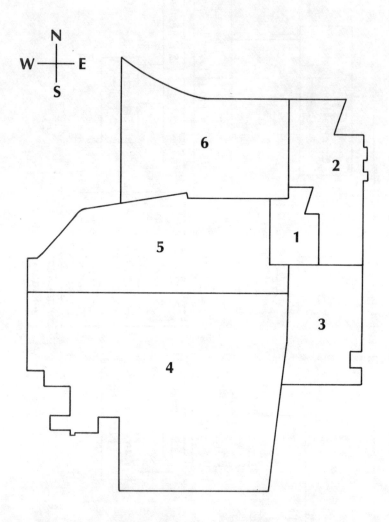

Figure 4-2. Champaign Police Beats

similarity or dissimilarity with departments serving other cities comparable to Champaign. Although an in-depth comparison would be beyond the scope of this analysis, some very general comparisons between Champaign and other Illinois cities of similar size are possible and would be useful in putting the present analysis in comparative perspective.

Table 4–1. Average Officer Days Allocated by Beat and Shift

Shift	Beat					
	1	2	3	4	5	6 (White Working-Class)
				(Southwest Mixed)		
	(Downtown)	(Northend)	(Campus)	Mixed)	(Mixed)	Class)
1 (7 A.M.–3 P.M.)	0.75	2.21	1.30	0.96	0.98	0.98
2 (3 P.M.–11 P.M.)	1.33	2.34	1.86	1.27	1.06	1.32
3 (11 P.M.–7 A.M.)	1.01	1.93	1.77	1.62	0.44	1.65
4 (7 P.M.–3 A.M.)	0.28	0.40	0.52	0.14	0.48	0.09
Average officer day allocated (sum of columns divided by 3)	1.12	2.29	1.82	1.33	0.97	1.35

Tables 4–2 and 4–3 present information on selected financial and manpower indicators. The former shows that although per capita expenditures on police in Champaign are just about average for the group of cities chosen, Champaign police officers do relatively well. Champaign's beginning and maximum salaries, and its percentage increases since 1971, are higher than the mean. In terms of manpower ratios (Table 4–3), however, Champaign is consistently below the mean for these cities with respect to the number of sworn officers, per capita officers, percentage increase in force since 1971, ratio of supervisory personnel to total force, and minority representation. With the exception of the size of the supervisory force, however, Champaign cannot be considered statistically deviant (as could, for example, East St. Louis).

BRIEF NOTES ON ORGANIZATIONAL-POLITICAL HISTORY: STEPS TOWARD INDEPENDENCE

It may be overstating the case to call this section a history of the Champaign Police Department. A history of a police department that has existed for over a century would require a book in itself. In any case, a

Table 4–2. Comparative Police Financial Data in Selected Illinois Cities, 1976

	1976 Per Capita Police Expenditure	1976 Starting Salary, Patrolman	Percentage Change Since 1971	1976 Maximum Salary, Patrolman	Percentage Change Since 1971
Aurora	$39.45	$11,075	48.86	$13,835	40.26
Belleville	23.51	11,100	—	11,473	—
Bloomington	28.77	10,006	41.09	12,122	62.93
Champaign	31.87	11,901	52.54	13,344	52.54
Danville	39.11	10,188	41.43	12,427	51.18
Decatur	21.93	10,970	38.45	13,334	40.27
East St. Louis	—	—	—	—	—
Elgin	31.49	11,274	28.70	13,956	27.80
Joliet	52.26	—	—	—	—
Moline	33.34	11,832	49.39	14,076	62.92
Quincy	20.78	9,520	35.61	11,849	47.19
Rock Island	28.33	—	—	—	—
Springfield	34.01	10,404	33.38	12,468	—
Average	$32.07	$10.827	41.03	$12,888	48.14

detailed treatment would go far beyond the needs of the present analysis. This section presents a brief overview of the development of the police department, its relationship with the political environment, and the events that have affected these things over the years. The focus of this overview will be on the notion of independence, since this concept is thought to be particularly relevant to an understanding of how an organization operates within its sociopolitical environment.

In this respect, the history of the Champaign police shows a shift from a politically vulnerable department to one essentially free from direct intervention by political officials.[2] Throughout much of its early history, the department was subjected to the direct political influence characteristic of that era. Initially the Champaign police marshal was an elected official; later the police chief was a political appointee of the mayor (Neumann 1974, pp. 16–18). During this era direct political interference with police affairs, especially in the areas of recruitment and vice, was not uncommon in Champaign and elsewhere in the country (Fogelson 1977). Perhaps the most visible instance of direct interference in Champaign occurred in 1935, when a police captain refused to adhere to a strict policy on vice-related arrests, to which the mayor was politically committed. The captain was demoted to a patrolman but was later reinstated when newspapers carried stories that the demotion was merely an attempt by

Table 4-3. Comparative Police Manpower Data in Selected Illinois Cities, 1976

	Actual Number of Full-Time Sworn Officers	Ratio of Actual to Authorized	Full-Time Officers Per Capita	Percentage Manpower Increase Since 1971	Supervisory Personnel (Captain to Sergeant) as a Percentage of Force	Minority Members as a Percentage of Force
Aurora	152	100	1.97	199.04	21.05	7.89
Belleville	61	100	1.39	—	26.32	0
Bloomington	65	100	1.56	136.84	27.69	3.08
Champaign	86	97	1.48	123.07	17.43	5.81
Danville	64	91	1.53	107.14	20.31	6.25
Decatur	107	100	1.19	105.83	15.86	7.47
East St. Louis	114	76	1.97	—	36.84	62.28
Elgin	91	96	1.52	111.00	20.88	5.50
Joliet	156	100	2.10	—	19.87	10.90
Moline	66	100	1.48	122.86	28.78	1.51
Quincy	63	100	1.44	115.25	20.64	0
Rock Island	78	99	1.59	—	36.17	5.13
Springfield	155	100	1.77	121.20	19.36	14.84
Average	96.77	96.85	1.61	126.91	23.93	10.05

the mayor to promote a political supporter to the vacated position (Neumann 1974, p. 31). A number of developments—some precipitated by actions outside the department and others by actions taken within—have resulted in more independence for the police department.

External Steps Toward Independence

Two major externally initiated efforts have helped reduce political influence on the Champaign Police Department. The first occurred in 1903, when the state mandated local boards of fire and police commissioners. These boards, designed to administer a merit system of recruitment, were an outgrowth of the first wave of police reform in the United States (Fogelson 1977). The three board members are appointed to staggered terms by the mayor, with the appointments subject to council approval. Although specific information on this board's activities is unavailable, it appears that the board initially played a limited role. In recent years, however, it has administered the civil service system for the department and acts as a buffer between police personnel practices and politics. The fact that board members are appointed by the mayor and approved by the city council does, however, leave open an avenue for possible indirect political influence.

Another reform that has affected the relationship between the police and local politicians was the adoption of the city-manager form of government in 1955. That change placed the police chief, as well as the police department's budget, under the control of the city manager. Although there was little initial change, the early 1970s saw the recruitment of a progressive, active city manager. His efforts in recruiting a professionally oriented police chief in 1974 did have a significant, although indirect, impact on the department's operations and ultimately on its relationship to the local political setting.

Internal Steps Toward Independence: Professionalization

Despite the external changes that occurred after the Champaign Police Department began as a one-man force in 1857, one hundred years later the department was still very much a product of Champaign's individualistic political culture; it has not really established its own independent organizational identity. In the late 1950s the department resembled Wilson's (1968) "watchman style" department in many important respects.

An extended excerpt from an interview with a twenty-year veteran of the force illustrates this quite nicely:

Interviewer: When did you come on the force?

Veteran: I came on the force in 1957.

Interviewer: What was the reputation about that time, what was the pay like relative to today; the type of people, for example were they mostly local folks on the force, a lot of part-time jobs, and so on?

Veteran: When I came on I knew, I didn't know them real well personally, but I knew who a lot of the officers were, they had been on [the force] several years when I was a kid growing up. . . . As I recall the police department had something like thirty-six–thirty-seven officers. . . . The chief of police here at that time was Clyde Davis, and Chief Davis had been Chief for God only knows how many years, I think thirty some years when he retired. He had come up through the ranks, but for twenty years or so he had been chief of police. The situation at that time, although it was just rumors, was that . . . the chief of police and some police officers were on the take; there were several houses of prostitution in the North-end primarily, gambling, after-hour joints, even as there is now. There were more of them then, they were more open; you know it was no trick at all to find a place to buy booze at night, it was no trick at all to find a house of ill-fame. There was several of them almost advertised. I think every kid that went through high school here knew where they were, so to speak. So, in all, the reputation of the department may not have been great, although I didn't really look at it as that bad. . . .

So far as coming on the police department, I needed a job. I can't say that I wanted to be a policeman all of my life, I didn't. Probably the farthest thing in my mind after I reached a certain age in childhood of playing cops and robbers, was being a police officer, but something occurred. Oh, I know what it was, I took my mother to the laundromat to do the laundry for some reason, and the guy that ran it was some kind of police commissioner or something, and he asked me if I was working, and I said no and he said why don't you go in to see Chief Davis and see if he won't put you to work; he needs policemen. I made some comment about that is the last thing in the world that I want to do, and I thought about it a couple of days and I came in and saw the Chief and he was very, oh he wasn't a strange character, but he was a character and he was very gruff, grouchy. It had been my experience, even then, that if you growled back usually you didn't have too much trouble out of these types; so when he growled at me, I growled back. He asked me "Do you know what you want to be a cop for?" "What the hell," I said, "is there anything else to do, you know, show me a better job and I will take it." He said, "What are you doing Sunday," and I said "Nothing." He said, "Why don't you come in to see me Sunday about noon?". . . . So Sunday at noon I came in, and I recall he gave me a hat that didn't fit and a gun that was all rusty and a holster that went on my left side instead of my right. He told me to put all that stuff on, as he wanted to see how it looked. I put it all on and he said, "It looks real good, here's your badge, come on out with me." We got in a car in the garage and we drove out to the mayor's office. The mayor was cleaning up his office and we walked in the backdoor and he said "Mayor, I want you to meet my new policeman" and that was it; I went to work.

Interviewer: That was it, no training?

Veteran: Hey, I hadn't even filled out an application yet!. . . . [In terms of training] the theory was "Do you know right from wrong" and when you said yes I do, then they said all right you go out on the street and if you see anybody doing anything wrong you bring them in and call us and then the sergeant will come in or the lieutenant will come in and we will sit down and figure out what law he broke, don't you worry about the law. If he is doing wrong you bring him in. That was your training session.

In addition Chief Davis had a system where, are you familiar with Crazy Corner? Main, Neil, Hickory, and Church Street all come together up there and we called it Crazy Corner, that is our name for it because there are five streets coming in instead of the regular intersection and there used to be a traffic signal out in the middle of the street. . . . What you did was the first few days Chief Davis would walk downtown with you. . . . Of course on Sunday there wasn't anybody there so he put you in a car and drove around the community and every time he would see somebody he would talk to them and introduce you to them. And then for the first week or so you would stand on one of the corners of Crazy Corner. You weren't allowed to go in any direction, you just stood on that corner and spoke to people as they walked by so they would get to know you as a policeman and be able to talk to you.

Interviewer: That was your human relations program?

Veteran: Yes, and they would get to look at their new police officer which had clothes on that didn't fit and no uniforms. Most of the guys would wear just street clothes with a badge on their shirt. . . . What we did, most of the guys, was if we were in the army wore our Ike jackets and our wool OD uniforms and had it dyed dark blue. . . . Then after the week he let you change corners every hour. You could walk when the light changed. After you had been on the corner for an hour you could walk to the other corner and then stand on that corner for an hour. And then after two or three days of that , then you could walk twenty-five or thirty feet each way from that corner. After about two weeks he would give you a beat assignment to walk. At that time we usually had three or four beat officers.

Interviewer: Officers walking, no cars?

Veteran: That is right, we had a North beat, a South beat, an East side beat, and a Campus beat. I knew right away I had problems the first time I walked Campus beat. I walked into a store and they took me into a back room and showed me where the refrigerator was and asked me what brand (of beer) I liked and told me they would make sure it was well stocked for me; all I had to do was keep coming into their store and be nice to their customers, etc.

Interviewer: What kind of equipment did you have back in those days?

Veteran: They furnished a badge, a whistle, a gun, a flashlight that didn't work, and a hat (cap), and that was about it. Well, they gave you a holster usually, of some sort. But it was practically guaranteed after you were equipped and got out on the street that you were going to buy new equipment because everything that they had given you was a mess. It looked like Salvation Army.

Interviewer: And what was the starting pay in those days?

Veteran: $320.00 a month. You had to kind of dedicated because you could go almost any place and make $100.00 a week. So you either really had to want to be a police officer or you had to have some other reason for it.

Interviewer: No education incentive pay or anything like that?

Veteran: No nothing like that. As a matter of fact $320.00 a month was it as I recall. The fact that you had twelve years seniority made no difference.

Interviewer: Very little differential?

Veteran: No differential. Sergeants were probably making $400.00, the lieutenants may have made $450.00.

Interviewer: What about squad cars?

Veteran: The squad cars they had when I came on weren't too old; they had just traded. They had three cars as I recall. But it wasn't unusual. . . . before the city-manager form of government in '59 or '60 . . . . for a car to have 100,000 miles on it. You could actually check the street for potholes by looking through the floor boards, because most of the time there was holes in the floor boards, big enough rusted out places, where you could see the street. Tires were bald, the cars would hardly run.

Such observations no longer characterize the Champaign Police Department. Like many other departments across the country, Champaign underwent some fundamental changes in the late 1960s and early 1970s. A police officer was no longer recruited from a laundromat and handed a gun before he had completed an application form. Instead, officers must now pass through a series of tests and interviews and must then attend a six-week session at the University of Illinois Police Training Institute. Later, selected field-training officers provide new recruits with on-the-job training.

Another consequence of professionalization is that since the early 1970s there has been a good deal of emphasis on education. A conservative estimate—no exact figures are available—is that about half the Champaign police force has at least an associate of arts degree and that many have bachelor's degrees. This is partly because a large proportion of the newer officers have some college background. But it is also because of Champaign's generous educational-incentive program ($42,000 was budgeted for educational incentives in 1976 alone). Officers are also given flexibility to pursue course work. Moreover, despite the emphasis on formal education, practical training has not been ignored. The budget for training programs went from $6,850 in 1973–1974 to $15,000 in 1974–1975 and to $31,400 in 1975–1976. These programs ranged from courses on criminal law and criminal investigations to courses on traffic control and management by objectives.

Beyond changes in recruitment and education, professionalization has brought about improved police technology, a variety of special programs, and increased efforts to obtain outside sources of funding. The present department has more and better-equipped patrol cars than those of earlier years. Most are traded in annually—it is no longer possible to check for potholes through the floor boards. In 1977 computers were introduced into the department, significantly enhancing its technological capacity in such areas as record keeping and personnel management. An Urban High Crime Program was established in 1975 and the department had a STEP program (Selective Traffic Enforcement Patrol) from 1976 until 1979. It also experimented with a team-policing program in the Northend between 1977 and 1979.

In addition to such local programs, the Champaign department engaged in several innovative metropolitanwide programs. One was a Metro Police Social Services program, which coordinated social service activities in Champaign, Urbana, and the University of Illinois. Another was Project LOCATE, which from 1977 until 1979 provided limited crime-analysis capabilities for the entire metropolitan area. Finally, in 1979 a METCAD (Metropolitan Computer Aided Dispatching) program was instituted, which provides centralized computerized dispatching for the entire metropolitan area on a closest-car basis.

The expanded operations of the Champaign department have been made possible in part by real increases for the police in the city budget. But many of these innovations (STEP, team policing, Metro Police Social Services, Project LOCATE, and so on) have been made possible mainly by the department's aggressive pursuit of state and federal law-enforcement funds. Indeed, the amount of outside funding rose from $3,864 in 1973–1974 to $125,480 in 1975–1976 and to $258,562 in 1976–1977. In proportional terms the percentage of the police budget derived from external funds went from 0.3 percent in 1973–1974 to 9.1 percent in 1976–1977.[3]

These significant advances made by the Champaign Police Department were largely the result of the efforts of the new police chief, who arrived in 1975. He was the first chief to be recruited from outside the department, and his professional orientation was a reflection of the new city manager's own inclinations. Although the winds of change had begun to blow before the arrival of these two individuals—had, in fact, precipitated their recruitment—the city manager and the chief certainly had an impact on the pace and direction of change. The most important point here, however, is that these changes had an effect on the relationship between the department and its political environment. The department was still constrained by the local political culture, but its new professional makeup added a new dimension to its organizational identity.

Because of the department's newly acquired technology and orientation and its sensitivity to professional criteria, it was no longer wholly legitimate for personnel to rationalize practices by reference to local custom or habit. Budgetary requests could be justified through references to national standards or by output and activity data made possible by the department's improved technological and record keeping capacities. Resources were no longer dependent on traditional political considerations. Finally, the department's newly acquired experience and success in generating outside funding for programs of its own initiation enhanced both its independence and its stature in the local community.

THE POLICE AND THE COMMUNITY

Today the Champaign Police Department is a modern, fairly professionalized force. The new chief is committed to the idea of using advanced technology, innovative police programs, high recruitment and behavior standards for staff, educational incentive programs, and so on. At the beginning of the period covered by this study, however, he had been in office only a little over a year. It is also important to note that of the nineteen chiefs who have headed the department since its inception in 1857, he was the first to be recruited from outside the department and the first to have been trained as a police administrator. Before the mid-1970s Champaign had no crime-analysis or computer facilities, and its record-keeping facilities were outdated. Moreover, many people—especially blacks in the Northend and students—saw the department as staffed with bigoted and easily corrupted ruffians. Indeed, although the present police chief is black, Champaign had no black patrolmen before the mid-1960s.

These observations are important because an understanding of an organization like the police that provides largely citizen-initiated services requires some insight into how the community views the organization. Moreover, much of what the community knows or feels about an organization is formed more by historical events than by service provisions made in day-to-day contacts. Thus, this section will outline the sources of some of the general image problems that have plagued the Champaign police over the years. In addition, it will review in some detail problems encountered in the Northend and student communities. Finally, it will present some survey data on citizen evaluations of police services and attitudes toward the police in the various subcommunities discussed in Chapter 3.

General Image Problems

The Champaign police have long suffered from a poor reputation among certain segments of the community. They have been viewed as corrupt, overly prone to physical and verbal abuse, and insensitive to various subcultures. Local conventional wisdom holds that they fare poorly when compared with the adjacent Urbana Police Department; proponents, however, are quick to point out that Champaign has a much more heterogeneous population than Urbana and that the police are routinely confronted with more difficult problems. Nonetheless, there is some historical basis for cynicism.

In its early history, the department suffered from occasional scandals, with chiefs being indicted or forced to resign. The early part of the twentieth century was marked by the transgressions and charges that plagued many departments during the Prohibition era. Bootlegging, gambling, and call houses were common in Champaign; and, although vice raids were made daily, suspicion of police corruption was widespread. This period is also memorable for a scandal that only indirectly involved the department but that tainted it nonetheless. In 1926 it was discovered that a former police marshal, who was then selling insurance, had been involved in a murder scheme with a prominent real estate saleswoman. This realtor would arrange for blacks to be moved into Champaign homes that she sold to them. As collateral she would have them purchase an insurance policy from the former marshal, with herself as beneficiary. The former marshal would then arrange for their murder, and the proceeds would be split. As many as twenty people had been murdered in this scheme. When the investigation led to the realtor, the former marshal killed her. He subsequently killed himself while under investigation for her murder.

The next major scandal came in 1962, after a lengthy period of relative calm. The incident is referred to as "Burglars in Blue in '62," and resulted in the resignation of virtually the entire night shift—eleven officers, including two lieutenants. Seven were indicted but were never brought to trial. The scheme involved night officers burglarizing commercial establishments and then reporting the crime. The story was widely covered in the local press, and community respect for the department hit a low point. The corrupt image that emerged from this incident was reinforced when just a year later it was revealed that a long-time veteran of the force had embezzled $20,000 from the Champaign Police Benevolent and Protective Association. The entire fund amounted to only $21,600 and had been accumulated since 1937.

Although such scandals have been relatively infrequent, they have done much to tarnish the image of the police. Of equal importance are the problems the police have encountered in the Northend and student communities and how they have handled them.

The Police and the Northend

The relations between the police and the Northend community have never been as good as those with the rest of Champaign. Nonetheless, they were not overly hostile until 1962—the year of the burglary scandal. Until the 1960s, in fact, few officers had reservations about walking the night beat in the Northend. Two factors changed this situation. The first was heightened civil rights activity in the black community. The second, and more significant, was the emergence of two black street gangs—the "Satan Lovers" of Champaign and the "Crabs" of Urbana.

In 1963 and thereafter Champaign experienced some conventional civil rights activity—mainly open-housing demonstrations—without much hostile police-community contact. A notable exception was an open-housing demonstration that resulted in the arrest of several demonstrators. Another notable incident was termed the "Spotlight Cafe Riot." The cafe, a known gambling and bootlegging center in the Northend, was largely tolerated by the police and local officials. On December 11, 1965, while several officers were attempting to arrest an intoxicated person, a crowd of about fifty people gathered. After a confrontation the crowd began to shower four officers with debris, injuring them all. They were rescued by three black patrons of the cafe. The incident received much press coverage, and the Champaign Human Relations Commission later laid much of the blame on the conduct of the officers. Although police abuse was cited, no formal charges were ever made.

Despite these serious occurrences, the issue of gravest concern to the police centered on gang activity, which peaked in the late 1960s. At the outset of that decade there had been some "harmless" gang activity, such as firing shotguns at rival gang members from a "safe" distance or over their heads. Events took a serious turn in 1969, when twenty members of one gang attempted to assassinate the unarmed leader of another. Fear of civil war led to a merger of the gangs, involving about 160 youths. The new structure even had a central committee known as the "Main 21."

One result of the merger was that the gangs turned their hostilities outward. A prime target was Champaign's police officers. Patrol cars were repeatedly attacked by snipers, even around the downtown area. Commercial establishments along University Avenue—the southern boundary of the Northend and a main drag in town—were "shook down" for protection by the gangs. Others were burned out in a series of fire-bombings. The area became known as "Warzone Charlie." One officer was sniped at six times. The gang merger was short lived, however, and by

1970 a splinter group emerged and inevitable conflicts ensued. The headquarters of one gang was firebombed and burned while snipers kept firemen at a distance. In another incident a gun battle along the railroad tracks left seventeen gang members wounded.

Two events in the early 1970s brought the years of violence to a virtual end. On April 29, 1970, a police officer stopped a black youth for traffic violations and for suspicious conduct. The youth fled, and the officer gave chase. During the chase the youth was shot and killed. The officer contended that his weapon discharged accidentally. This event was followed by days of riots culminating in an attack on a patrol car by seventy-five black youths just blocks from the police station near downtown Champaign.

The other incident occurred on August 8, 1971, and involved an ambush on a rival gang in a public housing project. A black resident who saw what was about to occur called the police. Twenty officers arrived, and a large-scale gunbattle ensued. One observer reported that several hundred shots were fired. When it was over, one black youth—armed with a stolen shotgun and a bandolier of ammunition—was dead. This incident ended most visible gang activity and capped a decade of hostility between the police and large segments of the Northend community.

The Police and the Student Community

The location of the main campus of the University of Illinois in Champaign-Urbana creates special problems for the Champaign police. The existence of approximately 34,000 young people, with diverse and frequently distinctive life styles and vulnerable to all sorts of problems often handled by the police, gives rise to a disproportionate level of demand. Since the 1920s (and perhaps even earlier) students have been toppling cars, conducting panty raids, having egg fights, and engaging in various other forms of quasi-deviant behavior that occasionally brought out the police but rarely resulted in serious confrontations. Although such incidents did little to improve police-student relations over the years, there were few overtly hostile incidents in Champaign until about twenty years ago.

The change came with a water riot that occurred in May 1957. A favorite summer activity of University of Illinois students was opening up fire hydrants and aiming streams of water at one another. When several students were injured during such a water fight, the police moved in. In the ensuing melee, tear gas had to be used to subdue the students. The next major student-police confrontation came in 1964 as a result of a three-hour panty raid, when ended with over 400 students pelting the police with rocks and bottles. Thirty students had their ID cards taken away. This decade of relative tumult ended with a demonstration by a large number of black students who were part of a relatively new educational-opportunities program. What began as a protest against inadequate housing facilities for some members of the program ended in a disturbance that caused extensive damage to two lounges in the student union. Although criminal charges were filed against 300 black students, all charges were later dropped.

The antiwar protests of the 1970s brought a marked change in the nature of student-police encounters. Although campus demonstrations at the University of Illinois were not as violent as those in Berkeley and Madison, they were extremely explosive by east-central-Illinois standards. Following a series of minor disturbances (including a firebombing of the Champaign Police Department on January 14, 1970), a major incident began on March 2, 1970, with the simultaneous cancellation of William Kunstler's appearance and the presence of General Electric recruiters on campus. Two thousand students demonstrated on the first day, and six officers were injured. The following day, as 5,000 students "trashed" campus buildings and Campustown establishments, the governor called in the National Guard. Troops and a Jeep with a six-foot-square barbed wire "cow catcher" imposed a 10:30 P.M. curfew. The disturbances ended on the third day with the departure of the General Electric recruiters. Nine students were suspended. This was followed several months later by large-scale demonstrations and "trashing" to protest the bombing in Cambodia. A less serious demonstration occurred on May 6, 1971, to protest the presence of Marine recruiters. Thirty-nine students were arrested, but the disturbances were handled solely by local authorities.

Drugs were another problem that plagued police-student relations during the 1970s. Although no major incidents occurred, numerous smaller ones caused tension. The university actively cooperated with the police in some drug raids involving major suppliers, but by the mid-1970s users of marijuana were largely ignored. In recent years there have been highly publicized and organized "Hash Wednesdays" on the campus. These, too, have been largely ignored by authorities.

This greater sensitivity to student lifestyles, in conjunction with increasing student conservatism, led to a general improvement in relations between students and the law-enforcement community during the mid-1970s. Other factors also contributed to this improvement. One was an effort by the university police to upgrade their department. In earlier days the university police suffered from a poor reputation among the students—at one point it was common for the students to refer to the "Illi Cops" as "Silly Cops." This situation changed as the university police raised their standards and updated some of their practices. In addition they instituted an "Officer Friendly" program—in collaboration with the Champaign police—which stressed crime prevention, including reduction of theft from dormitories and muggings on campus. The women's movement also inadvertantly had a positive impact on relations. Women's groups and others were very concerned about the rape problem on campus, and their efforts found eager allies in the local law-enforcement community.

The two issues of crime prevention and women's security finally put the students and police on the same side of the fence, and with one exception these improved relations continued up to the period of this study. The exception was a Halloween disturbance in the fall of 1976. The celebrations, held in Campustown, got out of hand; students spilled out into the streets, effectively closing them. The chief was out of town, and the night-shift commander made the decision to reopen the streets. This led to a confrontation between approximately 50 officers and 500 to 1,000 students. Some property damage was incurred, some minor injuries were sustained, and some arrests were made. All in all, however, this more closely resembled a 1950s event than a demonstration of the 1960s or 1970s. Moreover, careful plans were made for subsequent Halloweens with the result that in recent years there have been successful celebrations with no confrontations.

Champaign Neighborhoods and the Police: A Quantitative Assessment

Earlier sections have outlined different neighborhoods in Champaign and have briefly described historical relations between some of these communities and the police. The purpose of these descriptions was to provide some background for understanding the operations of the police service-delivery system in the context of this specific setting. The aim of this section is similar but more direct. It reports the results of a survey of Champaign citizens concerning their evaluations of police services and their attitudes toward the police that was conducted in January 1977.[4] Because police services are citizen activated, citizen perception of the police—like the history of relations between the police and a specific community—is important. Citizen attitudes may affect both the inclination of a citizen to request services and the police response to such requests; an understanding of these perceptions thus may be helpful in interpreting patterns of demands and responses.

A series of questions contained in the 1977 survey were factor analyzed to create a "service-quality" factor and a "personal-assessment" factor. The first factor contained items in which citizens evaluated the courtesy, speed, and overall quality of police services; the second factor contained attitudinal items in which citizens assessed the personal qualities of Champaign police officers.[5] A breakdown of these constructed variables according to the neighborhoods described in Chapter 3 will provide some insights into how these communities view the police. Before the results of this analysis are reported, however, it should be emphasized that the design of the survey did not permit a precise identification of all subgroups. The Northend and the student communities could be precisely identified. It was also possible to isolate respondents roughly in the white working-class neighborhood, although residents of the westernmost part of this neighborhood were systematically excluded.[6] Beyond this, the most significant problems were encountered in attempting to differentiate between residents of Southwest Champaign and those in the mixed district. In order to differentiate between these two groups, all cases *not* identified as belonging to one of the previously mentioned categories were isolated. The respondents in this residual group, who identified themselves (or another member of the household) as professionals or managers-proprietors, were grouped separately to approximate opinion in Southwest Champaign. Finally, all remaining respondents were lumped together to represent opinion in the mixed district. Although this grouping captures many respondents who actually live in the mixed district, it also undoubtedly includes residents of Southwest Champaign as well as those in the western part of the white working-class section. It is, however, the best approximation possible under the circumstances.

The results of the breakdowns of the composite service-quality and personal-assessment indexes are reported in Table 4–4.[7] An analysis of variance reveals that there is significant variation across these groups; the Fs are 25.08 and 36.44 for the service-quality and personal-assessment factors, respectively. Each is significant well beyond the .001 level.

The results reveal, not surprisingly, that on both dimensions Northend blacks give the police the lowest score. The next lowest on both is that of the working-class whites in the northern part of the city, followed by that of the students. The scores for the professional/manager and mixed

Table 4–4. Breakdown of Service and Attitudinal Measures

	Mean of Service-Quality Factor	Mean of Personal-Assessment Factor
Professional/managers	0.16 (173)	0.10 (175)
Northend blacks	0.59 (237)	0.85 (237)
Students	0.20 (161)	0.24 (161)
Working-class whites	0.15 (218)	0.24 (218)
Mixed groupings	0.02 (206)	0.03 (206)

groupings were the highest on both dimensions and were virtually identical. As tentative as these results are, it does appear that citizens in the northern sector of the city do not evaluate the police or police services as highly as do those living elsewhere. Whether these results are caused by actual differences in services or by the conditions of life in these different areas, or some other factor is not clear at this point. Later analyses may, however, shed some light on this.

NOTES

1. The data for the computations come from twelve weeks of 1976 daily logs (the first two weeks of every other month). The daily logs revealed which officers were assigned to each beat on each shift. The data for each shift-beat were then used to obtain the average number of officers assigned to each beat for each shift. If an officer was assigned to patrol two beats, his time was equally allocated to each; two-man cars were weighted accordingly.
2. Much of the information for the following sections will be derived from an historical account of the Champaign Police Department by Patrolman William H. Neumann. Officer Neumann prepared two separate reports on the Champaign police—"A Historic View of the Champaign Police Department: 1857 to 1958" and "A Historic View of the Champaign Police Department: 1958 to 1975"—in fulfillment of course work at the University of Illinois. I appreciate the Champaign Police Department's making these materials available. They will be supplemented with information obtained through personal interviews where appropriate.
3. The data on the changes in the proportion of external funds came from an untitled report in the files of the East Central Illinois Criminal Justice Commission.
4. The survey was part of an evaluation of a team-policing experiment that was located in the Northend community as well as in part of the adjacent white working-class neighborhood. It began in May 1977, several months after the period covered by this study. The survey was funded by and conducted for the Champaign Urban High Crime Program. The evaluation entailed the use of two samples—one for the "target area" (the Northend and the largely white working-class neighborhood to its west) and one for Champaign outside the target area. In addition, a general sample—one in which all Champaign residents had an equal probability of being included—was also available.
5. A detailed description of the questions and the method used to construct the service-quality and personal-assessment measures would require more space than is justified by their rather limited role in this analysis. Interested readers, however, can refer to Nardulli (1980) for complete documentation on these matters.
6. The Northend community and the eastern part of the white working-class community were easy to identify because these two groups constituted the experimental area covered by the team-policing experiment. Students were easy to identify because of a question asked on occupation.
7. The results in Table 4–4 appear somewhat odd because they are so low. Because factor-score composite indexes are simply weighted z scores one would expect a more even distribution in terms of negative and positive means. The reason that these means are skewed in a negative direction is that the scores for most of the Northend black and white working-class groups were derived from the target-area sample. The scores in

this sample were uniformly lower than those in the general sample, which was used to conduct the factor analyses. The application of the factor-score equations derived from the general sample (where all Champaign residents had an equal probability of representation) to the target-area respondents resulted in the weighting of the merged samples in a negative direction. This accounts for the negatively skewed means in Table 4-4.

REFERENCES

Fogelson, Robert. 1977. *Big City Police.* Cambridge, Mass.: Harvard University Press.

Nardulli, Peter F. 1980. "Police Deployment Strategies and the Delivery of Police Services: An Experiment in Team Policing." *Law and Policy Quarterly* 2:420–444.

Neumann, William. 1974. "A Historic View of the Champaign Police: 1857 to 1958." Unpublished manuscript on file at the Institute of Government and Public Affairs, University of Illinois.

_____. 1975. "A Historic View of the Champaign Police: 1958 to 1975." Unpublished manuscript on file at the Institute of Government and Public Affairs, University of Illinois.

Wilson, James Q. 1968. *Varieties of Police Behavior.* Cambridge, Mass.: Harvard University Press.

III: THE DEMAND FOR
POLICE SERVICES

Chapter 5

Understanding and Analyzing the Demand for Police Services

It is noted in Chapter 1 that an understanding of what was termed the citizen-assistance function of the police patrol division—as distinguished from their crime-deterrence or traffic-control functions—requires a two-pronged analysis. One needs to analyze both the demand for citizen-assistance services and the response of the police to those demands. These phenomena require separate analyses because although the responses to requests for assistance are governed largely by factors flowing from and through the police bureaucracy, the requests for assistance are determined by factors largely outside and independent of that bureaucracy. This distinction has a number of analytical implications. The most important, however, is that although many of the ideas developed in Chapter 2 are relevant to an understanding of police response, they are not relevant to an understanding of the demand for citizen-assistance services. One must look beyond the notions of bureaucratic decision rules, resource constraints, and other bureaucratic considerations to develop an understanding of why consumers register demands for services.

Because much of the theoretical discussion up to this point has not been relevant to an understanding of the notion of demand, the following section will be devoted to an analysis of factors affecting demand. A preliminary model of the demand process will be presented, followed by some suggestions for how this model might be operationalized and tested. The final section will outline the research design and available data for the demand analysis. In Chapter 6 these data will be employed, in conjunction with the model, to assess empirically variations in the demand for police services in Champaign during 1976.

DEMANDS FOR CITIZEN-ASSISTANCE SERVICE: A PRELIMINARY MODEL

In sketching a model of the demand for police services, a number of different approaches are possible. For example, one might begin with the internal psychological makeup of individual consumers. Or one might start with the socioeconomic characteristics of these individuals or their immediate environment. Although each of these factors must eventually be considered, it is more useful to begin with a basic conception of the role of police within society. This approach is more fruitful because it focuses on what is unique about police functions and thus offers more direction and specificity in the development of a theoretical framework. Once the foundations of this framework are established, it will be possible to integrate psychological and socioeconomic considerations in a more meaningful way.

The only serious problem with building a model of the demand for police services around the basic notion of the police role is that most discussions of this concept are wholly inadequate. Traditional conceptions of the role of the police have focused on their crime-deterrence or peace-keeping functions, although what the police are called on to do, and what they actually do, encompasses a much broader range.

One police scholar who has not limited himself in this way is Egon Bittner. He addressed the broad question of the role of police in society and has offered a definition that provides a useful starting point for this analysis. Bittner suggests

> that police are empowered and required to impose or, as the case may be, coerce a provisional solution upon emergent problems without having to brook or defer to opposition of any kind, and that further, their competence to intervene extends to every type of emergency, without any exceptions whatever. This and this alone is what the existence of the police uniquely provides, and it is on this basis that they may be required to do the work of thief-catchers and nurses, depending on the occasion. And while the chances that a policeman will recognize any problem as properly his business depends on some external regulation, on certain structured social interests, and on historically established patterns of responsiveness and responsibility, every structure arising out of these factors is

defeasible in every specific case of police work. This means that the appropriateness of police action is primarily determined with regard to the particular and actual nature of the case at hand, and only secondarily by general norms. [Bittner 1974, p. 18]

In Bittner's view, then, the police, in response to a request or on their own initiative, rush to the scene of an occurrence that involves "something-that-ought-not-to-be-happening-and-about-which-someone-had-better-do-something-now" (Bittner 1974, p. 30). Once they arrive at the scene, police officers assess the situation, and in accordance with canons of common sense, devise and impose short-term solutions without regard to resistance. Thus, the special competence of the police revolves around the fact that "the policeman, and the policeman alone, is equipped, entitled, and required to deal with every exigency in which force may have to be used to meet it" (Bittner 1974, p. 35). The exercise of this capacity constitutes the bulk of what the police service-delivery system contributes to the community.

Although Bittner is concerned with the police service-delivery mechanism in general, his analysis seems even more appropriate for understanding citizen-assistance services provided by patrol divisions. It should be stressed, however, that although Bittner places a good deal of emphasis on the notion of coercive force, he does not mean that police routinely employ coercion, or that they are all called on only in situations in which coercive force may be required. Rather, he is saying that in most instances the police department is the only institution that can respond in situations where force *may* be required. The police are normally called on in situations where someone desires a coercive resolution to something, but they are also called on in a variety of other situations for a variety of reasons.

The main point of Bittner's analysis is that before the police are called, *something must happen*. Moreover, not only must something happen, but also *someone* must define that happening as within the realm of policing. These two steps are reflected in the first two stages in Figure 5–1. A burglary, a lost child, a rabid dog on the loose, an automobile accident— all these are considered by most people to be within the realm of policing. But to some people an extinguished pilot light, or the need for a ride to the hospital, or the belligerence of an undisciplined neighbor may also be defined as within the police realm. On the other hand, few would call the police to report that their child was getting the mumps or to complain that their garbage had not been removed or that they had just been fired.

The social determinants of "happenings" that give rise to calls for police services are difficult to specify and undoubtedly vary by type of demand. Commercial consumers are most apt to register calls about

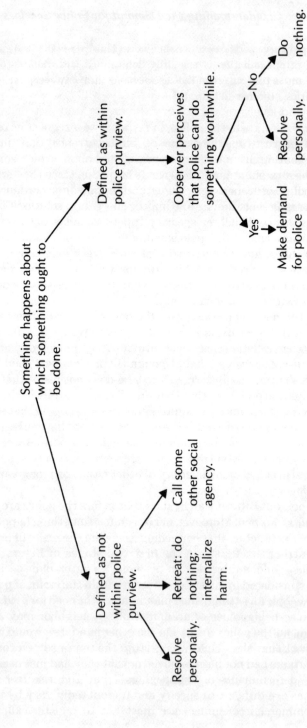

Figure 5-1. Preliminary Model of Demand-Making Process

thefts and perhaps about vandalism. Apartment dwellers may account for most burglary calls, whereas those living in high-density areas may register the most parking complaints. People living near centers of group activity (parks, commercial areas, busy streets, schools) may have higher overall demand levels merely because things are more apt to happen in such areas.

It is also difficult to specify what accounts for variations in people's decisions about whether a happening falls within the purview of the police. Political or governmental sophistication certainly plays a role, but can cut both ways. One might argue that more sophisticated citizens would be more likely to activate the public sector to resolve certain types of problems and would therefore have higher demand levels. However, one could also argue that more governmentally sophisticated citizens might well look beyond the police for the resolution of problems, whereas the less sophisticated "call the cops" for virtually every annoyance. Another factor that may influence someone's perception of an event is what might be called local custom. If police officers are routinely called into a neighborhood on a variety of matters, then this may in itself generate new demands. On the other hand, if the police are not routinely called, there may be greater general hesitancy to call them. A higher value may be placed on restraint or on handling the matter "among neighbors." This will tend to suppress demand levels.

The third step in the model depicted in Figure 5-1 is the determination by the potential caller that the police can do something about the situation. It should be stressed that the impact of this consideration is likely to vary according to the situation. Most citizens (except for the assailant) feel compelled to report a murder even when it is clear that the police can do little to uncover the criminal. They might not feel so compelled, however, if the incident in question involved a minor vandalism. This factor must be considered because, as with any meaningful action, there are costs and benefits involved when a citizen initiates a contact with the police. In most situations the citizen making the call would have to determine that the benefits outweighed the costs of requesting specific police services.

Examples of the costs involved would include waiting for the police to arrive, answering questions, filling out forms, going to the police station, and later going to court. In addition, there might be such costs as permanently damaged relationships with neighbors or family members and/or possible subjection to countercharges or some other type of retaliation or revenge. It should also be stressed that there might be costs involved in *not* calling the police. One is legally required to inform the police of certain types of accidents. Moreover, one is often under a social or moral, if not legal, obligation to inform the authorities of illegal conduct; failure to comply with this obligation could result in various types of psychic harm.

The benefits of calling the police would, of course, include the possibility of recovering lost or stolen property, of receiving restitution for damaged goods, and of retaliating against someone who did harm to you. In addition, it could result in having some continuing dispute resolved in one's favor or merely in enhancing the resources available to enable one to do something (such as find a lost child). There may also be psychic benefits available to one who enlists the help of the police to aid another.

ASSESSING THE MODEL

Although the model depicted in Figure 5-1 is a plausible reflection of the demand-making process, it is very rough and undoubtedly in need of the type of refinement that only careful empirical examination can provide. However, a "purist" test of the model would entail a major research effort beyond the present capabilities of social science. Just the problem of viewing individual responses to "something happening" would prove insurmountable. It would entail the assignment of observers to randomly selected individuals who would then wait for "something to happen"—an incredibly expensive, possibly invalid, and certainly socially unacceptable technique.

More indirect assessments are possible, of course. Service surveys could be conducted in a manner similar to crime-victimization surveys. Instead of defining certain crimes, the service survey could define different situations in which the police are frequently called on to act. Each respondent would then be asked a series of questions concerning a given situation, what he did about it, and why. Questions on general attitudes, orientation toward the police, and personal characteristics could also be asked. This would be valuable in determining the types of people who are most frequently involved in the different types of situations, as well as how they respond to them. This, in turn, could lead to insights into who benefits from this facet of police patrol services and why.

As desirable as these more direct research strategies may be, the resources needed to implement them were simply not available for this study. Thus, a more indirect assessment of the model (it cannot be called a test) must be undertaken. The basic data source for this study—to be described in the following section—is simply information on calls for services. These data were arranged so that they could be aggregated by block in order to determine demand levels and patterns throughout the city. It is this change in the level of analysis (from the individual level to the block level) that makes as assessment of the model depicted in Figure 5-1 less direct than other strategies.

Despite the indirect nature of the present research strategy, it does permit a rough examination of the model presented here and a general statement about patterns of demands. This is because blocks differ along certain dimensions that are meaningful in light of the model. Two general types of block characteristics are important for this analysis: physical-structural characteristics and sociopolitical characteristics.

As noted earlier, police services are usually requested because some event involving people has occurred. This means that the occurrence of police-related events is likely to be affected by human activity patterns. For a block-level analysis this means that the greater the density of human activity on any one block, the greater the probability that events will happen that require police assistance. Thus, the physical structuring of the environment is expected to affect the incidence of events. The existence (on a given block) of commercial centers, main intersections, apartment buildings, or congregating areas such as schools will be likely to produce more police-related events than will residential streets.

Once events occur, individuals must then determine whether or not it is appropriate or important or necessary to call the police for assistance. At this point it becomes necessary to understand the factors that might affect an individual's inclination to call the police for assistance. Two factors that appear to be significant in this respect are conceptions of the appropriateness of having a public agency resolve or deal with an event, and skill or sophistication in dealing with public agencies.

The first factor has to do with whether individuals believe that they should resolve their own difficulties, or whether they think it is more appropriate for the police to intervene. Americans differ in this regard (Sniderman and Brody 1977) in ways that tend to be associated with class variations and the area of activity involved. In the area of police services, these differences in self-reliance should become important as the "seriousness" of the incident declines. That is, there appears to be a general consensus that an incident involving a murder, mugging, robbery, or traffic accident should be reported; here self-reliance is likely to have little significance. As the incidents become less serious, or as it becomes less agreed on that the police should become involved, differences in demand levels should begin to show up. In areas such as family or neighborhood disputes or difficulties in lighting stoves, significant variations in demand should show up. The primary difference here should be across class lines.

The other factor that should affect demand levels is the experience or sophistication that individuals have in dealing with public agencies. Well-educated people, for example, will generally have more of the verbal skills necessary to make requests (Verba and Nie 1976, pp. 125–137) and therefore areas with such populations should be more inclined to make requests they deem appropriate. Previous experience with such matters should also play a role. Thus, areas with large numbers of local businessmen, who are used to interacting with public organizations such as the police, will probably make more requests than others, holding other factors constant.

DATA SOURCES AND DESIGN

To examine, even in a preliminary and indirect manner, the plausibility of the model developed here, requires the use of several different types of data. One type includes the kinds of calls for assistance that come into the Champaign Police Department and their distribution across the city. The second type concerns the physical-structural and sociopolitical characteristics of the areas from which the calls come. These two types of data required a number of different collection procedures and resulted in several different data sets. Finally, a variety of manipulations were done on each to construct and integrate data files and make them suitable for the required empirical analyses. This section will review these sources and procedures. First the calls for service data will be outlined and discussed; then the political, demographic, and locational data will be described.

Information on Calls for Service

Calls-for-Service Data File. The calls-for-service file is the basic data source for this study. It contains essential information for both the demand and response analyses. It was collected by a team of researchers from the Psychology Department at the University of Illinois pursuant to a contract with the Champaign Urban High Crime Program. These researchers systematically collected data on every incoming call for service that resulted in a patrol car being dispatched (that is, calls that were handled over the telephone were not included) during the last eleven months of 1976.[1] The number of cases in this data base (the call is the unit of analysis) totaled 30,518.

The information collected in this file included the dispatch number (a central index number), street address, type of location, time of call, time of dispatch, time of arrival, time cleared, number of cars sent, shift, and date. In addition, each incoming call was categorized into one of seventeen types. These seventeen call categories and their operational definitions are reported in Table 5-1. Although this is not the only way to categorize incoming calls for service, and there are admittedly some incidents that could fall in more than one category, the scheme reported in Table 5-1 is an eminently reasonable first attempt at a categorization of requests for police services. One problem, however, is that it is unmanageable for most analytic purposes. Thus, a refined seven-category typology was constructed, which will be used for most analyses. Rape, robbery, and murder were merged into a "serious-crime" category; burglary, theft, and vandalism into a "common-crime" category; and personal-assistance, investigation, peace-and-order, cars-and-traffic, and animal calls into a "service" category. Assaults, parking, and auto-accident calls were kept as separate categories. Finally, the "miscellaneous" category was enlarged by adding sex calls and alarms, two relatively infrequent types of calls.

After this calls-for-service data base was assembled and cleaned, the address information (street number, name, and direction) was used in conjunction with a computer-matching program (similar to the Census Bureau's ADMATCH program), to assign each call for service a census tract and block number corresponding to the block from which the call or incident came. Of the total cases in the calls-for-service data file, 76 percent were successfully "matched" with a tract and block number. There were five basic reasons for "no matches": (1) the street number was not within the range of the Census Bureau's DIME file (a master list of street names and numbers, which corresponds to block and tract numbers); (2) no street number was given; (3) the street name was not in the 1970 DIME file; (4) the street name was missing or incorrectly spelled; (5) the street direction (N, S, E, W,) was missing.

Perhaps the most troubling problem related to no matches is the fact that new streets (those constructed between 1970 and 1976) were excluded from the matched file. A visual inspection of the other no matches showed that they were randomly distributed across city streets owing to such things as misspellings. The exclusion of the new blocks is somewhat troublesome because it is systematic. It limits our ability to say anything about the police needs and demands of new neighborhoods. This limitation is not of paramount concern, however, because such an inquiry is not central to the research. In practical terms this limitation means that the city must be defined in terms of its 1970 boundaries. This does not present insurmountable validity problems, because it is doubtful that the exclusion of a few blocks would disturb any patterns that may emerge from the analysis.

Block File. To facilitate the analysis of the demands for police services, a block file was created. The unit of analysis in this file is the census block; it contains a case for each Champaign census block that

Table 5-1. Operational Definitions of Initial-Call Categories

Type	Definition—Example
Sex call	Peeping tom; child molesting; flasher; prostitution
Rape	Rape; attempted rape
Robbery	Armed or forceful attempt to take something from someone
Assaults/battery/ weapons	Intent of hurting is present or possible; physically hitting or threatening; fighting; threat; weapons (carrying and possessing, pulling gun or knife on someone)
Murder/manslaughter	Homicide; killing
Burglary	Breaking and entering; forceful entry to steal; unlawful entry with inference of intent to steal.
Theft	Having, buying, or receiving stolen property; larceny, counterfeiting, forgery, fraud; shoplifting
Vandalism	Intentional as opposed to accidental destruction of property; destructive hell-raising (kids kicking over garbage cans, kicking cars, throwing bricks at house; criminal damage to vehicle; man breaking street lights)
Accidents	Traffic accidents; hit and run; personal injury
Parking	Illegally parked car; abandoned car; car on private property
Calls for personal assistance	First-party calls: person usually wants help; escort; assist for deposit; keys locked in car; assist motorist; sick person; lost person; missing person; standby, extra patrol; someone needs assistance with no apparent legal violation; lost wallet; report of lost or found items; lost child; attempted suicide; overdose (drugs)
Animal	Stray or loose dog, cat, or wild animal; dog chasing mailman; opossum in garage; rabid dog
Peace and order	Third-party complaints: mediation or intervention between people often required (person who is object of call often neither wanted nor asked for police service); loud noise; disorderly conduct; family fight or disagreement; runaway teenager; trespassing; drunkenness
Alarms	Alarm indication
Investigations	Investigate reports of suspicious unknown persons, activities, events, or things (strange man, open window, broken window, prowler); unknown trouble call that turns out not to be in another category—intervention or mediation usually not required; possible legal violation; bomb threat; arson; abandoned children

Table 5-1. *Continued*

Type	Definition—Example
Cars and traffic	Misuse of cars, motocycles, minibikes, go-carts; suspicious vehicles; drag racing; loud cars; speeding; reckless driver; lost single license plate
Miscellaneous	Others (man running around with no clothes on—"streaking"); power lines down; back-up—county; unknown; ambulance

existed in 1970 ($n = 874$). Included in this file is summary information for each block from the calls-for-service data. Although a number of different summary measures were computed for each block (median response time, median time out of service, mean number of cars sent, and so on), the most relevant for the purposes of the demand analysis are frequency counts for each of the seven categories of service calls. These data are important because they provide information on demand levels across each block in Champaign for each general type of call.

Demographic, Political, and Locational Data

To analyze factors associated with variations in demands for various types of police services, several sets of independent variables—relating to the sociogeographic nature of each block—were added to each of the files outlined previously.[2] One set of variables can be considered basic demographic data. It is essentially all the block-level data collected in the 1970 census. This set included information on total population, percentage black, percentage under eighteen, percentage over sixty-two, average home or rental value, percentage rented, housing conditions, total units, average number of rooms, and other standard census measures. For industrial or commercial blocks there was, of course, no census information. Thus, they will have to be dealt with separately in the data analyses.

A second type of data collected can be labeled political. It includes the number of various types of elites, loosely defined, residing in each block in Champaign. Three basic types were identified. One included government leaders in each of two categories: (1) elected officials and heads of administrative agencies and (2) members of local commissions. One measure was computed for each of these two categories at both the city and county levels. The second type was a commercial-elite measure, which included all owners or heads of local businesses as determined by listings in the local city directory. The last type concerned civil elites. These included

Table 5-2. **List of Locational Variables Constructed**

Proximate to a main street
Downtown
Proximate to downtown
Outlying commercial center
Proximate to outlying commercial center
Campustown (a commercial center surrounding the University of Illinois)
Proximate to Campustown
Hospital
Proximate to hospital
High school
Proximate to high school
Elementary school
Proximate to elementary school
Park
Proximate to park
Church
Proximate to church

---

individuals identified as influential through a series of conversations with knowledgeable persons in the community. In addition, it contained people who served on bank boards, hospital boards, or the United Way board, as well as owners of local media.

The final set of independent variables includes those related to the geographical setting and termed locational variables. It was noted earlier that many types of police activities are initiated in response to something that has "happened." Moreover, it was suggested that those happenings that require police attention are not all randomly distributed throughout a community. Instead, many are more apt to occur at or near centers of communal activity: downtown areas, shopping centers, parks, schools, main streets, and so forth. Thus, a set of dummy variables was created indicating whether such a center was located on a block or set of blocks, or was proximate to a block (that is, the block bordered the center.) Table 5-2 summarizes the variables created.

Because these three types of data—social, political, and locational—were all keyed to census blocks in Champaign, it was a relatively simple matter to integrate them with the block file. This augmented block file will be used to conduct the demand analysis.

NOTES

1. Data were collected on every call during 1976; the box of data with January calls was misplaced by those who collected it.

2. It was possible to integrate this information with the various types of police data because the matching program described earlier assigned census block and tract numbers to each case in the various files. This made it possible to merge census information, which was also indexed by block and tract numbers.

REFERENCES

Bittner, Egon. 1974. "Florence Nightingale in Pursuit of Willie Sutton: A Theory of the Police." In *The Potential for Reform of Criminal Justice*, edited by Herbert Jacob. Beverly Hills, Calif.: Sage. (Reprinted in Bittner, Egon. *The Functions of the Police in Modern Society.* Cambridge, Mass.: Oelgeschlager, Gunn & Hain, 1980.)

Sniderman, Paul M., and Brody, Richard A. 1977. "Coping: The Ethic of Self-Reliance." *American Journal of Political Science* 21(August):501–521.

Verba, Sidney, and Nie, Norman H. 1976. *Participation in America: Political Democracy and Social Equality.* New York: Harper and Row.

Chapter 6

The Demand for Patrol Services

We turn now to indirect assessment of the demand model presented in the previous chapter. The various types of data contained in the augmented block file will now be used to explain differences in demand levels across the 874 blocks in Champaign. Two different demand analyses will be presented. First, the determinants of total calls will be analyzed. Second, in an effort to understand the differences in the determinants of individual call categories, a disaggregated analysis will be conducted. Here the dependent variables will be the total number of calls on each block for the seven call categories outlined in Chapter 5—serious crimes, common crimes, assaults, service calls, auto accidents, parking calls, and miscellaneous.

In both the aggregated and disaggregated analyses a set format will be employed in the regression analyses. First, a pair of control variables will be entered. These comprise the total population on a block and a dummy variable depicting whether or not the Champaign police share jurisdiction on a block with the University of Illinois police (scored 0 if no shared jurisdiction, 1 if there is jurisdiction). It is essential that these variables be controlled because they are likely to have an impact on call levels and, if not included, may well confound the real effect of the variables of theoretical concern. After the control variables are entered in the regression, the locational variables described in Chapter 5 are allowed to enter. These too are dummy variables, scored 1 if some center of activity is located on the block and 0 otherwise. Finally, the sociopolitical variables —the elite measures, the demographic variables (percentage black, percentage under eighteen, percentage female heads of households), and the set of dummy variables depicting each of the neighborhoods discussed in Chapter 3—are allowed to enter. This order of entry will permit the more immediate determinants of demand, which might be called need indicators, to explain much of the variance in demand levels as possible. The sociopolitical variables will then be used to explain the residuals.

THE DEMAND FOR PATROL ASSISTANCE: TOTAL CALLS

Using multiple regression analysis and the augmented block file described in Chapter 3 with total calls for service as the dependent variable, the following equation explained 54 percent ($R^2 = 0.536$) of the variance in 814 cases.[1]

$$
\begin{aligned}
\text{Totals} = {} & -4.5 + 0.078*\text{TOTPOP} - 49.9*\text{UPJURIS} \\
& + 106.1*\text{CAMPTWN} + 34.6*\text{DWNTWN} \\
& + 24.2*\text{COMMDIST} + 8.0\ \text{MNSTRT} + 5.3\ \text{PCHRCH} \\
& + 15.5*\text{PHOSPT} + 25.9*\%\text{RNTED} + 18.8*\text{CITYELTE} \\
& + 6.5*\text{COMMELTE} + 7.3*\text{WRKCLS} + 11.9*\text{STDNT} \\
& - 5.8*\text{SW} \qquad\qquad\qquad\qquad\qquad\qquad\qquad (6\text{-}1)
\end{aligned}
$$

where   TOTPOP = Total population
UPJURIS = University-police jurisdiction
CAMPTWN = Campustown dummy variable
DWNTWN = Downtown-Champaign dummy variable
COMMDIST = Outlying-commercial-district dummy variable
MNSTRT = Proximate-to-a-main-street dummy variable
PCHRCH = Proximate-to-a-church dummy variable
PHOSPT = Proximate-to-a-hospital dummy variable
%RNTED = Percentage rented
CITYELTE = Elected city officials plus top city administrative officials
COMMELTE = Commercial-elite measure
WRKCLS = White-working-class dummy variable
STDNT = Student-district dummy variable
SW = Southwest Champaign dummy variable

Table 6–1 shows several additional pieces of information on the aggregated demand regression.

Table 6-1. Essential Regression Information

Variable	Beta Weight	F Value	Significance Level (at or Beyond)
TOTPOP	0.20	62.1	.000
UPJURIS	− 0.13	25.5	.000
CAMPTWN	0.37	205.9	.000
DWNTWN	0.16	41.3	.000
COMMDIST	0.13	26.9	.000
MNSTRT	0.17	33.1	.000
PCHRCH	0.05	5.3	.05
PHOSPT	0.06	4.3	.05
%RNTED	0.20	38.9	.000
CITYELTE	0.08	9.8	.01
COMMELTE	0.08	11.5	.001
WRKCLS	0.07	8.0	.01
STDNT	0.09	9.1	.01
SW	− 0.06	4.3	.05

The Control and Locational Variables

Equation 6-1 and Table 6-1 reveal significant but not particularly surprising information about the control and locational variables. It turns out that if we control for population and jurisdictional overlap, the most important characteristics of a block, for the purpose of explaining variation in aggregate call levels, relate to the nature and level of human activity centered on or about the block. These results lend indirect support to important facets of the model presented in Chapter 5: citizen calls for patrol assistance can largely be understood as a response to "something happening." Where there is more activity, there is a greater likelihood of something happening that could give rise to a call for police assistance. Although this is very commonsensical, even mundane, it it the type of observation too frequently overlooked in sociopolitical analysis. An in-depth analysis offers further insights not readily apparent from the raw statistics.

The strength of the locational variable depicting the student-centered commercial area called Campustown shows most clearly the impact of activity on demand levels. It is the area of greatest density in the city. A significant proportion of the 35,000 students and several thousand faculty and staff members interact within and around Campustown each day. On weekends they are supplemented by local teenagers, air force personnel from nearby Chanute Air Force Base, and out-of-town visitors. In this relatively small area (fourteen blocks), traffic is extremely heavy, many younger drivers tend to drive recklessly, parking is sparse, there is a heavy concentration of bars, and there are numerous retail shops offering a variety of small items. All these features lead to situations that are likely to result in calls for police assistance.

The fact that the two other locational variables depicting commercial areas have very significant impacts upon demand levels, although to a much smaller degree than the Campustown variable, reflects differences in the nature and levels of activity. It also emphasizes their importance. Neither of these other two areas has the density that surrounds Campustown. Nor do they have as many habitues inclined to be as reckless or thoughtless as are many students. The impact of differences in activity levels can even be seen in the differences in the strength of the downtown and outlying-commercial-district variables. The latter is weaker because activity is less dense. Fewer businesses are spread over a greater space, and there is often ample parking in the outlying centers.

One last point should be made with regard to these three commercial districts. The greater demand levels in these areas should not be attributed solely to differences in need. They may by partially attributable to the greater sophistication and knowledge of local merchants. Frequent interactions between merchants and the police may give these individuals a better idea of what the police are about and what they can be used for; this in itself may give rise to higher demand levels. Moreover, the position of merchants in the community may even make it possible for them to assure that certain of their needs are defined as within the scope of police responsibility (escorting store personnel making bank deposits, assisting in the removal of cars illegally parked on private property). Both factors could have signficant, if only incremental, impacts on demand levels.

In the case of the "proximity" variables (main street, hospital, church) such a "sophistication and knowledgeability" interpretation would seem to carry less weight. Their impact on demand levels is probably simply the result of relatively higher activity levels—more cars, more people, more interactions. Moreover, it should be noted that part of the impact of the hospital variable may be artifactual. Many hospital calls may be the result of incidents that occurred elsewhere. The victim of an assault, for example, may not report it until he or she discovers the severity and/or cost of the injury, or until someone else (a nurse, for example) suggests reporting it. A final point that should be made regarding these proximity variables is that although several others were entered into the regression analysis (parks, high schools, elementary schools), only those reported here had a significant impact. Although no theoretical explanation for this can be offered, later research may suggest a more refined categorization that may in turn explain these patterns.

The final locational variable that had a significant impact was the percentage of units on a block that were rented (%RNTED). Although this is correctly categorized as a locational variable, it is somewhat different from the others and merits special discussion. In bivariate terms, this variable was the strongest predictor of demand levels ($r = 0.51$); its intercorrelations with such things as population and the Campustown and main-street variables, however, reduced its ultimate contribution. The source of much of this variable's potency undoubtedly lies with the fact that the relatively high density of apartment life gives rise to more incidents requiring police attention. This is particularly true with regard to parking and traffic problems and may even extend to burglary and vandalism.

However, although the density of apartment life is an appealing explanation for the impact of the rental variable, one may have to look beyond it to understand the real effect of this variable on demand. The transient nature of much apartment living, its impact on the relationships among neighbors, and its relative social heterogeneity should also be considered. The notion of transiency emphasizes a fundamental distinction between homeowners and renters. Homeowners have usually invested more money, time, and energy in their homes than have renters; and it is generally more difficult for them to move. Many renters may, in fact, be renters primarily because they anticipate moving in the near future.

Because of their greater commitment to their immediate vicintiy, homeowners have more interest in maintaining a civil atmosphere. More specifically, homeowners are more highly motivated to develop and to use informal methods of handling disputes. Few things are more unsettling to neighborly relationships than a call to the police to intervene in a dispute. Such interventions have doubtless led to innumerable social ostracisms, boundary-line fences, and shouting matches. These things are more troubling to the homeowner than the renter because the costs of extricating oneself from the situation are so much greater. The notion of social heterogeneity may also have an impact on the development and use of informal modes of dispute resolution, which may be more commonly used in areas dominated by single-family dwellings simply because these areas enjoy greater social homogeneity than others. By the same token, the greater heterogeneity of apartment dwellers may be a factor that inhibits the development of communication patterns and leads to the greater use of third-party mediators such as the police.

The Elite Variables

Although the two elite measures that had a significant effect in the analysis did not make a large contribution to the explanatory power of the equation, they are extremely important theoretically.[2] Moreover, it should be noted that a variables's contribution to the R^2 is not the only measure of its importance, especially (as here) in the case of dummy variables.[3] The B coefficient is also important; it can reveal the size of the difference in the predicted value of the dependent variable across categories of the independent variable, while controlling for other factors.

Consider, for example, a wholly residential block in Champaign's mixed district (not proximate to any significant center of activity), which has an average population (76 residents) and an average proportion of rental units (38 percent). Equation 6–1 can be used to estimate the residual call levels that would be expected from such a block, on the average, in an eleven-month period, as well as the number expected if the block had one or more elites residing on it. (These are termed residual call levels because, although they are computed "net of everything else," everything else is not randomly distributed throughout the city.) With no elites, 11.2 calls would be expected; with one or more city elites (and no others) residing on it, 30.0 calls would be expected; with one or more commercial elites (and no others), 17.7 calls would be expected. In other words, the difference in call levels is substantively significant on blocks where political and commercial elites reside (168 percent and 58 percent higher, respectively) in comparison with blocks with no elites.

To interpret the meaning of those results, one must turn again to the notion of governmental sophistication and knowledgeability; traditional "power-differential" interpretations will simply not explain them. People call the police when something happens to them, or around them, that requires the sort of attention or resolution they think the police can provide. People who are intimately involved on a day-to-day basis with government or commerce have a fairly sophisticated understanding of the scope of police capabilities, which they may communicate to others (in this case neighbors) through informal interactions or through observations.[4] The net result is higher residual call levels on blocks where various types of elites reside. These higher demand levels cannot be attributed to "power differentials" because the Champaign police routinely respond to most incoming calls.

The Neighborhood Measures

The final set of measures entered into the regression analysis were the dummy variables representing each of the neighborhoods discussed earlier. Only three of the five had a significant effect. The variables depicting the largely white working-class area and the student district were both positively related to the aggregated-demand variable, whereas the variable representing Southwest Champaign was negatively related to it. Here again, although the contribution of these variables to the explanatory power of the equation was not great, an examination of the B coefficient reveals that neighborhood does make a substantive difference.

Consider again, for illustrative purposes, a wholly residential block with an average number of people living on it, but with no elites and with an average proportion of rental units. If this hypothetical block were in the student district, Equation 6–1 would predict an aggregate demand level of 20.3, whereas if it were in the white working-class area it would predict 18.5. The predicted level would be 5.4 in Southwest Champaign and 11.2 in the mixed district and the Northend.

The picture presented by these results is of relatively higher residual demand levels in the student and white working-class areas, with lower residual levels elsewhere, especially in Southwest Champaign. A number of factors could account for these patterns. The relatively high residual call level for the student area, for example, could be a reflection of lifestyle. Students spend a large part of their four-year stay in Champaign in a relatively circumscribed, densely populated area surrounding and including Campustown and the university. Personal and physical space is often hard to find. In addition, because of their age, they are more rambunctious, on the average, than citizens in other areas. The combination of these factors probably involves students in more situations that require outside intervention or assistance. Also, many students may lack the maturity or the social skills to deal independently with many problems and, hence, are more prone to seek outside assistance.

If the Northend is excluded, for the moment, the differences in residual call levels outside the student district can be viewed in terms of social class. As one moves from the largely white working-class area in the northern sector of the city, through the socially mixed district in the heart of the city, to the predominantly white middle- and upper-middle-class area in the southern part (Southwest Champaign), one finds decreasing residual (as well as actual) call levels.

A number of factors could plausibly explain this pattern. First, it may be that the differences are simply reflections of differences in the nature and level of activity in the areas (that is, there are more loud parties, more drunks, more traffic problems, more common crime, and so forth in working-class areas than in middle-class areas), even controlling for differences in the location of various activity centers. Although this might account for the observed pattern, an equally plausible explanation may lie in the differing veiws across class lines on the legitimacy of "calling the cops." Working-class people may see such a move as a perfectly acceptable tool in their arsenal of techniques for coping with social problems. In many noncoercive or nonthreatening situations, however, middle-class people may be more hesitant to call the police because they place a higher value on self-reliance. To call for a third party to intervene in nonthreatening situations could be an admission of defeat. Moreover, they would be calling on individuals who have historically been considered of lower status than themselves, thus presumably less intelligent and less capable of dealing appropriately with noncoercive situations. Finally, in middle-class neighborhoods there may be a certain stigma attached to calling the police routinely for all but the most pressing reasons.

Regardless of whether this class-based interpretation is appealing, race confounds it. If class had a simple and direct relationship with aggregate residual call levels, then one would expect residual call levels in the largely black Northend to be at least as high as, if not higher than, those in the adjacent white working-class area. Instead, the Northend has residual call levels comparable to those in the largely white mixed district. The reason for this discrepancy probably lies in the recent history of the relationship between the Northend community and the police, briefly described in Chapter 4. The hostility that characterized this relationship could well have suppressed demand levels in the Northend by leading people to resolve many problems internally rather than call on an outside agent that they regarded with some animosity.[5]

One last point should be made with respect to the findings on the effect of the neighborhood variables, as well as of the two elite measures. If one simply examined the bivariate relationships between these measures and aggregate demand levels (that is, if the role of the more immediate determinants of demand were ignored), a markedly different picture would emerge. Table 6-2 shows a breakdown in the total-calls variable and the neighborhood and elite variables. It suggests that if the more immediate determinants of demand had not been considered, one would have missed entirely the impact of race in placing demands for police services. Moreover, although the breakdown of the elite variables approximates the final results, the differences reported in Table 6-2 are not statistically significant. They do not become significant until the "percentage-rented" variable is entered into the regression analysis. Therefore, their impact would also have been missed if the locational factors had not been controlled for.

THE DEMAND FOR POLICE SERVICES: DISAGGREGATED

This section extends the model that emerged from the analysis of all calls for patrol services to the seven-fold categorization introduced in Chapter 5. That categorization included serious crime (murder, rape, robbery); common crime (burglary, theft, vandalism); assault (assaults,

Table 6-2. Breakdown of Total-Calls Variable by Neighborhood and Elite Categories

Independent Variable	Mean Number of Calls	N
Neighborhoods		
Southwest Champaign	10.2	(138)
Mixed district	18.2	(311)
White working-class area .	24.0	(148)
Northend	30.1	(56)
Student district	61.9	(95)
Commercial areas	46.7	(67)
Commercial elites		
None on block	23.4	(547)
One or more on block	31.4	(327)
City elites		
None on block	26.1	(855)
One or more on block	41.6	(19)

threats, batteries); service (personal assistance, peace and order, traffic, animal calls, investigations); automobile accidents; parking problems; and miscellaneous (calls not categorized elsewhere, alarms, miscellaneous sex calls). It is important to disaggregate this analysis because it is unlikely that calls as diverse as serious-crime calls and parking or service calls will be influenced in a similar way by a common set of determinants.

It is doubtful, for example, that the happenings giving rise to serious crimes will be accurately reflected in the locational variables used here. It is just as unlikely that the observations made with regard to the elite and neighborhood measures are relevant to serious offenses. On the other hand, the role of the elite and neighborhood measures may increase in areas such as service or parking calls.

Table 6-3 reports B coefficients and F values (in parentheses) for each variable across the total-calls variable and the seven component categories, as well as the R^2s. In comparing the R^2s across the component categories, it is evident that a good deal of variation exists. The model does most poorly with the serious-crime and miscellaneous categories. This is probably because the happenings that give rise to such calls are not well represented by the locational variables used here. These variables probably capture variation in activity *levels*, which do a better job of explaining more common and routine incidents such as parking problems and automobile accidents. Indeed, it is doubtful that an aggregated, block-level analysis such as this could produce a refined understanding of complex phenomena like murder and rape, since these

Table 6-3. Regression Information for Disaggregated Analysis

	Population	University-Police Jurisdiction	Campustown	Downtown	Outlying Commercial District	Proximate to a Main Street	Proximate to a Church	Proximate to a Hospital	Percentage Rented
Total calls	0.078	−49.9	106.71	34.6	24.2	8.02	5.3	15.53	25.94
	(62.1)	(25.5)	(205.9)	(41.3)	(26.9)	(33.1)	(6.3)	(4.3)	(38.9)
Serious crime	—	0.465	—	—	0.209	0.572	0.107	—	0.282
		(5.7)			(5.22)	(4.33)	(6.9)		(13.1)
Common crime	0.015	−10.0	17.44	—	—	1.43	—	—	5.2
	(33.61)	(17.8)	(74.9)			(14.5)			(22.3)
Assaults	—	—	5.8	1.77	1.97	—	—	2.4	1.2
			(121.5)	(21.5)	(35.9)			(20.4)	(20.8)
Service	0.034	−16.7	24.5	9.04	10.2	2.65	2.05	6.4	12.4
	(60.6)	(16.4)	(57.6)	(14.8)	(25.5)	(18.6)	(4.9)	(3.9)	(51.8)
Auto accidents	—	−4.3	17.1	2.94	3.95	1.8	—	3.2	2.6
		(9.98)	(242.4)	(13.5)	(33.0)	(78.6)		(8.3)	(21.6)
Parking	0.021	−14.64	28.1	4.2	—	7.2	0.99	—	3.27
	(112.7)	(51.5)	(335.7)	(14.5)		(6.3)	(5.4)		(16.1)
Miscellaneous	—	—	10.3	14.6	2.73	1.18	—	—	—
			(24.4)	(93.8)	(4.4)	(8.98)			

	City-Elite Measure	Commercial-Elite Measure	Southwest Champaign	Mixed District	Northend	White Working-Class Sector	Student District	Constant	R^2
Total calls	18.8 (9.9)	6.5 (11.5)	-5.8 (4.3)	—	—	7.31 (8.0)	11.9 (9.1)	-4.5 (4.34)	0.54
Serious crime	—	—	—	—	—	—	0.199 (6.6)	—	0.13
Common crime	—	1.67 (10.14)	-4.93 (20.9)	-4.2 (22.99)	-4.94 (15.1)	-2.23 (5.2)	—	2.8 (8.1)	0.38
Assaults	—	—	—	—	1.35 (21.3)	0.64 (12.95)	—	—	0.31
Service	5.7 (4.6)	3.14 (14.0)	-3.1 (6.23)	—	—	5.1 (20.54)	—	—	0.42
Auto accidents	—	—	—	—	-1.3 (4.2)	—	—	—	0.49
Parking	—	1.77 (3.9)	—	—	—	—	9.96 (151.0)	-2.46 (42.8)	0.57
Miscellaneous	9.4 (30.6)	—	—	—	—	—	—	—	0.22

are so dependent on immediate, situational factors such as an intense fight, the availability of a weapon, or the presence of an unaccompanied woman in a deserted area.

If the different sets of variables (control factors, commercial districts, proximate variables, elite measures, neighborhood variables) are examined across call categories, other important insights can be gained. With respect to the control variables, it is of some interest to note that population drops out as a predictor of serious crime, assaults, and miscellaneous calls. This is, of course, consistent with the previous observation that certain types of calls are largely attributable to unique factors, more immediate than those available for this analysis. The fact that population drops out in automobile cases is also not surprising, since one would not expect population to be a major factor in the location of accidents. Moreover, to the extent that it is relevant at all, one would think that accidents would be high both where population was low (commercial areas) and where population was high (apartment complexes).

If the three commercial-district variables are examined across each category, it becomes clear why the Campustown variable was so much stronger than the other commercial-area variables. Auto-accident and parking calls, two concomitants of congestion, are extremely high. The strength of the Campustown variable, however, is not entirely the result of these three categories. It also has the strongest effect of any variable on three of the remaining five categories: assaults, common crime, and service.

As for the proximate variables, perhaps the most interesting results pertain to the hospital variable. The greatest impact of this variable is in the assault and accident categories, reinforcing the possibility that the higher call levels are the result of incidents that occurred elsewhere, with persons being brought to the hospital for medical treatment. It is also instructive to note that, although the percentage-rented variable is significant in every category except one, its greatest impact is in the service area. Since this category includes personal-assistance and peace-and-order calls, these findings lend indirect support to the notion that the higher call levels in rental areas result partially from the effects of transiency and social heterogeneity on communication patterns among tenants.

The disaggregated view of the two elite measures is also revealing, especially with regard to the city-elite measure. Table 6–3 shows that there were only two categories in which the city-elite variable (depicting the residences of elected officials and heads of administrative departments) made a significant difference: the miscellaneous category and the service category. Both can be viewed as relatively discretionary types of calls, which supports the view that these higher residual call levels are at least partially due to greater governmental sophistication and knowledge. The case is somewhat less persuasive with regard to the commercial-elite variable unless parking calls can be viewed as discretionary, as is often the case.

Table 6–3 suggests two interesting things about the neighborhood variables. First, the overall impact of the student-district variable is almost wholly a reflection of its impact on parking calls. Second, with the exception of a very strong positive effect on assaults, the pattern of the Northend variable closely resembles that of the Southwest Champaign variable. This is important because, given its social composition, one would expect a pattern more closely resembling the variable representing the white working-class area. This pattern again lends support to the view that the history of hostile relations between the police and some segments of the black community has suppressed demand levels in the Northend.

In summary, a number of things can be said about the results of the two demand analyses. First, it is clear that activity levels—as indicated by both the control and locational variables—plays the dominant role in determining demand levels. Demands on the police are greatest in places where things are most likely to happen. Somewhat less conclusive is the observation that governmental sophistication and knowledgeability also affect demand levels—especially for the more discretionary types of police services. Lifestyle evidently also plays a role, as seen in the impact of the rental and student variables. Finally, social class appears to affect demand levels, at least for whites. Across the largely white neighborhoods in Champaign, there appears to be a greater hesitancy to call the police in more middle-class areas. A similar hesitancy (after locational variables are controlled) exists in the Northend, which is composed largely of blacks. This hesitancy may be the result of a number of different factors such as the recent history of animosity between blacks and the Champaign police, discriminatory treatment of blacks, and a general distrust of the police by blacks. The response analyses will shed light on some of these matters.

NOTES

1. There were 874 total blocks, or cases, in the block file. In the case of 60 blocks, however, nothing was known about them. They were uninhabited at the time of the 1970 census and were not part of a commercial area captured in one of the locational variables. Thus, the unidentified blocks could have been empty lots, new residential areas of unknown composition, light industry, or some combination. Because their composition could not be determined easily, they were excluded from the analysis. It should also be noted that there were 13 commercial blocks that had no residents and, hence, no census information. These 13 were given the mean score on the TOTPOP and %RNTED variables.

2. Several other elite measures did not have a significant impact. These included the measures of the civic elite, a measure of secondary city political elites (those appointed to part-time city commissions), and two measures of county political elites that were comparable to the two city measures. Why they were not as important as the commercial and primary city-elite measures will become clear in the interpretation of the results.

3. In the case of dummy variables a variable's contribution to the R^2 is dependent on its distribution as well as on the difference in the means of the two categories. A variable that is split evenly between the two categories will have a greater impact than one that produces a similar difference in means but is highly skewed in one direction or the other. This was the case with the city-elite variables where there were only 18 blocks with elites on them.

4. It should be stressed that these findings do not, indeed methodologically cannot, mean that elites themselves make extraordinarily large numbers of calls. They simply mean that, controlling for other factors, blocks where elites live have higher residual call levels. It is not possible with the available data to determine whether the calls are coming from the residences of elites or those of their next-door neighbors, or from persons wholly unknown to them. Nor it is possible to say anything about how, or even whether, the elites' greater sophistication is communicated to their neighbors.

   Another point is relevant here. The reason that the city political- and commerical-elite variables were significant, whereas the other elite measures where not, may lie in the fact that members of the latter group do not have as good or as broad a grasp of local affairs as members of the former. County governmental elites certainly would not be expected to understand city affairs as completely as do the elected and administrative city leaders; and members as part-time city commissions would also not be expected to have as broad an understanding. None would have as much contact with the police as would members of the commercial elite.

5. A survey conducted to gather baseline data for an evaluation of a team-policing experiment that ran in the Northend between May 1977 and March 1979 found that blacks called the Champaign police for "personal assistance" less frequently than whites. After the team-policing experiment had been deployed for a year and a half, however, a follow-up survey reported that this difference in the inclination to call had been eliminated. This change was accompanied by positive perceptual changes in blacks' views of the police. For a summary of these results, see Peter F. Nardulli, "Team Policing and Police Services: An Experiment that Works," Illinois Government Research, No. 48, April 1979, Institute of Government and Public Affairs, Urbana, Ill.; for a more in-depth discussion of team policing and its relationship to community relations and crime, see Peter F. Nardulli, "Police Deployment Strategies and the Delivery of Police Services," Law and Policy Quarterly 2 (1980):420–444.

IV: POLICE RESPONSE

Chapter 7

Analyzing Police Response

Although patrol divisions within urban police departments spend a good deal of time simply patrolling, another of their main activities is responding to and handling service calls. These calls range from simple service calls to traffic accidents to serious crimes, as was demonstrated in Chapter 5. The remainder of this book will be concerned with an understanding of police responses and their distributional consequences. It should be stated at the outset that police response is a complex phenomenon, and there are many ways to assess and evaluate it. Indicators of police response could include such diverse things as the number of squads sent to answer a call, the amount of time it takes to get to the scene, the extensiveness of the file report, whether or not a detective is assigned to a case, the demeanor of the officer, and the kind of official action taken (such as a ticket or an arrest). This section concentrates on three general dimensions of response: speed, effort, and outcome. Although some of the previously mentioned response indicators fall within one of these categories and will be used in the following analyses (response time, number of cars responding, number of tickets issued, and so on), others clearly do not (demeanor).[1]

How these three dimensions were operationalized and the types of factors affecting them will be clarified in the next three chapters. Before we turn to these tasks, however, we must say something about the approach and design employed in producing them. Because the paradigm used in most contemporary studies of service delivery was inadequate for present purposes, an alternative approach had to be developed. The following section will demonstrate the inadequacies of the prevailing paradigm. A proposed alternative, along with its limitations, will then be presented. Finally, the research design used to organize the response analysis will be discussed.

APPROACHES TO
ANALYZING POLICE RESPONSE:
THE PREVAILING PARADIGM

To achieve the objectives set forth here—to obtain a better understanding of police responses and their distributional consequences—it is necessary to go beyond the dominant paradigm in empirical studies of urban services. The paradigm directs researchers to select various indicators of a given service and then to compare them across neighborhoods or census tracts that vary in their social, political, and/or economic makeup. A brief example using police data on Champaign will illustrate the shortcomings of this approach.

Table 7–1 reports a breakdown of several indicators of police services across the various neighborhoods in Champaign.[2] The first two factors might be considered indicators of police response, and the last two could be considered measures of resource dispersion. A number of interesting observations can be made on the basis of these data. Perhaps the most striking is the contrast between the figures for Southwest Champaign and those for the Northend. They are uniformly the opposite of what one would expect on the basis of what Lineberry (1977) calls the "underclass hypotheses." Fifty percent more police respond almost twice as fast in the Northend as in Southwest Champaign. Calls per assigned officer are almost 2.5 times as great in Southwest Champaign, and the average number of blocks an assigned squad must cover is almost 3 times as great. Another point worth mentioning is that this rather crude breakdown is consistent with earlier service-delivery studies, which find that the underclass hypotheses are unconfirmed or reversed (Lineberry 1977; Mladenka and Hill 1978) or that find and inverse relationship between workload and service-delivery indicators (Jones 1980).

As clear as some of the differences in Table 7–1 seem, one should not accept these findings as indicative of real distributional patterns, nor should one be content with such a paradigm in this area of study, for several reasons. First, if the data in Table 7–1 are examined in light of some of the demand patterns discussed in Chapter 6, one could argue that they may simply be the result of differences in need. In other words, if

Table 7-1. Service-Delivery Indicators by Neighborhoods

Area	Average Median Response Time (Minutes)	Average Numbers of Cars Responding to Call	Average Call per Officers Assigned	Average Blocks per Squad Assigned
Southwest	9.5	1.1	4,208	325
Northend	5.3	1.5	1,748	114
Student district	6.3	1.2	3,984	88
Working class	7.5	1.2	2,917	196
Mixed district	7.6	1.3	4,411	268
Nonresidential areas	5.3	1.1	3,533	136

response time and the number of cars responding are related to the type of call, then differences in call patterns may account for the differences observed in Table 7-1. For example, it was noted in Chapter 6 that assault calls were disproportionately high in the Northend and that noncriminal service calls were disproportionately high in blocks inhabited by elites. Such differences may well account for the observed patterns. Moreover, if characteristics of the calls were controlled, one might even find that the pattern of findings is reversed, that is, in similar situations members of the underclass receive relatively worse service.

Even if one could overcome these objections and the findings in Table 7-1 could be accepted, a second criticism would be relevant to the approach employed in producing them: they do not tell us very much about the delivery of police services. Although the prevailing paradigm may (or may not, for reasons similar to those cited here) yield distributional insights (who gets what), there are other important questions to be asked in this area, which this approach is not well suited to answering. Most of these questions concern the structure of service delivery. It is, of course, interesting to know the impact of sociopolitical factors and whether or not class or racial discrimination exists. But these sociopolitical factors are not the only factors that influence the delivery of urban services. For example, although the racial composition of a neighborhood may affect the number of police squads sent to calls from that neighborhood, so might such things as the seriousness of the call, the number of witnesses present, or the presence of a weapon. In order to understand the service-delivery process, one must integrate the impact of these factors into some type of conceptual framework appropriate for analyzing the process.

One final point is relevant here. Even if one were interested only in addressing distributional questions, there are at least two reasons that a different, more inclusive approach to the service-delivery process would still be necessary. First, up to this point urban-service researchers have viewed discrimination almost wholly as an additive phenomenon. That is, they have hypothesized that race or class will have a direct linear relationship with whatever indicators of service are under scrutiny. However, it is wholly possible that the relationship between these variables might be more complex. If, for example, professional-rational criteria dominate the procedures for disbursing a service, it might be that race or class affects the implementation of those criteria—that is, that an interactive relationship exists between professional-rational criteria and sociopolitical criteria. Consider, for illustrative purposes, the amount of effort expended on the investigation of a burglary case. The primary criterion for expending effort might be the amount of evidence available. However, for a given amount of evidence more effort might be expended in cases where the victim is white or middle class than where the victim is black or lower class.

A second reason for approaching the service-delivery process from a more inclusive perspective in order to understand its distributional implications concerns the possible existence of statistical suppression effects (Cohen and Cohen 1975, pp. 87–91). Under certain circumstances the real relationship between two variables will be obscured unless another is controlled. For example, when X_1 is positively related to Y and to X_2 but X_2 is negatively related to Y, the real relationship between X_2 and Y will be suppressed unless X_1 is controlled. This is particularly relevant to the study of urban services because there are many instances in which professional-rational criteria (indicators of need, for example) may be positively related to both service measures and sociopolitical indicators such as class or race. If, in addition, a negative relationship exists between these sociopolitical indicators and service levels, that relationship might be obscured in statistical analyses unless professional-rational considerations such as need are controlled.

AN ALTERNATIVE APPROACH

To avoid the pitfalls noted previously, the traditional approach has been modified somewhat. First, the unit of analysis employed is the individual response, as opposed to the neighborhood or census tract. Second, whereas earlier studies have been concerned primarily with the impact of sociopolitical factors on the service process, the present study has a somewhat broader focus. A further discussion of these differences will underline their significance.

The Unit of Analysis

Earlier works have utilized an aggregated unit of analysis in their quantitative work primarily because they have been interested in the distributional facets of service delivery (Levy, Meltsner, and Wildavsky 1974; Lineberry 1977; Mladenka and Hill 1978; Bloch 1974). In other words, these authors wanted to know the impact of an area's sociopolitical characteristics on the level or quality of services it received. Although this approach may have been adequate for these limited purposes, once the focus of their interest shifted to the role of bureaucratic decision rules, their methodology became inadequate. It is virtually impossible to do more than speculate about the nature or content of bureaucratic decision rules when the data are aggregated from service disbursements or cases (police calls, housing inspections, environmental-code violations) to geographical locales (blocks, tracts, neighborhoods). This is because bureaucratic decision rules are sets of criteria used to routinize the handling of situations that vary in their makeup. If all service situations were the same or required the same handling, either there would be no need for decision rules or such rules would be trivial. But this is not the case. In many areas situations handled by service deliverers vary significantly, and decision rules provide cues for handling these situations that may lead to variations in service delivery. When these service units are aggregated to geographical units the distinctiveness of the situations giving rise to different service disbursements is lost; it then becomes difficult if not impossible to document empirically the criteria affecting disbursements. This in turn makes it difficult to assess the content and role of decision rules in the service-delivery process.

The importance of this last point—the need to assess empirically the content and role of decision rules in the service-delivery process—cannot be overemphasized. Up to this point the primacy of bureaucratic decision rules in the service-delivery process is no more than a hypothesis arrived at in a post hoc fashion (that is, after sociopolitical expectations were not realized). Moreover, it is a hypothesis that concerns merely a *source* of influence on the service-delivery process. Although this is important to note because it focuses attention on the internal facets of the service bureaucracy and service deliverers, the mere identification of these rules as a source of influence says very little about their *content*, as was argued in Chapter 2. Many different types of influences can be reflected in the decisional criteria embodied in decision rules. Thus, the next logical step in this area of inquiry is to focus on the content of these influences and to assess their meaning for the service-delivery process. To do this it is necessary, in most instances, to shift from aggregated units of analysis to those that capture the disbursement of services in individual situations.

Broader Focus

To take this next step in this area it is necessary to adopt a broader empirical focus. Because of the substantive concerns and the methodology of earlier researchers, much of their research efforts involved the collection of data on the sociopolitical characteristics of the geographic units with which they were dealing. This research effort differs in that equal (or more than equal) emphasis was given to collecting measures of resource constraints and situational variables tapping important differences in service encounters. Measures of resource constraints are important because they are thought to have an impact independent of the effect of bureaucratic decision rules. These constraints place an upper limit on what can be done. For example, a decision rule pertinent to pothole repair may be that large potholes get filled first. The quality and level of pothole repair in an area, however, will be dependent on the resources (materials, personnel, equipment) available to the street department. In the area of policing, it may be a decisional criterion to give priority to emergency calls. However, at a given point in time the speed of a response to an emergency call will be strongly influenced by the number of available squads.

Situational variables are important because they provide a means, albeit indirect, to assess the impact of different decisional criteria on the various dimensions of police response. It is important to assess the role and nature of these decisional criteria because of their prominence in the literature and because of the expected importance of decision rules in the determination of police response. These decisional guides are expected to be influential here because police response—unlike demand—is largely under the control of the police department and the responding officers. Moreover, despite the uniqueness of many police-citizen encounters, the range of possible responses and the acceptable criteria relating circumstances to responses are fairly limited. This permits a good deal of routinization in response behavior, thus making decision rules feasible tools in decisional activity.

The following attempt to outline the nature and role of different decisional criteria will be indirect and inferential. To uncover in a direct manner the content of relevant decisional criteria would require an extensive amount of field work. Agency handbooks would have to be analyzed, hierarchical and line personnel would have to be systematically interviewed and observed, and shift meetings and informal gatherings would have to be attended. Moreover, an assessment of the impact of the array of decisional criteria that these efforts would be likely to uncover would require observing police-citizen encounters, systematically interviewing police personnel, and collecting and analyzing police files on individual cases.

Since the extensive field requirements of this more direct approach were beyond the resource limitations of this study, a more tentative and indirect one was employed. Data on situational and sociopolitical factors were collected and will be used in an attempt to infer something about the content of the criteria used in responding to citizen calls for police services. Situational variables include such things as the seriousness of the occurrence (extent of injury, damage, or theft); the type and amount of available evidence; the relationship between the parties; and whether or not a weapon was used. Sociopolitical variables include such things as the characteristics of the parties involved in the incident (race, sex, age) and the characteristics of the block or neighborhood from which the call came (number of elites, identity of the neighborhood, racial composition). To the extent that such things as seriousness and evidentiary matters affect what happens in a case, it will be inferred that professional-rational criteria affect response; to the extent that such things as race and neighborhood characteristics affect what happens it will be inferred that sociopolitical criteria affect response.

Despite the fact that this approach does permit some specificity about the content of criteria affecting police response and will provide some insights into the police service-delivery process, its shortcomings should be underscored. First, this approach makes it impossible actually to *test* the impact of decision rules as a general source of influence on the service-delivery process. To the extent that the various situational and sociopolitical variables have an impact on the various dimensions of response, we will infer that the source of their influence on the process emanates from the abstract notion of "decision rules." But this is quite different from molding a set of decisional criteria into a decision rule on the basis of extensive field work, and then testing the impact of this set of criteria on a specific decision.

A second noteworthy shortcoming is that the limited approach outlined here constitutes only a partial operationalization of the ideas embodied in Chapter 2. Four general types of decisional criteria were discussed: professional-rational, environmental, work-group, and individual. Obviously, very little can be said about the role of work-group or individual criteria with the approach employed here. Virtually no information is available on work-group norms and values or on the attitudes, beliefs, or predispositions of police personnel. A final, related shortcoming concerns the interpretation of sociopolitical variables. In Chapter 2 it was argued that sociopolitical influences on the service-delivery process could emanate from several sources—hierarchical pressures, individual beliefs and attitudes, and work-group practices. However, given the rather crude methodology employed here, it will be possible only to determine whether or not a given set of sociopolitical influences has an impact on a given dimension of police response. Little can be said about the structure of the linkages between these influences and the service-delivery process.

THE DESIGN OF THE RESPONSE ANALYSIS

Although this book is designed as a fairly intensive study of the police service-delivery process in one jursidiction, it is evident that a comprehensive analysis of every facet of this process was not possible. Another limitation is that the response analysis will be conducted only in selected substantive areas. In Chapter 5 it was noted that calls for service were originally classified into seventeen different categories. For the demand analysis this number was reduced to seven: serious crime, assaults, common crime, service, auto accidents, parking, and miscellaneous. Of these seven, three were selected for the response analysis. These categories were chose because (1) each was reflective of a very different type of police activity, and (2) situational follow-up information was systematically collected by the police and available for analysis.[3]

The first category selected was assault cases. Here police are presented with situations that vary greatly in terms of seriousness and the closeness of the relationship between the parties, and in which a suspect is usually present, known, or knowable. The second category will be referred to as common crimes. It includes vandalism, burglary, and theft cases, broadly defined. The seriousness of these cases also varies a good deal. As distinguished from assault cases, however, the relationship between the parties is normally nil. Also unlike assault cases, most common-crime cases involve real ciminal violations as opposed to private disputes. It should also be noted that a suspect is seldom present or easily ascertainable in common-crime cases, with the notable exception of certain types of theft and some vandalism. The final type of call sample was automobile-accident cases. Although these again vary in seriousness, they seldom involved true criminal violations (drunk-driving cases being the notable exception), although they may involve civil liability. Traffic cases thus involve largely administrative tasks, unlike assault and common-crime cases.

Sampling

Although each of the three types of case files was filed sequentially (by date of occurrence) a slightly different sampling strategy was used to

Table 7-2. Breakdown of Sample Attrition in Response Data Files

	Assault	Common Crime	Auto Accidents
Original number sampled	636	2,659	1,751
Number with missing calls-for-service data (usually because event occurred in January 1976)	16	336	1,481
Total with call-for-service card that were not matched with census tract and block	143	485	270
Proportion without a calls-for-service card or without a census match	23%	21%	18%

select cases in each category, primarily because the size of the various files differed (for example, there were many more accident cases than assaults). Thus, every assault case during 1976 was selected; every other burglary, vandalism, and theft case; and every third auto-accident case ($n = 636, 2,659, 1,751$, respectively). Once these cases were selected they had to be integrated with the calls-for-service data set (described in Chapter 5) and then "matched" with census block and tract numbers. These procedures were necessary because the calls-for-service data set contained important measures of police response (response time, number of cars sent, time out of service) and because a census block and tract match was essential to describing the sociopolitical characteristic of the block or neighborhood from which the call came.

As essential as these two procedures were for obtaining information pertinent to the response analysis, each led to some sample attrition. This made it impossible to use all sampled cases in every analysis of response. This attrition is summarized in Table 7-2. The sampled cases were integrated with the calls-for-service data by a central dispatching number that appeared on both. Where this number was missing or was incorrect, the calls-for-service data could not be added to the file data. Much of the loss here occurred because all the calls-for-service data for January 1976 were missing. A second source of sample attrition was the fact that not all the addresses on the calls-for-service card could be matched with a census tract and block. These nonmatches are reported in row 3 of Table 7-2. They are largely the result of missing or incorrect addresses and of occurrences on "new" blocks, those that are not in the 1970 DIME file and that consequently have no census block and tract numbers or data. There were several reasons that cases that had valid information on a calls-for-service card were not matched with census tract and blocks. These are tabulated in Table 7-3.

Table 7–3. Breakdown of Cases That Had Call-for-Service Cards but That Were Not Matched with Census Information

	Assault	Common Crime	Auto Accidents
Total nonmatches	143	485	270
Total not matched because street number not in DIME range	53	220	NA
Total not matched because no street number given	8	19	NA
Total not matched because street name not in DIME file	25	98	NA
Total not matched because no street name given	25	47	NA
Total not matched because of inadequate street-direction information	15	61	NA
Total not matched for other reasons	17	40	NA

Types and Sources of Data

To conduct even the limited analyses described in the preceding section required a number of different types of data derived from several sources. In terms of dependent variables, the data on the three dimensions of police response (speed, effort, outcome) came from both the police file and the calls-for-service data. Speed, for example, will be measured by response time, which comes from the calls-for-service data. Various effort indicators will be used, although all are neither available nor relevant across all three case categories. These indicators include such things as time out of service and number of cars sent to the scene, which come from the calls-for-service data. Effort indexes from the police-records data include such things as the assignment of a detective, the thoroughness of the report, the existence of one or more supplemental reports, and the application of police technology. The outcome measures, the relevance of which also varies by type of case, all come from the file data. Included here are indicators of charge severity, the making of an arrest (where a suspect is identified), and the issuance of a ticket.

Three different general types of independent variables are required for the proposed response analyses; each was derived from a different source. The first type includes measures of resource constraints. The information generally used to construct these measures included the average number of calls for the last eleven months of 1976 in each beat-shift (Beat 6, morning shift, for example), the average number of officers and cars

Table 7-4. Resource-Constraint Variables by Beat

Beat	Calls per Average Assigned Officers	Calls per Average Assigned Squads	Blocks per Average Assigned Officers	Blocks per Average Assigned Squads
1	3,903	4,890	74	93
2	1,748	3,287	61	114
3	4,007	5,399	64	87
4	4,208	4,452	307	325
5	4,759	5,031	185	195
6	3,225	4,637	151	217

assigned to each beat-shift (computed by examining daily logs for the first two weeks of every other month beginning with January 1976), and the number of blocks in each beat. From these data four measures were computed: the average calls per officer for the shift-beat in which the call was reported; the average officers per block in the beat in which the call originated; the average number of patrol cars assigned per block in the beat in which the call occurred.

There was a good deal of variance in these measures, as seen in Table 7-4, which is a breakdown of the four measures by beat. The limitations of these measures cannot, however, be stressed too much. In most of the analyses what is important is the interplay between resources and demands at the time of the call; these measures are only crude approximations of that interplay. They are, however, all that is generally available.

The second type of required variable included situational variables. The data on these variables were derived wholly from police files. Although the situational variables available for the response analysis varies somewhat across the three types of cases, they included such things as the seriousness of the incident (nature of injury, amount of theft or damage); the existence of evidence; the type of location; road conditions; and the nature of the accident (rear ender, head-on collision). In addition there was information on the presence of the defendent at the scene, the time elapsed between the incident and the call, the nature of the relationship between the parties, and so on. The forms used to collect this information are contained in Appendix A.

The last type of independent variable to be used in the response analysis is the sociopolitical variable. One sociopolitical variable of interest here concerns the characteristics of those involved in the incident. Such information was found in police files. Included here are data on the race, sex, and age of the participants. Although not all of this information was available for traffic cases, a rough SES measure was devised using the type of cars involved in the accident. For assault and common-crime cases, another type of sociopolitical variable was considered: the characteristics of the neighborhood or block from which the call originated. This is considered irrelevant for traffic accidents because of the relative randomness of their location. Information on the block and neighborhood from which a call originated was available only for those cases that could be matched with a census block and tract (see Table 7–2).[4] Where block and tract could be identified, it was possible to categorize cases into one of the six neighborhood types described earlier. Cases that occurred in residential areas could also be categorized in terms of block characteristics, such as the number of elites residing on the block, percentage black, percentage rental housing, and so on.

NOTES

1. These three general dimensions of response were chosen because they could most easily be integrated within a single research design utilizing official police records. The inclusion of a "police-demeanor" dimension, although highly desirable, would have required the use of extensive observational or interview data and was beyond the scope of this study.
2. The data in Table 7–1 are "means of medians" or "means of means" and are from the block file described in Chapter 5. For example, the response time variable in the block file is the median response time for each call that came from a block during 1976. The figure reported in Table 7–1 is the average of the median time for all blocks within each neighborhood. The average number of cars responding is a mean of means. The calls-per-assigned-officer and cars-per-block data were computed by using information on the average number of cars and officers assigned to each beat and information on the number of calls for each block within a given beat as well as the number of blocks within each beat. This information was used to calculate the average number of calls per officer for, and the average number of cars assigned to, each block. These then were broken down by neighborhood.
3. It should be noted that the choice of cases to sample was limited because (1) the number of serious crimes (murder, rape, armed robbery) was too small to permit quantitative analysis; and (2) written police records are not systematically collected on parking, service, and miscellaneous calls.
4. Because of the correspondence between the neighborhood designations used in this study (Northend, student, Southwest, and so forth) and the police beats observed in Chapter 4, it was possible to identify the neighborhood even in some instances where a given case was not matched with a census block and tract.

REFERENCES

Bloch, Peter B. 1974. "Equality of Distribution of Police Services." Washington, D.C.: Urban Institute, February.

Cohen, Jacob, and Cohen, Patricia. 1975. *Applied Multiple Regression/ Correlation Analysis for the Behavioral Sciences.* New York: John Wiley.

Jones, Bryan. 1980. *Service Delivery in the City.* New York: Longman.
Levy, Frank S.; Meltsner, Arnold J.; and Wildavsky, Aaron. 1974. *Urban Outcomes.* Berkeley: University of California Press.
Lineberry, Robert L. 1977. *Equality and Urban Policy.* Beverly Hills, Calif.: Sage.
Mladenka, Kenneth R., and Hill, Kim Quaile. 1978. "The Distribution of Police Services." *Journal of Politics* 40:113–133.

Chapter 8

Responding to Violence: The Handling of Assault Cases

What many view as the unique competence of the police is epitomized in the handling of assault cases. Here the police are frequently called on to rush to a relatively undefined situation where something is "happening" and to impose some type of order, perhaps requiring the use of physical force. The police must also decide which party is to blame and whether formal (or informal) sanctions are to be initiated. In addition to its importance vis-à-vis various conceptions of the police role, the handling of assault cases has significance in its own right. These incidents involve situations in which fundamental social rights may be threatened or violated. The manner in which these situations are handled may have important implications for the future security of the individuals involved as well as for their perceptions of and orientations toward the police and other governmental institutions.

Despite the importance of police response in assault cases we know very little about it. Criminologists have reported that many cases of assault occur between people with prior relationships (spouses, lovers, coworkers). They have also reported in detail on the types of weapons used in assaults, the severity of injury, and the social characteristics of the parties. What has not been studied in detail is the way police respond to assault cases and how the previously mentioned characteristics, and others, affect that response. This chapter will attempt to shed some light on this issue. Elaborating the general perspective outlined in Chapter 7, it will examine variations in several dimensions—speed, effort, outcome—of police response in assault cases. This will include a look at the structure of police response as well as an assessment of the distributional facets of police actions. First, however, an overview of the assault cases examined will prove helpful.

CHARACTERISTICS OF ASSAULT CASES

Although there were 692 assault cases in the files of the Champaign Police Department for the year 1976, only 636 of these were included in this analysis. The 56 missing cases (8 percent) had such problems as missing files or garbled, unintelligible reports. Table 8-1 reports the main offense involved in each incident as well as its statutory classification and maximum possible penalty. Of the 636 cases, 458 (72 percent) were cleared by the Champaign police. However, not all were cleared by arrest. Of the 458, in fact, precisely half (229) were cleared by means other than arrest. Of the 229 cases that were not cleared by arrest, 209 (91 percent) were accounted for by "refusals to prosecute."

Although there is a good deal of variation, the median response time for assault cases in Champaign is about 6 minutes (median = 5.8). About 90 percent of all calls are answered within two hours, with the remainder requiring several hours. In over half of all cases (54.1 percent), only one car is sent to the scene, whereas in another 30 percent two cars are sent. Once at the scene, officers normally spend about 14 minutes (median) on an assault call, although extreme cases can take several hours to resolve. Most investigations (72.8 percent) are completed in one day and require no more than a routine report. Others are more complicated. In 30.6 percent of all cases, one or more supplemental reports were filed and the mean time required for an investigation to be completed was 2.7 days (some extreme cases required more than a month). Detectives were assigned to 30.2 percent of all assault cases.

The diversity in the responses by the Champaign police department is matched by, and in part is a reflection of, the diversity of situational factors embodied in assault incidents. For example, not all assault cases are reported immediately. Although 15 percent of all incidents are reported immediately and about half (48 percent) are reported within 10 minutes, other calls (about 14 percent) do not come into the police department until several hours after the incident. Another 6 percent are not reported until the next day, or later. A related fact is that in over 76 percent of all cases the defendant does not appear to be at the scene of the incident at the time of the call. There was also some meaningful variance in terms of where the incident occurred. Almost 40 percent of all inci-

Table 8–1. Offense Distributions and Possible Penalties

Offense	Relative Frequency (Percentage)	Offense Type	Maximum Penalty
Simple assault	5.0	Class C misdemeanor	$500 fine
Simple battery	38.7	Class B misdemeanor	6 months, county jail
Aggravated assault	12.7	Class A misdemeanor	1 year, county jail
Aggravated battery	41.8	Class 3 felony	1–5 years, state penitentiary
Miscellaneous	1.8		
	100.0		

dents, for example, occurred within a private residence; and another 37 percent occurred at a public location such as a school, park, or street. The remaining 23 percent occurred at commercial settings such as taverns or restaurants.

Table 8–2 reports data on two dimensions pertaining to the gravity of the incident,the extent of the injury, and the mode of attack. This data makes it clear that, although over 35 percent of all incidents involved weapons and over 20 percent resulted in some type of serious injury, a greater percentage involved physical or verbal abuse and resulted in minor injury, or none at all.

About 70 percent of the assault incidents analyzed here involved one assailant attacking one victim. The social characteristics of these participants introduce another dimension to this overview. Of the participants described as the assailant in these encounters, 85.3 percent were males and 54.3 percent were black. However, only 51.9 percent of the victims were males and only 40 percent were black, indicating a good percentage of intersexual and interracial conflict. Further analysis revealed that 42 percent of the incidents were intersexual and 22 percent were interracial. Eighty-eight percent of all intersexual incidents involved male defendants and female victims, and in 80 percent of all interracial incidents the black was labeled the assailant and the white was labeled the victim. It should also be noted that where the nature of the prior relationship between the victim and the assailant is known, 75 percent of male assailant—female victim cases involved close or personal prior relationships (husband-wife, boyfriend-girlfriend). However, in 54 percent of black assailant—white victim cases there was no prior relationship between the participants.

The last set of figures introduces a dimension that may be relevant to certain facets of this analysis—the nature of the relationship between the

Table 8-2. Nature of Injury and Mode of Attack

	Percentage
Nature of injury	
None (intimidated only)	34.8
Cuts and/or bruises—no medical attention required	42.4
Cuts and/or bruises—required medical attention	21.0
Injury requiring hospitalization	1.8
	100.0
Mode of attack	
Handgun or rifle	10.7
Other weapon	25.0
Body	60.2
Voice	4.1
	100.0

parties. Criminological research has long shown that in violent episodes such as assaults, there is a high probability that the participants have had some type of prior relationship. This is important here because what the police do may be tempered by this relationship. Table 8-3 presents data on these relationships. It is clear that where the relationship is known, it is fairly evenly divided among the personal, casual, and "none" categories.

SPEED

Several factors emanating from several different sources are considered relevant to an understanding of how long it takes the police to respond to a call for assistance (time of arrival at scene minus time of call). One important source of influence here concerns the policies and practices of the dispatcher's office. In Champaign during 1976, incoming calls were received and screened by a desk officer. Those meriting a response were transmitted to the dispatcher, who was in an adjacent room. The dispatcher used a simple rule of thumb for most cases—first come, first served. A caller's position in the queue determined how quickly a car was dispatched; this in turn influenced how quickly a call was answered by a patrol car. There were exceptions, of course. Emergencies, for example, were always given top priority. A serious accident, a violent assault, or a robbery in progress would always receive precedence over routine service calls. In extreme cases cars would even be pulled off routine cases to respond to an emergency.

Table 8–3. Nature of Prior Relationship Between the Participants

	Frequency	Relative Frequency
None	163	25.5
Casual (acquaintances, coworkers, landlord-tenant)	162	25.5
Close (boyfriend-girlfriend, neighbors, long-standing or recurrent relationships)	43	6.8
Personal (spouses, family members)	171	26.9
Unknown	97	15.3
	636	100.0

The problems involved in measuring the role of this decisional criterion —first come, first served, except in emergencies—would be enormous. An observer would have to spend large blocks of time watching the dispatching process and systematically recording responses. The effect of this criterion on response time will, therefore, be assessed indirectly. A surrogate measure, the elapsed time between the time a call was received and the time a car was dispatched (dispatch time), will be used. This measure, as well as being a component of response time, is also an excellent surrogate of car availability and the dispatcher's perception of the gravity of the incident, both of which are crucial for assessing the role of the first-come, first-served criteria.[1] Under normal circumstances, if a car is available it will be dispatched to a call immediately, since dispatchers do not normally "sit" on calls. In emergency situations available cars will be diverted from other assignments. A lengthy dispatch time would indicate that no emergency existed and no car was immediately available. Thus, a curvilinear relationship between dispatch time and response is hypothesized. It is expected that officers, once dispatched, will respond much more rapidly to calls that are immediately dispatched than to those that have lengthy intervals between the call and the assignment.

The dispatch-time variable is relevant to the response analysis because it captures—although it does not distinguish between—relevant conditions within the responding service agency (the availability of cars) and the situation giving rise to the call for service (the gravity of the situation). There are, however, other situational factors that are relevant to the response-time analysis but are not captured by the dispatch-time variable. One such factor is the alleged assailant's presence at the scene. Regardless of the gravity of the occurrence, the assailant's presence is apt to prompt a quicker response than would otherwise occur. If the officer can arrive at the scene while the alleged assailant is still there, it will save him a good deal of work, especially if an arrest is warranted.[2] A second situational factor that might be relevant here is the amount of elapsed time between the incident and the call to the police. The longer the time, the less apt the officer is to rush to the scene once dispatched. One final type of situational variable expected to be relevant here is the nature of the relationship among the participants. Here it is expected that the greater the distance between the participants, the quicker the response time. The greater uncertainty inherent in situations involving strangers prompts this hypothesis. Officers are expected to respond more quickly in order to prevent subsequent disruptions.

Another type of variable—related neither to the situation nor to the dispatching process—is the size of the beat that must be traversed in responding to a call. The number of blocks contained within beats in the newer part of the city, which had expanded into the cornfields surrounding Champaign, had increased in the years before 1976 with little concomitant adjustment in beat designations. The older beats (in the northern and eastern sections of the city) are relatively smaller. Because of the impact of different-sized beats on traveling time, it is expected that the number of blocks in the beat from which a call comes will be positively related to response time.

The final type of variable to be examined in the response-time analysis is the sociopolitical variable. The variables to be used here are standard ones that will be used throughout most of the analyses on police response (with the exception of the traffic-accident cases). They include a set of dummy variables representing each of the Champaign neighborhoods; a dummy variable depicting the existence of one or more "elites" on the block from which the call came;[3] and variables depicting the age, race, and sex of the participants.

With response time as the dependent variable, Equation 8-1 explained 92 percent of the variance ($R^2 = 0.917$) in 472 assault cases.[4]

$$\text{Speed} = 3.03 + 1.11*\text{DSPTCHTM} - 0.001*\text{DISPTCHTM}^2$$
$$+ 0.007*\text{BEATSIZE} - 1.23 + \text{PRES} - 1.04*\text{INTERVAL}$$
$$+ 0.72*\text{RELTYPE} - 0.58*\text{CPLTSEX} \qquad (8\text{-}1)$$

where SPEED = Response time (in minutes).
　　DSPTCHTM = Dispatch time (in minutes).
　　BEATSIZE = Number of blocks in the beat from which the call came.
　　PRES = Presence of the assailant (1 = present, 0 = not present).

INTERVAL = Length of time between incident and call
(1 = less than ten minutes, 0 = more than ten
minutes).
RELTYPE = Type of relationship between the participants
(1 = close or personal, 0 = none or casual).
CPLTSEX = Sex of the complainant (1 = male, 0 = female).

All variables in Equation 8–1 are significant beyond the .05 level and most well beyond that. Table 8–4 reports essential data on the regression analysis.

Although the regression analysis explained a high proportion of the variance, primarily because of the dispatch-time variable, not all of the hypotheses were confirmed. For example, although the beat-size and dispatch-time variables were significant and the relationship between dispatch time and response time was curvilinear, the squared-dispatch-time variable was significant in the wrong direction. The problem here was revealed by an examination of a scattergram between dispatch time and response time. For less extreme cases the curvilinearity between those two variables was in the proper direction. In cases where the response time was extremely long, however, the curvilinearity was reversed. Moreover, because these are extreme cases, they weight the squared term in a negative direction. What the data mean, substantively, is that there is a fairly low upper limit on traveling time within the city. Although this traveling time can be reduced somewhat for emergencies (which accounts for curvilinearity in the nonextreme cases), it cannot be extended proportionately for nonpriority calls. Thus, whereas traveling time for a call that is dispatched immediately is perhaps only two minutes, traveling time for one that is not dispatched for one hour is only eight minutes and is not apt to get any longer even if the dispatch time is one and one-half or two hours. This unforeseen complication obscured the hypothesized relationship.

The three situational variables discussed earlier—the presence of the alleged assailant at the scene, a dichotomized version of the interval variable, and a dichotomized relationship variable—all had mild effects on the dependent variable in the hypothesized direction. Although the results here do not merit further discussion, it should be noted that a more comprehensive and systematic analysis of situational factors might well lead to others that are important for understanding police response time.

The sociopolitical variables were the least successful of the various types of variables employed in the speed analysis. The only such variable that had a direct effect on response time was the sex of the victim. Calls from women received quicker responses. No other characteristics of the

Table 8–4. Essential Data on the Speed Regression

Variable	Beta Weight	F Value	Significance Level (at or Beyond)
DSPTCHTM	1.00	1,376.6	.000
DSPTCHTM²	− 0.09	11.9	.001
BEATSIZE	0.05	15.5	.001
DPRES	− 0.06	13.4	.001
INTERVAL	− 0.06	15.1	.001
RELTYPE	0.03	5.0	.03
CPLTSEX	− 0.03	4.9	.03

participants made a difference, nor, with one partial exception, did the neighborhood variables. A breakdown of the beat-size variable revealed that the number of blocks in a beat was linearly related to response except for the largest category of beat size, which included Southwest Champaign and the mixed district. To test the possible significance of this interaction effect, the Southwest and mixed dummy variables were merged into one dummy variable (a middle-class-neighborhood dummy variable), and an interaction term was created using this and the beat-size variable. Although both were entered and were significant beyond the .01 level, one must be careful in interpreting this finding.[5] The results do not support the conclusion that middle-class residents get absolutely faster service than others. Rather, considering the fact that the police travel across more blocks, they seem to respond to calls from middle-class neighborhoods more rapidly than to those from other areas.

One last comment is in order with respect to the speed analysis and the sociopolitical variables. One might contend that the dispatch-time variable was masking the true effects of these variables. If differential treatment is accorded cases by the dispatcher—dispatch delays in calls from black neighborhoods, for example—the powerful impact of the dispatch-time variable on response time would eliminate any effects the sociopolitical variable might have. To check this possibility, correlations were computed between the dispatch-time variable and all the sociopolitical variables. Only one significant relationship was uncovered. The correlation between dispatch time and the dummy variable representing the while working-class sections of Champaign was 0.18, which was statistically significant at the .001 level ($n = 555$). In the absence of more patterned results, however, this single finding cannot support the view that the dispatch-time variable "obscures" the true effect of the sociopolitical variables.

EFFORT

Effort is a more slippery notion than the other two indicators of police response used in this analysis. The concept of speed is straightforward and easily measured, as are outcomes such as arrests, tickets, and charging decisions. Effort, however, suggests a plethora of indicators. These include how many cars were sent to a call, "out-of-service" time for the officer(s), extent of the initial report, length of time before the report was completed, number of supplemental reports, whether or not a detective was assigned, whether any evidence was sent to the state crime lab, and so on.

Despite the abundance of such indicators, not all are equally meaningful. What does it mean, for example, that some reports are completed within three days, yet others are not completed for a week? Would such a finding have allocational implications? Correspondingly, of what consequence is not having evidence for a case sent to the state crime lab when local facilities suffice? Because of these difficulties, this analysis will be restricted to effort indicators with fairly straightforward interpretations. These are the number of cars responding to a call, the length of time spent on the call (time out of service), and whether or not a detective was assigned to the case.

It should be stressed that these three indicators are very distinct phenomena. Moreover, the decisions affecting them are made by different people in different contexts. The dispatcher, for example, will normally determine how many units are sent to a call, although the desk officers and/or the assigned officer will often make recommendations. Moreover, on rare occasions an officer riding a beat will radio in advice on the need for a backup. In contrast, the amount of time spent out of service is largely determined by the officer handling the call. In emergencies, however, the dispatcher, with the backing of the shift commander, could reassign an officer. The decision to assign a detective is determined largely by the assignment detective. He receives case files daily, evaluates them, and decides whether a detective will be assigned and who it will be.

Although decisions affecting these effort indicators are made by different individuals in different contexts, it is possible to identify certain general types of factors common to each. In terms of professional-rational considerations, one could view various situational factors related to the concept of need and resource constraints as the primary determinants of the amount of effort expended on a case. Situational variants such as whether or not the defendant is present at the scene, the number of participants involved in the incident, the number of available witnesses, the severity of injury, and whether or not an arrest was made seem relevant to an understanding of how much effort is expended. More serious or in-volved situations simply require more effort than do routine incidents. Resource constraints are also relevant here because, like all municipal agencies, police departments work with a fairly fixed amount of re-sources. Where extra cars or time or officers are not available, they cannot be utilized, regardless of the immediate requirements of an incident. Thus, holding other factors constant, it is expected that the amount of effort expended on cases arising in shift-beats with high service-call-to-resource ratios will be less than the effort expended on cases arising in shift-beats with low service-call-to-resource ratios.

In addition to the professional-rational factors mentioned here, socio-political considerations are also expected to be relevant to decisions affecting the amount to effort expended on a case. These concerns are rele-vant because the department, as well as individual officers, is expected to be much more responsive to demands from the upper strata of the com-munity than to those from the lower strata. It is easier, for example, to tell welfare recipients that no more can be done for them than to tell the same thing to the owner of a local bank or retail store. Moreover, even in the absence of demands by members of the upper strata of the community, one might expect these persons to receive disproportionate expenditures of effort. Extra effort may be expended in responding to calls in better neighborhoods simply to ward off complaints from people who may have the influence to act on their dissatisfaction.

Up to this point we have focused on professional-rational and socio-political considerations simply because the nature of this study makes it possible to assess their impact on the selected effort indicators, if only indirectly. Other types of factors that are also likely to affect the expendi-ture of effort merit discussion even though they are beyond the scope of this study. Following the framework briefly introduced in Chapter 2, two other types of considerations may be relevant to decisions affecting the amount of effort expended in a case. One type concerns factors emanating from the values, interests, and norms of work groups. For example, a well-understood norm might relate to the length of time it takes to handle a given type of call. Officers who routinely consume more time might develop reputations as loafers. On the other hand, those who routinely take less time may earn reputations as rate busters or "hot dogs," and the quality of their work may even be called into question.

In addition, there are factors emanating from the values, beliefs, and aspirations of individual officers that can also affect effort. One of these is very general. Younger, college-educated, or ambitious recruits may have aspirations for an ultimate position in the police hierarchy. They may therefore expend greater amounts of effort, across the board, than older, more cynical officers who are simply awaiting retirement. A second way in which the individual attributes of officers may affect effort concerns their assessment of different situations. One officer, for example, may have a great deal of empathy for the victims in wife- or child-beating cases. Thus, in such situations he might be expected to expend disproportionate amounts of effort. Other officers may have other priorities and would be expected to allocate their resources accordingly. To examine this further, of course, one would need information on the views of individual officers as well as relevant information on the situations.

The Number-of-Cars Regression

With the number of cars sent to a call as the dependant variable, Equation 8-2 explained 31 percent of the variance ($R^2 = 0.313$) in 486 assault cases,[6] and Table 8-5 shows other important information on the NUMCAR regression.

$$NUMCAR = 1.7 + 0.73*PRES + 0.51*INTERVAL$$
$$- 0.12*DSPTCHTM - 0.39*OFCRLOAD \qquad (8\text{--}2)$$

where   NUMCAR = Number of cars sent to the scene.
               PRES = Presence of the assailant
                           (1 = present, 0 = not present).
    INTERVAL = Length of time between incident and call
                           (1 = less than ten minutes, 0 = more than ten minutes).
  DSPTCHTM = Dispatch time (in minutes).
   OFCRLOAD = Total number of calls for service in the shift-beat from which the call came. Average number of officers assigned to the shift-beat from which the call came.

Even though only a moderate proportion of the variance in the NUMCAR variable was explained, it is clear that surrogates of considerations categorized as professional-rational dominate. Neither the neighborhood characteristics nor any of the social characteristics of the participants in the incidents affect the number of cars dispatched. In contrast, the presence of a suspect at the scene, the speed of the dispatch, and the length of time between the incident and the call all affect the NUMCAR variable in the expected direction. Where the defendant is present and where there is some evident urgency (as indicated by the INTERVAL and DSPTCHTM variable), more cars are sent. This is a rational

Table 8–5. Essential Data on the NUMCAR Regression

Variable	Beta Weight	F Value	Significance Level (at or Beyond)
PRES	0.33	63.2	.000
INTERVAL	0.27	42.7	.000
DSPTCHTM	−0.11	7.7	.005
OFCRLOAD	−0.16	16.8	.000

allocation because more manpower may be needed in such situations. The negative relationship between the OFCRLOAD variable shows that where resource constraints are greatest (in shift-beats where the call-to-manpower ratios are greatest), the number of cars sent is somewhat lower than would otherwise be the case.

The Time-Out-of-Service Regression

With the amount of time out of service (measured in minutes) as the dependent variable, Equation 8–3 explained 9 percent of the variance ($R^2 = 0.094$) in 423 cases,[7] and Table 8–6 reports essential data on the SERVTM regression.

$$SERVTM = 7.2 + 5.4*INJRY + 11.7*PHYSEVID + 7.3*GUN$$
$$+ 7.9*PRES + 8.7*SOUTHWEST \qquad (8-3)$$

where   SERVTM = Time out of service (in minutes).
             INJRY = Extent of injury (1 = none, 2 = minor, 3 = required medical attention, 4 = required hospitalization).
     PHYSEVID = Existence of some physical evidence (1 = 1 or more pieces of physical evidence, 0 = no physical evidence).
            PRES = Presence of the defendant at the scene (1 = present, 0 = not present).
             GUN = Presence of a gun in the incident (1 = present, 0 = not present).
    SOUTHWEST = Whether or not the call came from Southwest Champaign (1 = Southwest, 0 = all other neighborhoods).

Table 8-6. Essential Data on the SERVTM Regression

Variable	Beta Weight	F Value	Significance Level (at or Beyond)
INJRY	0.17	12.6	.000
PHYSEVID	0.16	10.0	.002
PRES	0.14	8.2	.004
GUN	0.10	3.6	.057
SOUTHWEST	0.10	4.6	.03

Although the proportion of variance explained is quite low, the factors affecting the SERVTM variable was somewhat similar to those in the NUMCAR regression, with one exception. The INJRY, PHYSEVID, GUN, and PRES variables are each positively related to how long it takes an officer to handle an assault call. Moreover, all these variables are reflective of complicating factors in a situation that requires greater expenditures of effort. This, of course, justifies their categorization as factors reflective of professional-rational criteria. For example, situations where the injuries are extensive may require some first aid, a ride to the hospital, or a wait for an ambulance. These situations may also require more attention to detail and/or more extensive interviewing—as might situations involving a gun or those in which physical evidence is available and needs to be catalogued. Finally, incidents where the suspect is still present are apt to require extensive arbitration on the part of the officer. Such arbitration is essential to good police work because the disputants frequently must deal with one another on a continuing basis.

The basic difference between the SERVTM and NUMCAR regressions is the role of the SOUTHWEST variable. Although its impact is not strong, it does appear that with the other factors controlled, officers tend to devote more time to calls in Southwest Champaign than to those in other areas of the city. The "other-factors-controlled" aspect of this finding should be stressed because the SOUTHWEST variable does not have a significant effect on SERVTM without controlling for its more immediate determinants. This also demonstrates the importance of including professional-rational factors in empirical studies of urban services.

The Detective Regression

With whether or not a detective was assigned to the case as the dependent variable, Equation 8-4 explained 13 percent of the variance

($R^2 = 0.132$) in 618 cases; and Table 8-7 reports essential information on the DETECTIVE regression.

$$\text{DETECTIVE} = 0.21 + 0.31*\text{CLEARED} - 0.21*\text{PRES}$$
$$+ 0.16*\text{JUVENILE} + 0.16*\text{EVIDLINK}$$
$$- 0.08*\text{ID\#S} + 0.09*\text{MIDCLASS} \qquad (8\text{--}4)$$

where DETECTIVE = Whether or not a detective was assigned (1 = assigned, 0 = not assigned).

CLEARED = Whether or not the case was cleared (1 = cleared, 0 = not cleared).

PRES = The presence of the suspect at the scene (1 = present, 0 = not present)

JUVENILE = Whether or not the suspect was a juvenile (1 = juvenile, 0 = adult).

EVIDLINK = The presence of a piece of evidence that is linked to a particular suspect (1 = evidence exists, 0 = no evidence exists).

ID\#S = Number of eyewitnesses (1 = 0, 2 = 1 or 2, 3 = 3 or more).

MIDCLASS = Whether or not the call came from a middle-class neighborhood (Southwest or mixed) (1 = middle-class neighborhood, 0 = all other neighborhoods).

The DETECTIVE regression is similar to the other two effort analyses in that the factors that do affect the assignment of a detective are reflective of professional-rational criteria. If one were to ignore the low proportion of the variance explained by Equation 8-4 and were to extrapolate a bit from the findings, it could be said that detective resources are used primarily where they can do some good or where they are needed. Consider, for example, the impact of the CLEARED variable. This indicates that detectives are more apt to be used where a suspect is known and where, therefore, some work presumably needs to be done on the case. This is, of course, not to say that detectives are not also employed in attempts to find an unknown assailant or that the work of detectives does not contribute to a case being cleared—it undoubtedly does. Usually, however, detective resources are not squandered on cases with no leads or suspects. This view is supported by the impact of the EVIDLINK variable, which showed that a detective was more apt to be assigned if existing evidence was linked to a particular suspect. Because detectives can "do some good" in a case where the linkage between evidence and a

Table 8-7. Essential Data on the Detective Regression

Variable	Beta Weight	F Value	Significance Level (at or Beyond)
CLEARED	0.31	47.9	.000
PRES	−0.19	19.9	.000
JUVENILE	0.15	14.7	.000
EVIDLINK	0.10	6.2	.01
ID#S	−0.11	5.2	.02
MIDCLASS	0.08	4.6	.03

suspect needs to be established or protected, they are far more frequently assigned to such cases than to others.

The negative effects of the PRES and ID#S variables shows that detectives are more apt to be assigned to cases where they are needed than to other cases. For example, where the suspect is present at the scene, there is less need for a detective (that is, no one needs to be tracked down). Correspondingly, detectives are less apt to be assigned where the police have already been in contact with the suspect. A similar interpretation holds for the number of eyewitnesses. The more there are, the stronger the case and the less need to expend detective resources.

The last point to be made about the DETECTIVE regression is that, as was the case in the SERVTM analysis, it appears that the better neighborhoods get slightly better service. The impact of the MIDCLASS variable in the DETECTIVE regression was, however, somewhat different from the impact of the SOUTHWEST variable in the SERVTM analysis. Whereas the SOUTHWEST variable was not significant until the more immediate types of factors were controlled, the impact of the MIDCLASS variable was much stronger before the other factors were controlled. Thus, the utilization of professional-rational factors also helps put the role of sociopolitical influences in their proper perspective.

OUTCOMES

Two outcome measures will be used here in an attempt to understand and assess this facet of the police service-delivery system. One is the severity of the charges filed; the second is whether or not an arrest was made, for cases that were cleared (that is, where an assailant was known). Although a dummy variable was used for the arrest decision (1 = arrest, 0 = no arrest), a scale had to be constructed for the charging decision. Four major charges are used in assault cases, and these were ranked in terms of their severity by reference to the legal classifications and maximum penalties reported in Table 8-1. Thus, simple assault was coded 1; simple battery, 2; aggravated assault, 3; aggravated battery, 4.

In analyzing these outcome decision, the notion of bureaucratic decision rules seems particularly relevant. Unlike the speed and effort analyses, where resource and situational constraints play a larger role, the making of an arrest or charging decision more closely resembles a situation in which the service deliverer weights and integrates a number of different criteria before taking some action. However, as was noted in Chapter 2, to say that bureaucratic decision rules are influential in a given area is not to say very much unless attention is paid to the types of criteria embodied in those decision rules. Moreover, with respect to outcome decisions, a number of different types of criteria appear relevant, although not all would be expected to be relevant to both indicators employed here.

Using again the categories introduced in Chapter 2, one relevant type of criterion would be professional-rational. These criteria relate such things as evidentiary and seriousness matters to outcome decisions. They are expected to be relatively influential in outcome decisions because they are quite visible compared with other decisions made by patrol officers. Charging and arrest decisions often require consultation with and the approval of the shift commander. Thus, professional-rational and other hierarchically imposed criteria are more easily implemented. A second set of criteria relevant to these outcome decisions, especially to the arrest decision, is work-group criteria, those emanating from the norms and values of the service deliverers as a group. These are important because arrests are widely considered the true "stuff" of policing and therefore become the subject of work-group norms and scrutiny.

Despite the fact that no data exist on the personal values, beliefs, or attitudes of individual officers, no discussion of the criteria embodied in outcome decision rules would be complete without mentioning the role of these individual criteria. Despite the importance just attributed to professional-rational and work-group criteria, no organization's control mechanisms are so effective that they completely neutralize the views and predispositions of the individuals who must carry out day-to-day tasks; and police departments are no exception. Even in charging and arrest decisions, which, as noted earlier, are among the most susceptible to departmental influence, there is room for the preferences of individuals. The source of this discretionary power comes, of course, from the individual's control over information flows. Departmental rules may exist, but they can never be completely inflexible; furthermore, information must be provided before these rules can be implemented. This permits individuals such as the arresting officer and the shift commander to influence outcome decisions. What becomes relevant here are such things as their views on the efficacy of arrest and punishment, their view on the appropriateness of arrest and punishment in a given case, and their faith in the judicial system. In addition, such things as racial and/or sexual prejudices may come into play as well as views on juvenile delinquents and sympathy, or lack thereof, for the poor and underprivileged.

In light of the previous discussion, the relevance of the sociopolitical factors to outcome decisions is obvious. Factors such as the type of neighborhood and the race or sex of the participants can influence the charging and arrest decisions in either of two ways. First, beliefs and norms concerning the proper treatment of different racial or sexual groups can develop and become part of the prevailing set of informal work-group practices within a department. These in turn are perpetuated and implemented through peer pressure. A second source of influence would be through the discretionary powers of individuals. By manipulating—consciously or unconsciously—information that they control, individuals can influence the outcomes of cases so that they become consistent with their individual beliefs or prejudices. Because no individual-level data on officers is available, it is not possible to determine the manner in which sociopolitical factors affect outcomes, if they affect them at all. It should be noted, however, that if these variables mainly influence outcome decisions through the exercise of individual discretion, then the mode of analysis used here will obscure the true impact of sociopolitical criteria.[9]

To state that these various types of criteria affect outcome decisions is much simpler than to assess their impact empirically. Moreover, some criteria are harder to assess than others. For example, although there were no data to assess the role of criteria emanating from individual attitudes and beliefs, a set of situational variables, hypothesized to reflect professional-rational concerns, were available. These include measures of the extent of injury; various evidence measures (number of witnesses, available physical evidence); mode of attack; and the nature of the relationship between the participants. The same approach will be used with respect to the standard sociopolitical variables introduced earlier.

An even more indirect and partial approach will be used to obtain some sense of the role of work-group criteria. The two variables that are relevant here—but only with respect to the arrest decision—are those concerning the number of cars responding to a call and the assignment of a detective to the case. The number-of-cars variable is relevant because where more than one officer is assigned, the discretion available to the officer in charge is both limited and influenced toward handling the case in a formal manner. Peer pressure influencing the officer to be tough, coupled with the value placed on arrests, might lead an officer to handle a situation more formally when more officers are present than if he were alone.[10] The assignment-of-a-detective variable is relevant because, within the organization, detectives are in a different position than patrol officers. They have already achieved elite-corps status, and an arrest is therefore less important to them. Moreover, they have more experience in dealing with criminal matters and are apt to scrutinize cases more rigorously. Thus, it is expected that, all other things being equal, cases in which a detective is assigned are less apt to result in arrest than those handled exclusively by patrol officers.[11]

Charge Severity

Equation 8–5 explained 28 percent of the variance ($R^2 = 0.284$) in 513 assault cases,[12] and Table 8–8 includes relevant data on the charge-severity regression analysis.

$$\text{CHRGSEV} = 3.23 + 0.51*\text{INJRY} - 0.45*\text{ATKMODE}$$
$$- 0.15*\text{RELTYPE} + 0.21*\text{SUSPRACE} \qquad (8\text{–}5)$$

where   INJRY = Extent of injury (1 = none, 2 = minor,
                    3 = required medical attention,
                    4 = required hospitalization).
     ATKMODE = Mode of attack (1 = gun, 2 = other weapon,
                    3 = body, 4 = voice).
     RELTYPE = Nature of relationship between participants
                    (0 = none, 1 = casual or close,
                    2 = personal).
     SUSPRACE = Suspect's race (1 = black, 0 = white).

Although the proportion of the variance explained in the crude charge-severity measure was not high, the results show that criteria relevant to the categories proposed earlier—especially the professional-rational category—do have an effect on the charging process. Both the injury and mode-of-attack variables are clearly within this category because the extent of injury and the method of attack are integral parts of the legal definitions of the various crimes. It is somewhat more questionable to treat the relationship variable as a professional-rational one. Although the analysis shows that the closer the relationship, the less severe the charge, this is susceptible to a number of different interpretations. It may be that experience has shown that individuals with close personal relationships will not follow through in assault cases when charges are severe. If so, then a conscious strategy to systematically charge less

Table 8-8. Essential Data on Charge-Severity Analysis

Variable	Beta Weight	F Value	Significance Level (at or Beyond)
INJRY	0.38	97.9	.000
ATKMODE	−0.33	73.6	.000
RELTYPE	−0.12	10.3	.001
SUSPRACE	0.10	7.2	.01

severely (in order to guarantee the complainant's cooperation) might be considered rational. If, however, the practice is based on the notion that it is more legitimate for spouses to abuse one another physically than for strangers to do so, then this finding might have sexist implications. In that case, the variable might reflect sociopolitical criteria. In any event, the suspect-race variable (blacks are systematically charged with more severe offenses) clearly reflects of sociopolitical influences.

The Arrest Decision

Equation 8-6 explained 31 percent of the variance in 375 assault cases,[13] and Table 8-9 includes further information on the regression analysis.

$$\begin{aligned} \text{ARREST} = \ & 0.37 + 0.13 \text{*ID\#S} + 0.29 \text{*PHYSEVID} \\ & - 0.05 \text{*RELTYPE} + 0.07 \text{*NUMCAR} - 0.09 \text{*DET} \\ & - 0.20 \text{*CPLTRACE} + 0.14 \text{*SUSPRACE} \\ & + 0.09 \text{*CPLTAGE} - 0.12 \text{*SUSPAGE} \\ & - 0.13 \text{*SUSPSEX} - 0.11 \text{*MIXDNBRHD} \end{aligned} \tag{8-6}$$

where
- ID#S = Number of eyewitnesses.
- PHYSEVID = Existence of 1 or more pieces of physical evidence (1 = 1 or more pieces, 0 = none).
- RELTYPE = Nature of relationship between participants (0 = none, 1 = casual, 2= close, 3 = personal).
- NUMCAR = Number of cars responding.
- DET = Assignment of a detective (1 = detective assigned, 0 = detective not assigned).
- CPLTRACE = Complainant's race (1 = black, 0 = white).

SUSPRACE = Suspect's race (1 = black, 0 = white).
CPLTAGE = Complainant's age (1 = under 20, 2 = 20–45, 3 = over 45).
SUSPAGE = Suspect's age (1 = under 20, 2 = 20–30, 3 = 30–45, 4 = over 45).
SUSPSEX = Suspect's sex (1 = female, 0 = male).
MIXDNBRHD = Mixed neighborhood (1 = blocks where percentage black > 5 and percentage black < 50, 0 = all other blocks).

Although the proportion of the variance explained in Equation 8-6 is again only moderate, the results are noteworthy because they illustrate the diversity in the types of criteria that might be incorporated in decision rules. For example, the impact of eyewitnesses, physical-evidence, and relation-type variables (the more evidence available and the more social distance between the parties, the greater the probability of arrest), suggests that professional-rational criteria figure prominently in the arrest policies of the Champaign police. The criteria mentioned here appear to be based on a desire to make good arrests that will be supported by the criminal law and will be successfully prosecuted in court. A more complete inventory of factors that are related to these professional concerns would undoubtedly enhance the predictive power of this analysis. It should be noted, however, that several such measures were analyzed here and were not found to have a significant impact. These included such things as the seriousness of injury, the method of attack, and the making of a statement by the defendant. More refined measures of these variables as well as of those found to have an impact may enhance our understanding of this facet of the arrest process.

Equation 8-6 also shows the possible relevance of work-group criteria in arrest decision rules. One could argue, on the basis of the impact of the number-of-cars variable (the more cars responding, the greater the arrest probability) and the detective variable (where a detective is assigned, the arrest probabilities are reduced), that such things as peer pressure and the organizational incentive structure could affect the arrest decision. The impact of the number of cars variable suggests that patrol officers are less likely to handle cases informally when their peers are present, whereas the detective variable suggests that—because of either inexperience or a desire to accumulate arrests—patrol officers are more apt to utilize arrest powers than are detectives. Because of their tentativeness and their susceptibility to alternative interpretations, the results of these two variables will not be dwelled on. Suffice it to say that these may illustrate systematic, internal influences on the use of bureaucratic power based on criteria derived from the values and interests of work groups.

Table 8–9.   Essential Data on Arrest Regression

Variable	Beta Weight	F Value	Significance Level (at or Beyond)
ID#S	0.25	27.9	.000
PHYSEVID	0.19	17.4	.000
RELTYPE	−0.12	6.7	.01
NUMCAR	0.13	7.4	.01
DET	−0.09	3.9	.05
CPLTRACE	−0.20	11.5	.001
SUSPRACE	0.14	6.3	.01
CPLTAGE	0.10	4.1	.04
SUSPAGE	−0.19	14.0	.001
SUSPSEX	−0.09	3.8	.05
MIXDNBRHD	−0.11	6.0	.01

The interpretation of the sociopolitical variables is not nearly as tentative as for those just discussed. There seems to be little question that the social characteristics of the participants influence how arrest powers are utilized. Race plays a crucial role here. The assailants of black victims were less apt to be arrested, whereas black assailants were more apt to be arrested. Similar findings were recorded for the age variables. The assailants of older victims were more apt to be arrested, whereas the younger the assailant, the greater the probability of arrest. Female assailants were less likely to be arrested than were men. Finally, in an attempt to unravel the role of race in the arrest decision, arrest rates were compared for neighborhoods with different racial compositions. It was found that in mixed neighborhoods, where the proportion of blacks ranged from 5 to 50 percent, arrest rates were systematically lower. This is reflected in the MIXDNBRHD variable. Although the meaning of this last finding is not altogether clear, it may suggest a desire on the part of the department—or on the part of the individual officers—to use more informal methods of handling incidents. This may be because of the existence of racial tensions in a neighborhood or because of a desire not to instigate such tensions.

Race Reexamined

One last comment is relevant to the sociopolitical variables. As mentioned before, it is not possible to determine whether they are relevant because of well-established informal norms within the department, because of the views of individual officers, or because of a combination of the two. However, if their primary source of influence is the discretionary power of individual officers, then the picture provided by the preceding analysis is not entirely revealing. In such a case the actual effect of sociopolitical variables will vary according to the views of the arresting officers. Officers who are racially prejudiced will arrest blacks at significantly higher rates than will white officers who hold more enlightened racial views. The latter may actually engage in compensatory arrest practices that result in lower arrest rates for blacks. Finally, some officers who are very professionally oriented may consider race a wholly illegitimate criterion; therefore, race may not affect their arrest practices at all. If this is the case, the impact of the race variable in Equation 8-6 may simply be an indication that the police department has a disproportionate number of racially prejudiced officers.

There is, of course, no valid way to determine whether the impact of sociopolitical factors varies with the individual attitudes and beliefs of service deliverers without having measures of the attitudes of these individuals. In an effort at least to probe the plausibility of this view, a somewhat crude and exploratory approach was used. First, a breakdown of arrest roles by race for each arresting officer was done. Three groups of officers were then constructed—a discriminatory group, a compensatory group, and a neutral-professional group. If the arrest rate of a given officer for black suspects was at least 20 percent higher than for white suspects (for example, 35 percent for whites and 65 percent for blacks), then the officer was placed in the prejudiced group. If the arrest rate of a given officer for black suspects was at least 20 percent lower than for white suspects, he was placed in the compensatory group. All others were placed in the neutral group. There were fourteen officers in the prejudiced group, nine in the compensatory group, and twenty-seven in the neutral group.

A racial attitude (RACATT) variable was then constructed. In each case where the arresting officer was in the prejudiced category, RACATT was scored 1; when the officer was in the compensatory category, RACATT was scored -1; neutral officers were scored 0. After the SUSPRACE variable was recoded so that whites were scored -1, an interaction term was created and added to the regression. The result is shown in Equation 8-7 ($R^2 = 0.33$, $n = 369$) and in Table 8-10.

$$0.34 + 0.14*ID\#S + 0.26*PHYSEVID - 0.05*RELTYPE$$
$$+ 0.05*NUMCAR - 0.09*DET + 0.07*CPLTAGE - 0.10*SUSPAGE$$
$$- 0.11*SUSPSEX - 0.12*MXDNBRHD - 0.10*CPLTRACE$$
$$+ 0.06*SUSPRACE - 0.04*RACATT + 0.13*SUSPRACE*RACATT$$
$$(8-7)$$

Table 8-10.   Essential Data on Second-Arrest Regression

Variable	Beta Weight	F Value	Significance Level (at or Beyond)
ID–S	0.26	31.0	.000
PHYSEVID	0.18	14.7	.000
RELTYPE	−0.12	6.4	.01
NUMCAR	0.10	4.56	.03
DET	−0.09	3.9	.05
CPLTAGE	0.08	2.6	.10
SUSPAGE	−0.16	9.8	.002
SUSPSEX	−0.08	2.8	.09
MIXDNBRHD	−0.11	6.7	.01
CPLTRACE	0.21	12.0	.001
SUSPRACE	0.11	3.7	NR
RACATT	−0.05	1.5	NR
SUSPRACE*RACATT	0.17	13.2	.000

From an exploratory perspective the results embodied in Equation 8-7 are quite interesting. Not only is the SUSPRACE*RACATT interaction term much stronger than either of the two individually, but in terms of its beta weight (0.17) and F value (12.7) it is one of the most powerful variables in the equation. This suggests that because of the role of decisional criteria derived from individual personality attributes, the role of sociopolitical factors in some studies of urban service delivery may have been underassessed. It should be stressed, however, that the results presented here merely suggest that future research should be sensitive to the role of individual-level factors; because of the approach used to derive them, no valid support for substantive interpretations can be claimed.

SUMMARY

Two main points about police response in assault cases should be stressed. First, the results reported here indicate that a number of different types of factors influenced police response. Resource availability affected the number of cars sent to an incident. Situational characteristics played a major role in a number of areas. Speed, for example, was affected by whether an assailant was present and by how long it took to report the incident. This indicates that police response varied with the urgency of the situation. The police also took into account the severity of injury in allocating time to cases. Race, sex, and age also played a role, indicating the relevance of sociopolitical criteria. Finally, some indirect evidence was offered to show that the preferences of an individual officer may also be important.

Second, the results suggest that the type of criteria affecting response seemed to vary with the different stages of the process. The earlier phases of the process were dominated by professional-rational concerns, whereas sociopolitical considerations were more likely to show up in the later phase. The reasons for this are not entirely clear. They may have something to do with the amount of information available to the responding officer. It is not possible to react to someone's social characteristics until one is apprised of them, and this may not occur until the later stages of the service encounter. More will be said about this in Chapter 11.

NOTES

1. Response time, as used here, is measured as the interval between the time the call was received and the time the car arrived. Dispatch time is the interval between the time the call was received and the time a car was assigned to it.
2. The presence of a defendant at the scene was inferred from a reading of the narrative in the police report. Especially important here was whether or not the assailant was present when the police arrived. It should be stressed that the information on this point is only indirect. There may be instances in which the defendant was present at the time the call was made but left by the time the police arrived. Such instances may obscure the true impact of this variable.
3. In Chapter 5 it was noted that information was collected on several different types of elites (political, commercial, civic) by block. Unfortunately, for the assault analysis the distribution of cases for each individual category was so small that they had to be merged into one elite variable depicting the existence of any type of elite on the block from which the call came. It should be stressed, of course, that this variable *does not mean* that the call came from the household of that elite; and inferences must be tempered accordingly.
4. Only 472 of the total 636 cases were used in this analysis because of missing data, primarily on the dependent variable and the dispatch-time variable. Apparent keypunch errors led to extremely long values for some of these cases, often in excess of eight or ten hours. These were excluded. In addition to these, eleven deviant cases were excluded. These cases had very short dispatch times (less than 3 minutes) but extremely long response time (three to four hours). They were either keypunch errors or cases in which some extraordinary intervening event occurred.
5. The regression equation with the MIDCLASS*BEATSIZE interaction term is: $2.19 + 1.1*DISPTCHTM - 0.001*DISPTCHTM^2 + 0.01*BEATSIZE - 1.24*DPRES - 1.03*INTERVAL + 0.63*RELTYPE - 0.63*CPLTSEX + 2.02*MIDCLASS - 0.13*MIDCLASS*BEATSIZE$.
6. Here, as in the case of the speed regression, the primary reason for the missing cases in the data analysis is that there are missing values on the DSPTCHTM variable. One other point needs to be made here. For the NUMCAR analysis, it may have been better to use TOBIT analysis. TOBIT is useful for cases in which most of the values of the dependent variable cluster at one value. This would have been valuable

because in most cases only one car was sent to an incident. TOBIT fits a regression to such skewed distributions. Unfortunately, no program was available to conduct this analysis. The significance of this is that the resulting R^2 are lower than they would be with TOBIT programs.

7. Most of the missing cases in this analysis were the result of missing values on one of the time variables needed to compute the SERVTM variable. Some also existed because addresses could not be matched and assigned a block and tract number, essential for determining the values on the neighborhood variable.

8. The analysis for the assignment of a detective could also have been done using PROBIT. Unfortunately, a multivariate PROBIT program was not available to both authors (the analyses were done at separate locations), so linear regression was used instead. Although PROBIT would have been a better means of analysis, regression produces results very similar to PROBIT results in that the relative magnitudes of the coefficients are the same when the distribution of the dependent variable is not extremely unbalanced between 0 and 1. Thus, the results presented here can be accepted as reasonable estimates of the significance of variables. See John Aldrich and Charles Cnudde, "Probing the Bounds of Conventional Wisdom: A Comparison of Regression, Probit, and Discriminant Analysis," *American Journal of Political Science*, 19 (1975):571–608.

9. For an interesting analysis of this problem in another area see James L. Gibson, "Race as a Determinant of Criminal Sentences," *Law and Society Review* 12 (1978):455–478.

10. One might well argue that any positive relationship between the number of cars responding and the use of arrest would be the result of an intervening variable: the seriousness of the offense. More cars would be sent to more serious situations, and an arrest would be more likely. To counter this possibility, the number-of-cars variable will be used only while controlling for seriousness indicators.

11. Here again it might be argued that any negative relationship uncovered between the assignment of a detective and arrest might be the result of the circumstances surrounding the assignment of a detective. That is, cases may be given to a detective only when there is some evidentiary problem that needs to be resolved. If it cannot be resolved, then the defendant is released. To counter this possibility, the detective variable will again be used only in conjunction with evidentiary variables.

12. The main reason for the missing cases in this analysis was the missing values on the racial makeup of the participants.

13. The reason there are only 375 of the 636 cases is that only 458 cases were cleared. Uncleared cases were eliminated because the analysis only makes sense when there is a known suspect. The difference between 375 and 458 is the result of missing values on some variables, primarily the two race variables.

Chapter 9

Attacks on Property: Handling Common Crimes

Offenses against property account for the most frequent crime-related situations requiring police action; the most common of these are vandalism, burglary, and theft. Vandalism (an attack resulting in damage to property) affects mainly cars, homes, and businesses. Burglary involves illegal entrance into a house or building with the intent of taking something. Thefts involve situations in which some property has been stolen, either from an individual or from an institution.

Although common crimes are not as life threatening as assaults, they have a special importance to the general public and to a police department's image. Unlike many violent crimes, property crimes are normally perpetrated by strangers. They threaten the security and peace of mind of victims, especially in the case of home burglaries and vandalisms. Moreover, this anonymity makes it especially difficult for the police to solve the crime or repair the damage. However, this does not make police response unimportant. A police report may be necessary in order for someone else (such as an insurance company) to undo the damage, and the presence of an officer may be useful in permitting the victim to vent his anger or frustration. In addition, a prompt and attentive response by the police may be reassuring, enhancing the victim's sense of security and persuading him or her that everything possible will be done.

In this sense, the role of the police is likely to be somewhat more symbolic in the area of common crimes than in assault cases. This

Table 9-1. Offense Distributions and Possible Penalties

Offense	Relative Frequency (Percentage)	Offense Type	Maximum Penalty
Burglary— structure	16.1	Class 2 felony	1–20 years, state penitentiary and $10,000 fine
Attempt	2.2	Class 3 felony	1–10 years, state penitentiary and $10,000 fine
Burglary—auto	18.6	Class 2 felony	1–20 years, state penitentiary and $10,00 fine
Attempt	1.2	Class 3 felony	1–10 years, state pentitentiary and $10,000 fine
Theft— over $150.00	13.9	Class 3 felony	1–10 years, state pentitentiary and $10,000 fine
Theft—less than $150.00	27.4	Class A misdemeanor	1 year, county jail and $1,000 fine
Vandalism	21.5	Class 4 felony or Class A misdemeanor	1–3 years, state penitentiary and $10,000 fine or 1 year, county jail and $1,000 fine
	100.0%		

difference is important because where symbolic action is relevant, political factors may result in differential response times, efforts, and outcomes in different areas of the city. The police may, for example, devote more time to cases in Southwest Champaign, or may be more inclined to assign a detective to cases from this area compared with those in other areas as an indication of the effort being made on the case. This chapter will examine these possibilities along lines similar to those followed in Chapter 8.

CHARACTERISTICS OF COMMON CRIMES

Within the common-crime category there were 907 burglaries, 545 thefts, and 1,107 cases of vandalism. Within each of these broad categories there were a number of different specific offenses, as shown in Table 9-1. The ranges in statutory penalty provide some insight into legal judgments concerning the relative seriousness of the different offenses, with burglary clearly the most serious of the lot. Another way to view the seriousness of these offenses is to look at the amount of property stolen or damaged in each. There was a good deal of variance in this respect, also. Amounts ranged from nothing (in attempts) to several

Table 9–2.   Source of Common-Crime Calls

	Burglary (Percentage)	Vandalism (Percentage)	Theft (Percentage)
Individuals	88.2	91.5	52.9
Institutions	11.5	8.1	47.1

thousand dollars. The mean estimated values were quite high, ranging from $195 in thefts to $413 in burglaries to $515 in vandalisms.

Most of the common-crime cases were the result of calls from private citizens, as demonstrated in Table 9–2. However, a large proportion of thefts were from institutions. The calls unaccounted for by these categories were made by police officers. Where the call for assistance came from individuals, most were from males, with the proportions ranging from 58 to 74 percent. Calls from minorities were roughly equivalent to their proportion in the population, with the proportion from blacks varying from 11.3 to 16.0 percent.

Considering each of the three types of common-crime cases, only 11.5 percent of burglaries, 39.3 percent of thefts, and 16.5 percent of vandalisms were cleared by the police. Moreover, clearances by arrests accounted for only 9.0 percent of burglaries, 29.9 percent of thefts, and 11.7 percent of vandalisms. Perhaps the primary reason that the police fare so poorly in common-crime cases—compared with assault cases, where more than 70 percent of cases are cleared—is that these crimes normally occur when no one is around. Consequently, it seldom happens that a perpetrator is viewed by a complainant. This was true for 4.5 percent of burglary cases, 13.0 percent of vandalisms, and 29.3 percent of thefts. In cases where a suspect was identified, a prior relationship existed between suspect and victim in only 30.4 percent of burglary cases, 44.1 percent of vandalism cases, and 23.2 percent of theft cases. Even perpetrators who are seen cannot always be identified. As shown in Table 9–3, in the vast majority of cases complainants could not specify a time at which the crime occurred. Most could only indicate a range of hours or days within which the crime might have occurred. (The sole exception is theft cases, where many shoplifters are spotted on the scene.)

The fact that common crime-calls are not normally life threatening and are usually "cold" has a number of implications for police response. First, fewer cars are normally sent in response to common-crime calls. In contrast to assault cases, where only one car was dispatched in response to about 54 percent of all calls, only one car was sent to about 89 percent

Table 9–3. Complainants' Report of Time Frame for Crime

	Burglary (Percentage)	Vandalism (Percentage)	Theft (Percentage)
Over several days	16.3	9.8	11.8
Over several hours (24 or less)	65.7	53.1	38.9
At a specific point in time	18.0	37.1	49.3

of all common-crime calls. Moreover, median response time is somewhat slower in common-crime cases (median = 7.8) than assault cases (median = 5.8), and median time out of service is shorter (median = 12.0 for common crime; 14.0 for assaults). Finally, detectives were assigned in about one-half as many common crime cases as assault cases (16 percent compared with 30 percent).

SPEED

As with the speed analysis for assault cases, the concern here is with the time it took the police to arrive at the scene of an incident from the time a call was received. The structure of the analysis is also very similar, although some of the relevant situational characteristics vary. The dispatch-time variable (the amount of time elapsing between the call and the dispatch of a car) will again be used as a surrogate for the first-come, first-served criterion employed by police dispatchers. As a surrogate it is, of course, subject to all the shortcomings noted in Chapter 8. Nonetheless, it is expected to be the most important determinant of response time. Also relevant to this analysis are resource constraints; the very rough measures of these constraints discussed in Chapter 7 will again be used. Other professional-rational factors thought to be important here include beat size, the amount of time elapsed between the incident and the call for service, and whether or not a suspect was present at the scene.

The sociopolitical variables are again the social characteristics of the caller (age, race, sex); the neighborhood from which the call came; and the elite measure. In addition, whether the call is from an individual or an institution will be considered, a variable that was not relevant to assaults because institutions cannot be "assaulted" according to the criminal code. Since local commercial establishments can, however, be burglarized, vandalized, and robbed, it becomes important to compare the treatment these establishments receive with that accorded individuals.

With response time as the dependent variable, Equation 9–1 explained 85 percent of the variance ($R^2 = 0.849$) in 1,764 common-crime cases.[1]

$$\text{SPEED} = 3.1 + 1.17\,\text{DSPTCHTM} - 0.002\,\text{DSPTCHTM}^2$$
$$+ 0.0015\,\text{OFCRLOAD} - 0.50\,\text{CPLTYPE} \qquad (9\text{–}1)$$

where   SPEED = Response time (in minutes).
   DSPTCHTM = Dispatch time (in minutes).
   CPLTYPE = Whether complainant is an institution
        (1 = institution, 0 = individual).
   OFCRLOAD = Average number of cases handled within hour
        of call, adjusted for average manpower levels.

All the variables in Equation 9–1 are significant at or well beyond the .05 level. Other essential data on the speed regression are reported in Table 9–4.

The results reported in Equation 9–1 and Table 9–4 show some of the similarities and differences between this analysis and the assault speed analysis. The most marked similarity concerns the impact of the dispatch-time variable. The B coefficients are virtually identical in both equations, suggesting again that conditions within the service agency (such as the availability of a car) and the nature of the situation (such as the dispatcher's perception of its urgency) are the primary determinants of response time. It should also be noted that the squared-dispatch-time term again had an unanticipated negative impact time. This occurred for the same reason noted in Chapter 8—there is an upper limit on how long it takes a car to arrive at the scene once it is dispatched.

The OFCRLOAD variable shows that resource constraints, beyond those implicit in the dispatch-time variable, have an impact on response time. This was not the case in the assault analysis and may be a reflection of the priorities accorded different types of cases. Another difference in the two analyses is that in the case of assaults situational factors such as the presence of the assailant, the length of the interval between the incident and the call, and the relationship between the parties affected response time. None of these are significant here for a number of reasons. First, as was noted earlier, there is little variance in the type-of-relationship variable, since most perpetrators are not related to their victims. Also, in property-offense cases few perpetrators are present at the time the call is made. Moreover, their presence may not mean what it would in an assault case, where a personal attack has taken place and another may be imminent. Where a perpetrator is present at the scene it is often a youth picked up for a minor theft or vandalism. The fact that the presence of the perpetrator is not always very significant may also

Table 9–4.   Essential Information on Speed Regression

Variable	Beta Weight	F Value	Significance Level (at or Beyond)
DSPTCHTM	1.01	2,800.4	.000
DSPTCHTM^2	−0.12	37.3	.000
OFCRLOAD	0.05	24.8	.000
CPLTYPE	−0.05	13.9	.001

account for the failure of variables depicting the time span between the incident and the call.

Some statistical reasons also account for the failure of some of these factors to affect response time. The variable depicting the presence of a defendant at the scene was slightly correlated ($r = -0.11$) with the dispatch-time variable, as was a variable indicating that the call reporting an offense was reasonably proximate to the commission of the offense ($r = -0.14$).[2] These indicate that some of the considerations represented by these variables were reflected in the dispatching decision. The correlation between them and the dispatch-time variable, and its strong correlation with the dependent variable, negated their impact on response time.

The only variable having any sociopolitical connotations as well as an impact on response time in common-crime cases was the complainant type variable. Neither the neighborhood variables nor the elite measure had an effect. Moreover, as was true for the data presented in Chapter 8, none of the sociopolitical variables was related to the dispatch-time variable; consequently, it did not obscure their impact. With respect to the complainant-type variable, the analysis revealed that calls from institutions (primarily commercial establishments) received more prompt responses. This could, of course, be interpreted as supporting the view that regular users with some political clout receive preferential treatment and that this is a conscious strategy pursued by the police bureaucracy. Although such an interpretation might be justified, it should be tempered by the realization that most commercial establishments have a locational advantage that may be of even greater import. Unlike residences, most commercial establishments are located on main streets that are well known and well paved. Also, those in downtown Champaign are located in a very small police beat. Both factors may lead to reduced response times. This does not entirely discount the sociopolitical interpretation. However, a more consistent pattern of sociopolitical influences needs to be established before much reliance can be placed on it.

EFFORT

The same relationships are expected in the case of common crimes as with assault cases. The effort analyses of assault cases showed that need-related factors and, to a lesser extent, resource constraints were the primary determinants of the amount of effort expended. Among the most important need indicators are such things as the seriousness of the incident (measured in dollars of damage or theft), whether any information is available on the identity of the suspect, the availability of physical evidence, whether a suspect is present on the scene, and whether the incident involves a "real" crime or simply a personal dispute. Three indicators of effort will be examined empirically—the number of cars responding to a call, the time spent out of service, and whether or not a detective was assigned to a case.

The Number-of-Cars Regression

With the number of cars sent to the scene as the dependent variable, Equation 9-2 explained 12 percent of the variance ($R^2 = 0.123$) in 1,967 cases.[3] Table 9-5 reports other relevant information on the regression.

$$NUMCAR = 1.07 - 0.0001*OFCRLOAD + 0.09*AWARE$$
$$+ 0.16*PRES + -0.004* DSPTCHTM$$
$$+ 0.11*PERPDESC + 0.08* VAND - 0.07* COMELTE$$
$$- 0.03*CPLTYPE + 0.11* BLCKIND \qquad (9-2)$$

where   NUMCAR = Number of cars dispatched to scene.
OFCRLOAD = Average number of calls in beat-shift of
call, adjusted for average manpower levels.
AWARE = Interval between incident and victim's
awareness of it (1 = a matter of minutes,
0 = a matter of hours or days).
PRES = Presence of the defendant at the scene
(1 = present, 0 = not present).
DSPTCHTM = Length of time bewteen call and dispatch of
a car (in minutes).
PERPDESC = Availability of a description of the perpetrator
(1 = a description, 0 = not present).
VAND = Vandalism call (1 = vandalism call, 0 = other
type of call).
COMELTE = Existence of one or more commercial elites
residing on block from which call came
(1 = existence of commercial elite, 0 = none).

> CPLTYPE = Complainant type (1 = institutions,
> 0 = individuals).
> BLCKIND = The existence of a black complainant
> (1 = black complainant, 0 = white
> complainant or institutions).

Although the explanatory power of the NUMCAR regression is not even half of that in the assault analysis, its structure is remarkably similar in some respects. In assault cases, PRES, DSPTCHTM, OFCRLOAD, and INTERVAL were the only determinants of the number of cars sent; here PRES, DSPTCHTM, OFCRLOAD, and AWARE are the most important determinants. This suggests that the most influential factors in the allocation of police squads are resource constraints and some sense of urgency or need. Where more cars are normally available, more are sent to a scene. Where a suspect is present, or where the information conveyed in the call leads to a quick dispatch, or where the incident is relatively "hot" (current), or where a perpetrator can be described, more cars are sent. These results are, of course, reflective of professional-rational criteria.

What makes the common-crime NUMCAR regression different from the assault regression is the impact of several variables whose interpretation is somewhat problematic. The first is the VAND variable, which indicates that somewhat more cars are routinely sent to vandalism cases than to burglary and theft cases. The meaning of this is not at all clear, although it probably has something to do with the situational characteristics of vandalism cases.

The interpretation of the COMELTE, CPLTYPE, and BLCKIND variables are not as problematic, but they are somewhat involved. The impact of the commercial-elite variable (COMELTE) indicates that *fewer* cars are normally sent in response to calls coming from blocks on which at least one commercial elite lives. The joint impact of the CPLTYPE and BLCKIND variables (which form an interaction term) is that where the complainant is an individual and the individual is black more cars are sent than would otherwise be the case. If viewed in sociopolitical terms these results are puzzling, as one would expect the opposite impacts— more cars (better services) for elites, whites, and commercial establishments. The first temptation is to interpret these results in light of the greater allocation of police cars to the largely black Northend beat. However, when a variable depicting the average number of cars assigned to the block from which the call came is entered into the regression, the results do not change.

This suggests that one must look beyond sociopolitical considerations to organizational ones to understand these findings. The history of poor relations between the police and certain segments of the black commun-

Table 9–5. Essential Information on NUMCAR Regression

Variable	Beta Weight	F Value	Significance Level (at or Beyond)
OFCRLOAD	−0.11	22.9	.000
AWARE	0.12	20.3	.000
PRES	0.11	15.9	.001
DSPTCHTM	−0.08	13.4	.001
PERPDESC	0.11	12.8	.001
VAND	0.07	7.9	.01
COMELTE	−0.06	7.7	.01
CPLTYPE	−0.05	3.3	NS
BLCKIND	0.07	8.5	.01

ity may lead to a greater sense of insecurity on the part of the police when responding to calls from black households. This in turn may lead to a tendency to assign more cars to calls from certain sections of the Northend (housing developments, for example).

The Time-Out-of-Service Regression

With the amount of time out of service (measured in minutes) as the dependent variable, Equation 9–3 explained 9 percent of the variance ($R^2 = 0.094$) in 1,770 cases.[4] Table 9-6 reports other important information on the regression analysis.

$$\text{SERVTM} = 20.47 + 4.43*\text{PHYSEV\#} + 2.81 \text{ SUSPECT}$$
$$+ 5.83 \text{ SIGHTED} - .1.11 \text{ HRLYCALL}$$
$$-2.47 \text{ VAND} \tag{9-3}$$

where SERVTM = Time out of service (measured in minutes).
PHYSEV# = Number of pieces of available physical evidence.
SUSPECT = A specific suspect exists (1 = a suspect exists, 0 = no suspect exists).
SIGHTED = A perpetrator was sighted at the scene (1 = sighted, 0 = not sighted).
HRLYCALL = The average number of calls during the hour in which the call came.
VAND = A vandalism call (1 = a vandalism call, 0 = a burglary or theft call).

Table 9-6. Essential Information on SERVTM Regression

Variable	Beta	F	Level of Significance (at or Beyond)
PHYSEV#	0.15	20.9	.001
SUSPECT	0.09	12.6	.01
SIGHTED	0.11	11.9	.01
HRLYCALL	−0.06	5.9	.02
VAND	−0.06	5.5	.02

Even though the regression analysis explains only a small proportion of the variance, the interpretation of the findings is quite straightforward. Although resource constraints (represented by the HRLYCALL variable) are somewhat important, need-related factors dominate. All three of the most significant variables (PHYSEV#, SUSPECT, SIGHTED) reflect work requirements. Where there is more physical evidence to process, more time is required to handle it. Where information on a suspect exists more time is required to elicit it and perhaps pursue it.

The only variable that does not fit the need–resource-constraint category is the VAND dummy variable. Although it indicates that less time is normally spent on vandalism cases than on burglary and theft cases, its interpretation is somewhat unclear. It may reflect a lower priority assigned to vandalism cases within the department, or it may simply mean that vandalism cases are somewhat more straightforward than other types of common-crime cases. On the other hand, it may be necessary to interpret this finding in light of the impact of the VAND variable in the NUMCAR analysis. There it was found that more cars were assigned to vandalisms than to other types of common-crime cases. Thus, more manpower might well account for the lower average service times.

The Detective Regression

The final effort indicator to be examined here is whether the department assigned a detective to investigate the case, as occurred in 16 percent of the common-crime cases. The results of the DETASGND regression are reported in Equation 9-4; other relevant information is included in Table 9-7. The equation explained 12 percent of the variance ($R^2 = .116$) in 2,559 cases.

$$DETASGND = 0.06 + 0.09* OPEN + 0.22* PHYSEV\#* OPEN$$
$$+ 0.05* SUSPECT* OPEN + 0.12* ID* OPEN$$

Table 9-7. Essential Information on DETASGND Regression

Variable	Beta	F	Significance Level (at or Beyond)
OPEN	0.06	4.3	.05
PHYSEV# * OPEN	0.17	52.2	.000
SUSPECT* OPEN	0.06	8.5	.01
ID* OPEN	0.06	7.1	.01
EVIDLINK	0.10	10.3	.001
VALUE	0.09	25.5	.000
PERP#	0.06	9.4	.01
RELTYPE	0.09	17.3	.001

$$+ 0.4\ \text{EVIDLINK} + 0.19*\ \text{VALUE} + 0.09*\ \text{PERP\#}$$
$$+ 0.15*\ \text{RELTYPE} \tag{9-4}$$

where DETASGND = The assignment of a detective (0 = none assigned, 1 = detective assigned).

OPEN = Suspect not apprehended on the scene (0 = apprehended on scene, 1 = not apprehended on scene).

PHYSEV# = Pieces of physical evidence.

SUSPECT = Existence of a suspect (0 = none, 1 = a suspect).

ID = Existence of a witness who could identify the perpetrator (0 = none, 1 = 1 or more).

EVIDLINK = Existence of some evidence that is directly linked to a suspect (0 = none, 1 = some).

VALUE = Value of property damaged or stolen (0 = less than $500, 1 = $500 or more).

PERP# = Number of perpretators suspected or sighted.

RELTYPE = Existence of a prior relationship between the parties (0 none, 1 = prior relationship).

The results here are somewhat more complicated than in most of the earlier analyses. The complication is the result of the fact that a conditional relationship exists between some evidentiary considerations, the apprehension of a suspect at the scene, and the assignment of a detective. Given the earlier results, it was expected that detectives would be assigned to cases in which they could do some good, that is, where some evidentiary leads existed. However, unlike the situation with assault cases, the apprehension of a suspect at the scene obscured the relationship between evidentiary matters and the assignment of detectives in common-crime cases. The difference in the impact of the evidentiary variables in the two types of cases is probably the result of the fact that assault cases are normally much more complex than common crimes. Apprehending the suspect in assault cases is often not as great a problem as unraveling what happened, determining who is to blame, and establishing the appropriate course of action. In any event, a conditional analysis was necessary in order to depict accurately the relationship between the evidentiary variables (PHYSEVID, SUSPECT, and ID) and DETASGND in common-crime cases.

Despite these complications, the interpretation of the results is quite straightforward. Although detectives are less often assigned where someone is apprehended at the scene, their allocation in other cases is directly tied to the existence of evidentiary leads. Sociopolitical considerations played no role; but the existence of physical evidence, the existence of a suspect, and the number of witnesses able to make an identification were all positively related to the assignment of a detective. In addition, two indicators of the case's gravity—the value of the property stolen or damaged and the number of perpetrators involved—had a positive impact on the DETASGND variable. Both sets of variables, evidentiary and seriousness, are indicative of the significant role played by professional-rational considerations in the allocation of detective resources.

The interpretation of the last variable—RELTYPE—is not quite as straightforward but may also be reflective of professional-rational criteria. The regression shows that situations involving perpetrators and victims who have some personal relationship to one another are more apt to have a detective assigned than other types of cases. This may indicate that these cases involve more complex situations that are not really appropriate for criminal resolution or that require mediation of some sort. The assignment of a detective may well perform this mediating function. Some indirect support for such an interpretation is provided in the following analysis of the arrest decision.

OUTCOMES

In Chapter 8 two aspects of case outcomes were examined—the charging decision and the arrest decision. Here, however, only the arrest decision will be examined because of the relatively large number of offense types involved, and because their determination is largely the result of a mesh of legal and situational factors that are not of interest here. A building burglary differs from an auto burglary solely on the basis of the target of attack. Vandalisms differ from thefts because property is

Table 9-8. Essential Information on Arrest Regression

Variable	Beta	F	Significance Level (at or Beyond)
SIGHTED	0.30	70.8	.000
PHYSEV#	0.14	15.5	.001
RESTORE	− 0.30	66.5	.001
RELTYPE	− 0.15	20.5	.000
RESOLVE	− 0.11	9.8	.01
BURG	0.13	17.7	.001

damaged rather than stolen. In short, an analysis of the charging decision with respect to common-crime cases would not make much sense in light of the overall nature and purpose of this inquiry.

With respect to the arrest decision, the analyses here will proceed much as before. Arrest decision in common-crime cases go through the same stages as assault arrests. The visibility and importance of these decisions and the fact that they are amenable to bureaucratic control suggest the importance of decision rules. Here again, however, the primary interest is with the nature of the criteria embodied in those decision rules. Evidentiary considerations, the seriousness of the offense, efforts toward an informal resolution, and the sociopolitical characteristics of the participants are expected to be of primary significance.

The Arrest Regression

Equation 9-5 explained 46 percent ($R^2 = 0.463$) of the variance in 629 cases in which an arrest decision was made (that is, the case was cleared). Arrests accounted for 76 percent of these clearances. Table 9-8 reports other essential information on the statistical analysis.

$$\text{ARREST} = 0.55 + 0.25\,\text{SIGHTED} + 0.07\,\text{PHYSEV\#}$$
$$- 0.37\,\text{RESTORE} - 0.16\,\text{RELTYPE} - 0.15\,\text{RESOLVE}$$
$$+ 0.15\,\text{BURG} \tag{9-5}$$

where   ARREST = Whether an arrest was made (1 = arrest, 0 = no arrest).
   SIGHTED = Suspect was sighted at the scene (1 = someone sighted, 0 = no one sighted).
   PHYSEV# = Number of pieces of physical evidence.

RESTORE = Whether a restoration of some type was made between the parties involved (1 = restoration, 0 = no restoration).

RELTYPE = Evidence of a previous relationship between the parties involved (1 = previous relationship, 0 = no evidence of a previous relationship).

RESOLVE = The existence of a private resolution (1 = resolution, 0 = no resolution).

BURG = Case involved burglary.

The analysis shows that the dominant considerations in common-crime arrest decisions include available evidence and efforts toward a private resolution. The only factor to have an impact was a dummy variable depicting whether or not a case involved a burglary; this may be considered a seriousness indicator since burglaries are viewed with much more concern than other offenses. The SIGHTED and PHYSEV# variables are, of course, the evidence variables. The regression indicates that the existence of an eyewitness identification and the amount of available physical evidence is directly and positively related to the decision to arrest a suspect.

Perhaps the most interesting variables in the regression are those suggesting efforts at a private resolution—the RESTORE and RESOLVE variables and, to a lesser extent, the RELTYPE variable. The findings indicate that where there has been a private settlement of a dispute—or where there is a good chance of one, as in the case of RELTYPE—the police are much less likely to initiate formal proceedings. These results could be reflective of both professional-rational considerations and, in a more general sense, sociopolitical ones. Professional-rational considerations would play a role since the pursuit of cases in which a private settlement has been reached is often a poor investment of resources. Victims have little motivation to pursue the case, and court proceedings would prove difficult. For the police to push such cases would merely undermine their credibility with local prosecutors. One could also view these findings in a sociopolitical light. What they indicate, of course, is a preference for informal dispute processing. In communities where cultural preferences lean toward more formal dispositions, one might not find such a strong relationship.

Arrests Reexamined

A significant difference between Equations 9-5 and 8-6, the initial arrest analysis for assault cases, is that the various sociopolitical variables that played a discernible role in the assault arrests (race, age, neighborhood)

Table 9-9. Essential Information on Second-Arrest Equation

Variable	Beta	F	Significance Level (at or Beyond)
SIGHTED	0.29	69.6	.000
PHYSEV#	0.13	14.1	.001
RESTORE	−0.29	63.9	.000
RELTYPE	−0.16	21.8	.000
RESOLVE	−0.10	8.4	.01
BURG	0.14	19.8	.000
OFFGRP	0.13	20.7	.000

do not make much difference in common-crime cases. The reasons for this difference are not at all clear. They may have some relation to the complexity and intensely personal nature of many assault cases and/or to the way participants and situations fit the stereotypes held by police officers. Whatever the reasons—the determination of which is beyond the scope of this study—the differences in the two equations give rise to other questions. More specificially, they raise the possibility that the results obtained in the second-assault arrest regression, which suggest indirectly that the attitudes of individual officers played a role in arrest decisions, may be idiosyncratic to assault cases.

To examine this possibility, a similar but somewhat simpler technique than that used in Chapter 8 was employed. An OFFGRP variable was created by assigning a 1 to officers in the common-crime sample who had arrest rates above the mean, and a 0 to those below the mean. This variable was entered into the arrest regression after all the other variables had been entered. The results are reported in Equation 9-6 ($R^2 = 0.48$, $n = 629$) and Table 9-9; they are similar to those obtained in Chapter 8. Grouping officers by arrest inclinations leads to enhanced explanatory power above that provided by situational factors (the B coefficients of these variables remained largely unchanged). What these results suggest is that the views of individual service deliverers may be an important factor in service delivery and a source of sociopolitical influence. However, the crudeness of the approach used here prevents any definitive statements. Later efforts incorporating the views of service deliverers could shed light on these matters.

$$\text{ARREST} = \quad 0.55 + 0.25\,\text{SIGHTED} + 0.07\,\text{PHYSEV\#}$$

$$- 0.36\,\text{RESTORE} - 0.17\,\text{RELTYPE} - 0.14\,\text{RESOLVE}$$

$$+ 0.16\,\text{BURG} + 0.12\,\text{OFFGRP} \qquad (9\text{-}6)$$

where all variables have the same meanings and codings as previously discussed.

SUMMARY

The analysis of police response in common-crime cases again demonstrates that a variety of influences affect police response, as was also the case with assaults. The results indicate that police behavior was affected by the amount of resources available and the extent of competing demands. Situational factors such as the presence of a perpetrator, the availability of physical evidence, or a description also influence the police to respond more rapidly, to devote more cars and time to a case, to assign a detective, and to make an arrest. Some indirect evidence also suggested that the attitudes of the responding officer play a significant role in response. In many general ways, then, the results here are similar to those reported in Chapter 8.

In one respect, police response in common-crime cases seems to differ from that in assaults. There is less evidence that sociopolitical factors play a role. In the final stages of a case (assigning a detective and making an arrest), they play no role at all. The reasons for this are not at all clear. It may have something to do with the differences in social settings in the two broad types of cases. The passion and hostility involved in assault cases may highlight the salience of the personal characteristics of the parties. Another alternative is that the real relationship between these factors and arrest is obscured. There may be complex interactions occurring between the wishes of the victims, the views of the officer, and the sociopolitical characteristics of the perpetrator that we are unable to untangle with the available data.

NOTES

1. Most of the 795 missing cases in this analysis are the result of the missing data on the SPEED and DSPTCHTM variables.
2. It should be noted that severe problems were incurred in estimating intervals between incidents and calls. In many cases, the offense occurred when the victim was gone; in others, the victim did not notice the damage or missing property for several hours or days. In such cases it was impossible to specify the time of the incident, as could be done in assault cases. It was, however, possible to isolate cases where the victim could specify a point in time at which the incident occurred. This information was then used to differentiate "stale" calls from "fresh" ones.
3. Most of the missing cases in this analysis, as with the SPEED analysis, are the result of missing data on the DSPTCHTM variable.
4. Of the 785 missing cases, approximately 49 percent were the result of missing information on the dependent variable, SERVTM. Most of the remaining missing cases resulted from obviously erroneous data on SERVTM. Many indicated extremely long service periods extending far beyond a day or a shift; others were negative values.

Chapter 10

Cars and Cops: Accident Cases

Although auto accidents can be among the more routine types of encounters handled by the police, they also represent an important set of situations in which public resources are expended. Even in a city the size of Champaign, the police receive thousands of auto-accident reports each year. For the purposes of this analysis, the significance of these contacts is not solely a reflection of their number. They are important also because of the nature of the clientele the police are likely to encounter in accident cases and because of the possibility of significant variations in police response. In terms of clientele the police are much more apt to encounter a cross-section of the community in auto accidents than in any other reactive situations that might entail formal sanctions. With respect to consequences, it should be stressed that differences in police response can have both real and symbolic effects: a slow response may prolong suffering or even result in irreparable damage. In routine cases the impact of response time is largely symbolic—it leaves an impression about the level and quality of services in a community. Much the same can be said for effort. Variations in effort, however, can also have real consequences: more effort may lead to more complete information and, hence, to more equitable outcomes.

Before the three response analyses are presented, it should be mentioned that there are several important distinctions between this chapter and the earlier ones. Because accident records were kept separately and

Table 10–1. Extent of Injury to Drivers

Injury	Relative Frequency	
	Driver 1	Driver 2
None apparent	89.9	85.7
None visible but complaining of problem	4.2	5.4
Some visible injury	2.4	3.6
Bleeding wound, distorted member	3.3	5.1
Dead	0.1	0.1

on different forms, the data base for these cases is quite different. Much situational information was available; this included data on the extent of personal injury, vehicular damage, where a car was hit, road conditions, the number of units involved, evidence of drinking, and so on. Information on the personal characteristics of the drivers was scarce, however. Only age, sex, and address were available. This precluded some sociopolitical analyses, such as an assessment of the impact of race. However, other, more indirect social indicators were available. These were data on the make, size and year of the cars involved in the accident.

A second important distinction here is that the location of the occurrence does not have the same impact as it did in earlier chapters. It meant something to compare the handling of a Northend burglary or assault to a Southwest Champaign burglary or assault. But the location of accidents is almost random and has no meaning in the recent analyses. Thus, instead of matching the address of the *accident* with a census tract and block, the address of each *driver* was matched. Although this matching was not as successful as it was with the other data bases, it did provide some information on the drivers.

CHARACTERISTICS OF ACCIDENT CASES

Most traffic accidents involve only two cars (86.5 percent) and are not viewed by any bystanders (76 percent). Moreover, most do not involve serious personal injuries. This latter statement is supported by the data in Table 10–1, which, for the sake of simplicity, includes information only for the first two drivers listed on the accident-report form. It shows that apparent injuries occurred in less than 9 percent of the cases, considering each driver separately and based on the fact that drivers were only infrequently taken to the hospital. This occurred in 4.4 percent of the

Table 10–2.   Damage to Vehicles

	Relative Frequency	
Damage	Car 1	Car 2
None	6.2	4.9
Minor damage	68.7	64.5
Substantial damage	22.0	20.5
Very substantial damage	2.5	2.3
Totaled	0.5	0.3
Unknown	—	8.5

cases for Driver 1 and 7.6 percent for Driver 2. The more likely outcome of an accident is that there will be damage to the vehicles involved. This information is given in Table 10–2, again only for the first two cars. As this information indicates, almost all cars suffered some damage; and a considerable proportion were extensively damaged. The damage was significant enough to result in the car being towed away in 18.8 and 16.5 percent of the cases for Drivers 1 and 2, respectively. A final relevant point here is that, although accidents involving drinking tended to be more serious, most accidents involved no evidence of drinking. There was evidence of drinking on the part of Driver 1 in less than 5 percent of all cases and in less than 3 percent for Driver 2.

With respect to the personal characteristics of drivers involved in accidents, males accounted for 69 percent of those designated as Driver 1 and 68 percent of those designated as Driver 2. The average age of these drivers was approximately thirty-two years. The socio-economic status of these drivers is difficult to assess. The only information on this is from census data, and this was available only for drivers whose addresses could be matched. Using the data on the median value of homes for the block the drivers lived on gives some indication of the distribution of drivers. This information is shown in Table 10–3. As noted earlier, a large proportion of matches could not be made. The figures in Table 10–3 are based on 575 cases for Driver 1. The results for Driver 2 were very similar but were based on an even smaller subsample. Despite these deficiencies, the figures clearly suggest that drivers involved in accidents tend to come from a cross-section of economic strata within the city.

One last area that deserves comment, especially for the outcome analysis, is ticketing. The relative frequencies of tickets given out are shown in Table 10–4. Again, only Driver 1 and Driver 2 are shown. Unfortunately, the picture presented in Table 10–4 is somewhat deceiving. It leaves one with the impression that, in the modal situation, the police do not allocate blame or responsibility through ticketing decisions. That this is not the

Table 10-3. Breakdown of Median Home Value, for Driver 1 Only

Median Home Values on Driver 1's Block	Relative Frequency
$0–10,000	2.4
$10,001–20,000	55.7
$20,001–30,000	31.7
$30,001–50,000	11.5

case is demonstrated by the cross-tabulation in Table 10-5. By summing the calls in which one driver was given at least one ticket and the other was given none, it can be seen that in almost 80 percent of the cases the police clearly indicate culpability. In only 3 percent are both parties ticketed.

With the nature of accident cases clarified, it is now possible to present the speed, effort, and outcome analyses. Although these will be somewhat different from the earlier analyses for the reasons already given (limited data on participants, limited role of locational indicators), the concerns will be largely the same.

SPEED

As in earlier chapters, the concern here is with those factors affecting the length of time it took the police to arrive at the scene once a call about the accident was received; the results are shown in Equation 10-1. The five variables explained 69.7 percent of the variance for 1,695 cases; only 56 cases were lost because of erroneous or missing data. Additional information on these results is contained in Table 10-6.

These results indicate that dispatch time again plays a very prominent role in explaining variations in response time. As before, however, there is an upper limit on its effect, as indicated by the squared term. Two other factors also play a role. The impact of the OFCRLOAD variable shows that the greater the call load per officer, the longer it takes for the police to get to the scene. The other is the amount of damage and injury to the drivers. These two indicators represent the seriousness of the accident; their negative relationship to speed suggests that the more serious the accident, the quicker the police response. In general, these relationships provide support for the idea that resource limitations and seriousness play a major role and that professional-rational criteria dominate the response process. None of the personal or sociopolitical variables had an

Table 10–4. Ticketing Frequencies

Number of Tickets Received	Relative Frequencies	
	Driver 1	Driver 2
0	51.0	63.7
1	44.6	34.4
2	3.8	1.7
3 or more	0.6	0.2

impact. But this is not surprising, given that such information is not normally provided to responding officers.

$$\text{Speed} = 2.80 + 1.27 \text{ DSPTCHTM} - 0.006 \text{ DSPTCHTM}^2 + 0.007$$
$$\text{OFCRLOAD} - 0.67 \text{ TOW1} - 0.91 \text{ HOSP1} \qquad (10\text{-}1)$$

Where   SPEED = Time in minutes to arrive at scene.
    DSPTCHTM = Time in minutes to dispatch a car to scene.
    OFCRLOAD = Average number of calls handled within hour of call adjusted for average manpower levels.
    TOW1 = Was Car 1 towed away (1 = yes, 0 = no).
    HOSP1 = Was Driver 1 taken to hospital (1 = yes, 0 = no).

EFFORT

The Number-of-Cars Regression

With the number of cars sent to the scene as the dependent variable, Equation 10-2 explained 13 percent of the variance ($R^2 = 0.133$) for 1,751 cases. Additional information on this equation is reported in Table 10-7.

$$\text{NUMCAR} = 0.87 + 0.14 \text{ TOW1} + 0.19 \text{ DRINK1} + 0.095$$
$$\text{INJURY1} - 0.00012 \text{ OFCRLOAD}$$
$$+ 0.04 \text{ DAMAGE1} \qquad (10\text{-}2)$$

Where   NUMCAR = Number of cars sent to the scene.
    TOW1 = Was Car 1 towed away (1 = yes, 0 = no).
    DRINK1 = (1 = no evidence, 2 = some, 3 = evidence of impairment).
    INJURY1 = Injury to driver 1 (0 = none, 2 = complaint of

Table 10–5. Ticketing Cross-Tabulation by Driver

Number of Tickets for Driver 1	Number of Tickets for Driver 2	
	0	1 or more
0	308 (17.7%)	581 (33.3%)
1 or more	803 (46.0%)	52 (3.0%)

           injury, 3 = visible injury, 4 = serious injury,
           5 = dead).
OFCRLOAD = Average number of calls received in hour of
           incident adjusted for manpower levels.
 DAMAGE1 = Extent of damage to Car 1 (0 = none,
           4 = totaled).

Although Equation 10–2 does not explain a large proportion of the variance, the results are consistent with those reported earlier. The basic determinants of NUMCAR are seriousness or need indicators (TOW1, INJURY1, DAMAGE1, DRINK1). DRINK1 is included in this category for a number of reasons. Driving while drinking is a violation of law. When there is evidence of such an infraction, the police may need more personnel to make a more thorough report for future purposes. It is also likely that when a driver has been drinking and has become physically impaired, additional personnel will be necessary to handle the driver while other officers handle the accident. The only other variable with a significant effect on NUMCAR is OFCRLOAD, a measure of resource constraints. It shows that the greater the manpower constraints, the fewer cars sent to an accident. This again is consistent with the earlier NUMCAR analyses.

The Service-Time Regression

If seriousness and need criteria are adhered to, the amount of service time that the police devote to an accident should be a function of some of the same factors just discussed in the NUMCAR analysis. However, once the police arrive at the scene, their awareness of the social characteristics of the drivers involved may affect their behavior. To assess this, two indicators of the socioeconomic status of the drivers involved were created. One involved the status of the driver's car, and the other was derived from census data on median home values on the driver's block. Each was a dichotomous variable. For the CARSTAT variable, Oldsmobile, Buick,

Table 10-6. Essential Information on Speed Regression

Variable	Beta	F	Significance Level (at or Beyond)
DSPTCHTM	0.96	1443.39	.001
DSPTCHSQR	−0.16	39.72	.001
ORCRLOAD	0.05	16.06	.001
TOW1	−0.05	11.95	.001
HOSP1	−0.04	7.21	.0025

Cadillac, Lincoln, Chrysler, Volvo, Saab, and Porsch/Audi were considered high status. All others were coded as low status. For the HMESTAT variable, cases in which the driver came from a block with median home values of $20,000 or greater were considered high; all others were considered low.

The crudeness of these measures will undoubtedly dilute whatever effect socioeconomic status may have on this facet of police response. Unfortunately, this problem cannot be dealt with given the existing data. However, a second problem that also exists can be dealt with. This concerns the fact that in accident cases—which often have no well-defined aggressor or victim—the police may be responding to the joint status of the parties involved. For example, if both parties are of high status, the response may be fundamentally different than if both parties are of low status. A wholly different response might emerge from mixed-status (one high, one low) accidents. In order to examine these possibilities, a series of dichotomous variables was constructed to capture each of the possible combinations for both SES variables.

Equation 10-3 explained 8 percent of the variance in SERVTM for 1,247 cases. The missing cases were largely the result of missing information on the type of car. Further information on the regression is reported in Table 10-8.

$$
\begin{aligned}
\text{SERVTM} = {} & 27.7 + 2.85 \text{ DAMAGE1} + 6.67 \text{ TOW1} + 2.03 \\
& \text{INJURY1} - 1.76 \text{ HRLYCALL} + 3.57 \text{ NOTOWNR} \\
& + 2.72 \text{ CAR\#} + 8.89 \text{ CARSTAT1} \tag{10-3}
\end{aligned}
$$

Where   SERVTM = Time out of service at scene (in minutes).
           DAMAGE1 = Damage to Car 1 (0 = none, 1 = minor,
                   2 = substantial, 3 = very substantial,
                   4 = totaled).
           TOW1 = Was Car 1 towed away? (1 = yes, 0 = no).
           INJURY1 = Injury to Driver 1 (0 = none,
                   1 = complaint of nonapparent injury,

Table 10-7. Essential Information on NUMCAR Regression

Variable	Beta	F	Significance Level (at or Beyond)
TOW1	0.14	19.52	.001
DRINK1	0.16	46.49	.001
INJURY1	0.17	59.57	.001
OFCRLOAD	−0.11	23.50	.001
DAMAGE1	0.07	4.90	.025

2 = visible injury, 3 = serious injury, 4 = dead).

HRLYCALL = Average number of other calls within hour of incident.

NOTOWNR = Driver of car was not owner (0 = owner driven, 1 = not owner driven).

CAR# = Number of cars involved in accident.

CARSTAT1 = Both cars of high status (0 = low status, 1 = high status).

These results indicate that very different types of factors influence the allocation of service time to an accident. First, the seriousness of the accident plays a role, with DAMAGE1, TOW1, and INJURY1 being positively related to SERVTM. In addition, more involved accidents, indicated by the CAR# variable, also received more time. This is to be expected, since accidents involving several cars require gathering more information and may present additional physical problems. Another situation that probably requires more information, and thus more service time, occurs when the driver of a car is not the owner. This is reflected in the positive correlation between NOTOWNR and SERVTM. A third type of influence on the SERVTM variable is resource constraints, as evidenced by the significant effect of the HRLYCALL variable.

The final type of influence shown in Equation 10-3 is sociopolitical, the CARSTAT1 variable. It demonstrates that when both drivers are driving high-status cars, the police tend to spend more time on the scene. It should be stressed that it was necessary to consider the joint status of the parties: variables depicting the status of one car or another did not have a statistically significant effect. One last point should be made here. One of the HMESTAT variables also had a statistically significant effect on SERVTM. When both drivers cam from low-status blocks, the police spent *less* time at the scene. However, the relatively small number of cases (about 475) for which there was good data on median home values

Table 10–8. Essential Information on Service-Time Regression

Variable	Beta	F	Significance Level (at or Beyond)
DAMAGE1	0.11	11.69	.001
TOW1	0.14	24.12	.001
INJURY1	0.08	8.23	.005
HRLYCALL	−0.07	6.57	.01
NOTOWNR	0.06	4.77	.05
CAR#	0.06	4.22	.05
CARSTAT1	0.08	8.47	.005

made it impossible to enter this variable into the regression. Despite this, there is evidence to suggest that sociopolitical influences do play a role here—even if they are not as significant as professional-rational considerations.

OUTCOMES

The most important outcome indicator in accident cases is the ticketing decision. It is important because it often has economic implications. A ticketed individual may have to pay a fine and may even have to spend some time in jail. Also, the ticketed party may be subject to civil liability and/or license revocation. The importance of this decision as an indicator of police response is enhanced by the fact that this is one of the few areas in which recipients of police sanctions are apt to include the entire social spectrum in a community. A middle- to upper- class citizen is far more likely to be involved as a wrongdoer in an accident case than in an asault or burglary case.

These considerations underscore the importance of understanding the criteria embodied in ticketing decisions. Here again, the primary concern will be with both professional-rational and sociopolitical considerations. Two basic types of professional-rational factors were examined here. One consisted of "fault indicators," a set of situational variables that shed some light on which party was to blame for the accident. Fault indicators included such things as whether the driver was hit while stopped, whether there was evidence of intoxication, and whether the car was hit from behind. Each is important because it provides the responding officer, who in all likelihood did not see the accident, some rational basis for allocating fault. The second category of professional-rational criteria concerned the seriousness of the accident and included both personal and property damage. These were considered important because responding officers may feel more compelled to give tickets in situations where the stakes are high than where they are low.

As noted earlier, information on sociopolitical characteristics of accident participants was limited. Despite their shortcomings, several sociopolitical indicators were available, including the status and age of the car, the neighborhood in which the drivers lived, and whether or not they were local residents.

Before the quantitative analysis is presented, an analytical problem not encountered in earlier analyses must be discussed. Most of the outcome analyses undertaken in Chapters 8 and 9 involved situations where there was a well-defined victim and/or perpetrator. This is not the case in traffic-accident cases. The individuals involved are simply identified as Driver 1 or Driver 2. This creates an ambiguity in the quantitative assessment of the ticketing decision. Should one focus on the tickets given to Driver 1 or on those given to Driver 2? There is no good resolution to this problem. Fortunately, however, empirical analyses demonstrated that it does not matter. Regression analyses done on each driver produced very similar results. That is, the statistical impact of a rear-end collision is similar whether the tickets given to Driver 1 or those to Driver 2 are analyzed. Thus, for purposes of simplicity, only the results for the tickets given to Driver 1 are reported.

The Quantitative Analysis

With the number of tickets given to Driver 1 as the dependent variable, Equation 10-4 explained 19 percent of the variance ($R=0.187$) in 1,093 cases (the missing cases were largely the result of missing data on the age-of-car variable and the residence-of-driver variable). Other information on the regression analysis is reported in Table 10-9.

$$\text{NUMTICK} = 0.03 + 0.66 \text{ DRINK1} - 0.17 \text{ REARHT1} - 0.39$$
$$\text{CAR1STOP} + 0.27 \text{ CAR2STOP} - 0.25 \text{ DRINK2}$$
$$+ 0.24 \text{ DR2HOSP} + 0.09 \text{ REARHT2} + 0.017$$
$$\text{AGECAR1} + 0.10 \text{ NONLOC} \qquad (10\text{-}4)$$

Where NUMTICK = Number of tickets given to Driver 1.
           DRINK1 = Evidence of drinking by Driver 1 (1 = no, 2 = some evidence of impairment, 3 = definite impairment).
       REARHT1 = Car 1 was hit in rear (1 = yes, 0 = no).
    CAR1STOP = Car 1 was stopped when hit (1 = yes, 0 = no).
    CAR2STOP = Car 2 was stopped when hit (1 = yes, 0 = no).

Table 10–9.   Essential Information on Ticketing Regression

Variable	Beta	F	Significance Level (at or Beyond)
DR1DRINK	0.26	87.09	.001
REARHT1	−0.15	25.96	.001
CAR1STOP	−0.15	27.44	.001
CAR2STOP	0.10	13.37	.001
DR2DRINK	−0.11	15.50	.001
DR2HOSP	0.09	11.53	.001
REARHT2	0.08	7.03	.005
AGECAR1	0.11	18.47	.001
NONLOC	0.07	6.85	.01

DRINK2 = Evidence of drinking by Driver 2 (1 = no,
2 = some evidence of impairment, 3 = definite
impairment).

DR2HOSP = Driver 2 was taken to hospital (1 = yes,
0 = no).

REARHT2 = Car 2 was hit in rear (1 = yes, 0 = no).

AGECAR1 = Age of Car 1 (in years).

NONLOC1 = Driver 1 was not from local area (1 = not,
0 = yes).

The results indicated by Equation 10–4 are very consistent with earlier analyses. Professional-rational considerations dominate, especially those variables considered as fault indicators. Drinking while driving, being hit (or hitting someone) in the rear, and being stopped when hit (or hitting someone who is stopped), all have the expected impact on the ticketing decision. Each of these is a reliable decisional criterion for the responding officer and permits him to allocate blame in a manner consistent with widely accepted societal norms of behavior. The interpretation of the one seriousness measure that had a significant impact, however, is not so straightforward. It appears that the more seriously Driver 2 is hurt, the more likely Driver 1 is to get a ticket, controlling for other situational factors. This implies that responding officers have a tendency to compensate for grievous injuries suffered by one party by ticketing the other, regardless of fault. The source of this influence could be either departmental policy, work-group norms, or individual beliefs.

Despite the straightforward interpretation given to the DR2HOSP variable, it should be cautioned that the regression analysis may be obscuring or oversimplifying a far more complicated phenomenon. It may be that the true relationship between the seriousness of the injury to one party and the ticket given to another is a conditional one. The relationship may vary with the degree of fault attributable to the one being ticketed. Where the injury is serious and fault is not clear, ticketing may be light. But when injury is serious and fault is clearly attributable to the other party, the number of tickets issued might be far greater than in situations where injury was slight and fault was clear. In the latter situation the officers may consider the occurrence too routine or minor to warrant legal proceedings. It should be noted that these conditional relationships were examined with the available data, but none were uncovered. This should not, however, discourage future inquiries along these lines. The null results may simply be attributable to the crudeness of the present data.

The last two variables that had an impact on the ticketing decision—AGECAR1 and NONLOC—can be viewed as having sociopolitical implications. The age of the car driven by Driver 1 is a rough surrogate for social class. Although, older cars are driven by people from all social strata; it is certainly arguable that older cars are disproportionately owned and operated by members of the lower- and working-class strata, and that the positive relationship between car age and tickets at least suggests that social class has some impact on the ticketing decision. But as plausible as the social-bias argument may be, one should at least consider alternative hypotheses. The observed relationship may simply reflect variations in how people articulate their positions. On the other hand, it may mean nothing more than that older cars have more mechanical failures or difficulties, which result in more accidents for which they are accountable. On this latter point, however, it should be noted that some control variables on the condition of the cars were available. Their introduction did not affect the impact of the AGECAR1 variable.

The impact of the NONLOC variable shows that drivers from outside the Champaign-Urbana area are more apt to be ticketed in traffic accidents than local residents. This may have sociopolitical implications in that it suggests that people from outside the local political community receive different treatment than do those from within. Here again, however, alternative explanations should be considered. Strangers in the community may simply be unfamiliar with local situations, make a greater number of incorrect judgments, and end up in more auto accidents. In sum, then, although the data suggest that some sociopolitical influences operate in ticketing decisions, better and more complete data are needed before more confidence can be placed in these statements.

Ticketing Reexamined: The Role of Individual Officers

As indicated in earlier chapters, a primary concern in this study is with the influence that individual service deliverers have on the distribution of services. Ticketing decisions provide a unique opportunity to assess this influence. In considering the three types of cases analyzed in this section, the role of individual proclivities in affecting outcomes is expected to be greatest in accident cases. Although some accidents are serious, most are very routine. Decisional consequences are not normally as high as in "real" criminal cases. Although license revocation leads to inconvenience, there is seldom a threat of incarceration. These factors make ticketing decisions much less visible than arrest decisions; there is less scrutiny because the stakes are not as high. Moreover, the rules governing ticketable offenses are not nearly as well defined as those for criminal situations. All this is expected to lead to an enhanced role for the individual officer in defining situations and influencing outcomes.

Despite the expected importance of individual officer views in ticketing decisions, our efforts at examining them empirically were hampered by the same factors as before—the lack of data on the views of responding officers. The only alternative was to proceed with the same crude techniques used in earlier chapters. The ticketing tendencies of officers were examined by performing a breakdown of the NUMTICK variable by officer. The results were then used to group the officers into a trimodal OFFATT variable. Officers who gave, on the average, a large number of tickets were scored 2, those in the middle were scored 1. Officers were equally distributed across the three categories.

According to the same procedure used before, the OFFATT variable was entered into the NUMTICK regression after all the variables reported in Equation 10-4. The results, reported in Equation 10-5, are striking. The inclusion of the OFFATT variable doubles the proportion of variance explained in the NUMTICK variable with only modest changes in the coefficients of most of the other variables (see Table 10-10). The only exception is REARHT2, which drops out of the equation.

$$NUMTICK = -\ 0.17 + 0.54\ DRINK1 - 0.12\ REARHT1 - 0.24$$
$$CAR1STOP + 0.18\ CAR2STOP - 0.22\ DR2DRINK$$
$$+\ 0.21\ DR2HOSP + 0.012\ AGECAR1 + 0.06$$
$$NONLOC + 0.32\ OFFATT \qquad (10\text{-}5)$$

where all variables have the same meanings as before, and where OFFATT is the measure of officer ticketing inclinations.

It should be stressed that, despite the significance of the OFFATT variable, only limited conclusions can be drawn from Equation 10-5. They do support the contention that the views of individual service deliverers appear to be a powerful source of influence on the ticketing decision, indeed

Table 10-10. Essential Information on the Second-Ticketing Regression

Variable	Beta	F	Significance Level (at or Beyond)
DRINK1	0.21	77.54	.001
REARHT1	-0.09	12.86	.001
CAR1STOP	-0.10	14.26	.011
CAR2STOP	0.06	6.60	.005
DR2DRINK	-0.10	16.05	.001
DR2HOSP	0.08	11.84	.001
AGECAR1	0.09	12.45	.001
NONLOC	0.05	3.98	.05
OFFATT	0.46	330.77	.001

—as expected—of more influence than elsewhere. But much is still unknown about this source of influence. For example, what specific attributes of police officers lead to different ticketing tendencies? How do these attributes interact with situational factors to affect outcomes? Are there organizational structures or strategies that can eliminate or reduce these differences? Although it is possible only to raise questions at this point, Equation 10-5 suggests that the issue is important enough to warrant further consideration.

SUMMARY

Again, we find broad similarities between the determinants of response in accidents and those in assault and property cases. Workloads and the availability of resources affect the time it takes to get to an accident, the number of cars sent, and the amount of time devoted to a case. The seriousness of injury and damage involved in an accident, or the fact of a nonowner driving a car, have an expected effect on service time. Also, the fault indicators used had a marked impact on the ticketing decision. Sociopolitical influences also played a role in ticketing, as evidenced by the impact of the SES surrogate and the residence indicator (local, out-of-towner). This supports the observation made in Chapter 8 that these influences seem to be more important during the latter phases of the service process. Finally, although it is still indirect, this chapter presents some very strong evidence of the importance of individual influences. Moreover, because the impact is so much greater here, these results suggest that the impact of these influences is more significant in discretionary areas that are more routine and mundane.

V: CONCLUSIONS

Chapter 11

Toward Understanding the Service-Delivery Process

The dominant theme in the urban-service-delivery literature has been the importance of bureaucratic considerations vis-à-vis political ones as determinants of service levels or disbursements. It is interesting but of no great significance that this theme emerged largely from the inability of service scholars to reject the null hypothesis in empirical studies. It is important, however, to note the narrowness that the obsession with the politics-bureaucracy dichotomy has imposed on the study of urban services. That dichotomy is hardly the most important issue in this area. A fundamental refocusing of efforts is required. Concern should be with the development of a general framework for understanding how service-delivery organizations operate—that is, what affects how they disburse services. Such a focus would bring this whole area much closer to the study of organizations in general, which in turn would facilitate the cross-fertilization of knowledge and the development of theoretical insights. In addition, it would produce research with more direct policy implications, leading to a better understanding of how service delivery can be improved.

The present study, although limited, has something to say about the initial development of this general framework. First, any serious attempt to develop a conceptual framework for understanding service delivery must take into account the wide variety of existing service agencies and service tasks. Indeed, preliminary work needs to be done on developing a service-delivery typology that incorporates important characteristics of these phenomena. This is crucial because the determinants and dynamics of service delivery are apt to be very different across various types of agencies and tasks. Second, efforts toward theory development must be sensitive to the multiplicity of factors involved in service delivery. Service-delivery mechanisms will be fully understood only after a thorough consideration of all possible sources of such influence, as well as of the content of the influences emanating from various sources and the linkages between the sources and the service-delivery process. Following a consideration of these points, some directions for future research will be suggested.

THE DIVERSITY OF URBAN SERVICES

For purposes of theory development, it is important to consider the differences within and across service areas and service tasks. It is not very fruitful, for example, to talk about the distribution of sanitation services or police services or library services as if each were a unidimensional concept. Each general service area (police, library, sanitation) may involve several distinct kinds of service tasks (street paving, pothole repairs, street cleaning, police patrolling, criminal investigation, vice deployment) the assessment of which may require several different kinds of measures (speed, thoroughness, frequency). In addition, the provision of a general type of service may require a service-distribution center (a library building, a garbage dump, a fire station), which may have positive or negative sociospatial (distributional) consequences.

These distinctions are important because a given set of factors is not likely to have the same impact on service disbursement in different service areas. Indeed, it is very likely that the impact factors will vary even across different service tasks within a given agency. To grapple with these complexities, a good deal of work needs to be done on the development of service-task and service-agency typologies. From this may emerge a set of characteristics that can help distinguish among these various phenomena.

Because this study was limited to one service area, the police, it is not possible to refer to the empirical results for examples of how different approaches are needed in service agencies with different characteristics. However, it is possible to illustrate the importance of service-task characteristics. Moreover, an examination of the empirical analyses presented here suggests that in trying to understand the types of factors affecting the performance of service tasks, it is useful to focus on questions concerning the locus of decision making, the sources of relevant stimuli, and in some cases the identity of agents who filter plausibly relevant stimuli.

Perhaps the best illustration of the importance of these considerations is found in the contrast between the demand and the response analyses. In order to understand adequately demand levels across the city, it was necessary to look beyond the police department because the relevant locus of decision making lies in the community. Citizens were, by and large, responsible for initiating demands. The relevant stimuli were things that affected *their* homes or well being, and *they* were the agents who filtered and integrated these stimuli and made a decision about what to do. Thus, the focus had to be on such things as activity levels and citizen predispositions, with only indirect references to the service agency involved. This approach was justified by the empirical results. These showed, although necessarily in an indirect manner, that levels of human activity were the primary determinants of service levels, with political and social factors (the neighborhood and elite variables) playing a lesser role.

Both the approach used in the demand analysis and the empirical results obtained stress the importance of the relationship between the service agency and its environment, and work to dispel the overly simplistic image of the service agency "disbursing" services. However, it would be a mistake to think that an agency's environment is totally independent of the agency's actions and policies. It is not. At the time of this study, a department policy with very significant implications for the demand analysis was that the Champaign police would respond to virtually all requests for an officer. More restrictive screening policies could change the relationship between the department and its environment. Also, over the long run the action of the department could modify its relationship to various groups in more indirect ways. Their demeanor and the nature of their response to certain types of calls or people could affect citizen inclination to request police services.

These considerations notwithstanding, the service bureaucracy—its policies, personnel, and resource levels—was of much greater consequence for understanding police response than for understanding demand. This is, of course, because the police bureaucracy had much more control over the decisions and stimuli affecting response. Through policy formulation, information control, and policy implementation, they could determine how various stimuli were molded into responses. Perhaps the best example here is the car assignment procedure. The department established a "first come, first served, except in emergencies" policy. The dispatcher handles virtually all the stimuli and assigns cars on the basis of the established rule. This in turn had a marked effect on the speed of police response.

Another way to illustrate that service-delivery determinants will vary across service tasks is to compare the various response analyses with one another. To contend that a police department has more control over what its officers do than over what citizens demand of it is not to say that the impact of bureaucratic influences is equal across all facets of police work. Since police work is largely responsive, it is difficult to control, even in this age of sophisticated, two-way radio communications. When the "action" shifts from police headquarters to the field, a whole array of factors may enter into the decisional calculus. The police bureaucracy can do little directly to filter or control these stimuli. The interaction between the stimuli and departmental guidelines will, more often than not, determine what happens. The department has only limited and largely indirect control over how this integration takes place. The stimuli are filtered and integrated by responding officers and, as long as these officers are the primary source of certain types of information flowing into the bureaucracy, they will continue to exercise a healthy amount of discretion. One result of this considerable discretion is that in some situations the significance of factors unique to individual officers will be at least as important as those emanating from the police bureaucracy.

The general point that sources of influence on service tasks vary even where the service bureaucracy has some direct control can be illustrated by several empirical examples. Perhaps the best is the contrast between the speed analyses and the other response analyses. Speed, or response time, was determined almost totally by dispatch time and, to a far lesser extent, by such things as beat size, resource availability, and seriousness indicators. What is most striking when the speed equations are compared with the others is the minimal roles played by situational and sociopolitical factors. The reason for the difference lies in the locus of the decision making. The dispatch decision, which largely determines response time, is made in the rather sterile atmosphere of the dispatch room. Comparatively little information is available to the dispatcher, and some fairly simple decision rules are available. Moreover, the dispatcher is likely to transfer even less information to the responding officer.

Decisions concerning other facets of response (effort, outcome) are made in a wholly different milieu. Often both parties to the dispute are present, and the officer is inundated with contradictory information. Also, because the parties to the dispute are usually functioning human beings, they may have their own set of interests, priorities, and preferences. When these overlap, they may be able to impose an outcome that neither the officer nor the department may be able to prevent. This certainly appeared to be happening in many property cases, as the arrest regression in Chapter 9 suggests. In other instances, situational factors may emerge as controlling sources of influence. The total lack of evidence, the presence of a gun, the undeniable existence of intoxication, and the occurrence of serious injury are examples of such factors; evidence of their significance is demonstrated in the charge-severity analysis in Chapter 8, in many of the effort analyses, and in the ticketing analyses in Chapter 10.

Only indirect evidence was available on how an individual officer's predispositions and views will affect the delivery process. Although it seems clear that these considerations are important, their significance, like that of other factors, is apt to vary across the different dimensions of response. Consider, for example, the relationship between an officer's social views and response time. There is very little discretion involved in simply driving to a call; this is largely a mechanical act. Moreover, it is very likely that the responding officer will know very little about a wide array of possibly relevant social characteristics of the parties, or about their plight. Without this information, it is ridiculous to expect him to react to them. Once contact is made, it makes more sense to consider the impact of the officer's views. But even in this instance, the importance of these views is apt to differ across various situations. An officer would be expected to have more latitude in less serious traffic and misdemeanor encounters than in felony matters. Members of the departmental hierarcy, as well as prosecutors and judges, are apt to scrutinize more serious cases more closely than less serious ones. Some indirect evidence for this phenomenon can be seen by comparing the impact of individual officers in the ticketing analysis as described in Chapter 10 with the arrest analyses in assault and property cases in Chapters 8 and 9. Their impact is far greater on the less visible ticketing decision.

SOURCES OF INFLUENCE, CONTENT, AND LINKAGE

A truly comprehensive understanding of the service-delivery process will require more than simply a greater sensitivity to, or recognition of, the diversity of service tasks and agencies. Also needed is a greater awareness of the many and varied influences on the delivery process, what these influences consist of, and their linkage to service-related behavior. To some extent, this is an integral part of the previous discussion. By focusing on the different loci of decision making and the relevant sources of stimuli, one will become sensitive to some of the concerns that have been raised. These considerations are important enough to warrant further elaboration here.

Most studies of service delivery have involved efforts to relate geographic locales of varying sociopolitical composition to service levels in an attempt to assess the impact of politics. Since these have failed to establish any consistent relationships between politics and service delivery, researchers have adopted theoretical explanations that emphasize the centrality of bureaucratic decision rules. However, influences on service-delivery processes emanate from many sources other than politics and bureaucracies; there are sources of political influence that have little to do with the demographic makeup of a neighborhood; and there is no reason to view bureaucratic influences as either neutral or omnipotent. A greater sensitivity to the multiplicity of influences on the service-delivery process, and their limitations, would do much to dispel the false dichotomy often posed between political and bureaucratic influences as determinants of service levels. Neither of these very general types of factors is a unidimensional concept, and the fact that both types of influences, along with several others, may simultaneously influence service delivery, has been demonstrated throughout the empirical analyses presented in this book, especially in the outcome analyses. Although this analysis was not always sophisticated enough to isolate the various sources, the suggestion of a multiplicity of influences was quite strong.

A number of sources, such as the environment, the bureaucracy, the work group, and the individual service deliverer, have already been mentioned. But, such general categories are clearly inadequate as a basis for enriching our understanding of the service-delivery process. What is needed here is a good deal of first-hand observational work oriented toward an elucidation of relevant stimuli and their sources. The study of service delivery is at the point where further aggregate analyses, based solely on agency records and census data, are apt to contribute little to what is already known. Instead, observational techniques, or interviews and surveys where required for practical reasons, can provide researchers with insights unavailable from the more conventional techniques in this field.

First-hand knowledge of the stimuli that affect service-related behavior will not only illuminate sources of influence but may also have something to say about content. This is especially true if the research is carried out in a comparative framework. Consider environmental influences, for example. Research conducted in very different types of cities could provide insight into the range of influences emanating from political systems with very different characteristics, or working under very different types of constraints. Research conducted across very different types of service agencies (small versus large, professional versus traditional) could serve to illustrate the variety of organizational directives and concerns. Much the same could be said for other sources of influence.

Although the value of comparative, observational research should not be overemphasized, one last point needs to be made: Such a strategy can also serve to illustrate the relative importance of various sources of influence under different conditions, thereby touching on the question of linkage. For example, research conducted in cities with different formal political structures, political and social configurations, or levels of political-party strength could shed some light on the factors affecting the impact of environmental influences on service delivery. Research efforts focusing on similar types of service agencies with different fundamental structures (hierarchical versus decentralized, for example) could lend insights into factors influencing the strength of bureaucratic forces. Finally, studies involving similar cities but with agencies that differ in terms of their general orientation (professional versus traditional) or the strength of their control mechanisms could answer questions about the service agency's role as a conduit for environmental influences.

NOTES FOR FUTURE RESEARCH

As this study has shown, several areas are ripe for future research. Some of them are obvious from the foregoing. There is a dire need for comparative service-delivery research. Moreover, this research should have an observational phase and should be sensitive to questions concerning the level of analysis. Multiple levels should be used where appropriate and feasible. Where this is not feasible, the implications of ignoring a certain level should be addressed. The primary concern here, of course, is with the dearth of attention paid to the impact of service deliverers on the delivery process. The importance of the service deliverer as a source of influence will undoubtedly vary with the nature of the task performed. But the manner in which views of these individuals interact with task requirements, situational considerations, and the characteristics of the recipients could provide important insights into the nature of the service process. Their role can be lost in aggregate analyses.

Despite the importance of micro-level efforts, macro-level analyses should not be ignored. They can be useful in addressing significant questions that cannot be adequately handled through the other means alone. Among the more important of these is the relationship between the service agency and its consumers. Although this is apt to differ depending on who controls service initiation, both situations (citizen initiation, bureaucratic initiation) should be considered. Much work needs to be done on need determinants, agency efforts to manage and anticipate demand, and the impact of agency response patterns on demand. Finally, research needs to be done on the relationship between service agencies and the political system. The notion of bureaucratic independence must be carefully scrutinized, and relationships in different types of systems and agencies should be examined. Here again, a mix of observational and interview research strategies will enable researchers to overcome the sterility that has characterized so many studies of urban service delivery.

Appendix A

Data-Collection Forms

CRIME DATA SHEET - FINAL DRAFT

IDENTIFICATION INFORMATION

Variable   Columns

201   Dispatch Ticket Number   _ _ _ _ _   1-5

202   Which file was this case in?   6-7

                    Animal Bites   1
                    Arson.   2
                    Assaults   3
                    Bicycles   4
                    Burglary   5
                    Con.   6
                    Fraud.   7
                    Grand Theft.   8
                    Indecent Exp   9
                    Informations   10
                    Lost Articles.   11
                    Lost Licenses.   12
                    Miscellaneous.   13
                    Missing Persons.   14
                    Molest   15
                    Murder   16
                    Narcotics.   17
                    Obscene.   18
                    Petty Theft.   19
                    Rape   20
                    Robbery.   21
                    Runaways   22
                    Stolen Vehicles.   23
                    Suicide.   24
                    Threats.   25
                    Vandalism.   26
                    Not relevant   88
                    Missing.   99

203   What Number is this case within the file?   _ _ _ _   8-11

             INFORMATION ON INCIDENT

204   Number of Complainants (Code Direct)   _   12

                    8 or more.   8
                    Missing.   9

205   Type of Complainant
                                                                           13
                    Individual, not a policeman.   1
                    A policeman.   2
                    Corporation or Institution   3
                    A noncommercial entity (not profitmaking).   4
                    Unclear.   5
                    Missing.   9

206   Type of location where call originated:
                                                                           14-15
                    Residence - single family.   1
                    Residence - apartment.   2
                    Residence - don't know   3

175

```
                   School - elementary. . . . . . . . . . . . . . . . .     4
                   School - high school . . . . . . . . . . . . . . .       5
                   School - university. . . . . . . . . . . . . . . .       6
                   Auto - at home . . . . . . . . . . . . . . . . . .       7
                   Auto - away from home. . . . . . . . . . . . . . .       8
                   State, federal or municipal property (not a school). .   9
                   Street, alley, parking lot . . . . . . . . . . . .      10
                   Public park or recreation arena. . . . . . . . . .      11
                   Restaurant . . . . . . . . . . . . . . . . . . . .      12
                   Tavern . . . . . . . . . . . . . . . . . . . . . .      13
                   Theatre. . . . . . . . . . . . . . . . . . . . . .      14
                   Loan or finance office . . . . . . . . . . . . . .      15
                   Laundromat . . . . . . . . . . . . . . . . . . . .      16
                   Filling station. . . . . . . . . . . . . . . . . .      17
                   Chain store (grocery or convenience store) . . . . .    18
                   Liquor store . . . . . . . . . . . . . . . . . . .      19
                   Bank . . . . . . . . . . . . . . . . . . . . . . .      20
                   Retail store . . . . . . . . . . . . . . . . . . .      21
                   Hotel or motel . . . . . . . . . . . . . . . . . .      22
                   General commercial business. . . . . . . . . . . .      23
                   Industrial building. . . . . . . . . . . . . . . .      24
                   Other (Specify _____) . . .          25
                   Not relevant . . . . . . . . . . . . . . . . . . .      88
                   Missing. . . . . . . . . . . . . . . . . . . . . .      99
```

Complainant #1

207	Sex		16
	Male.	0	
	Female.	1	
	Not Relevant.	8	
	Missing	9	
208	Age	_ _	17-18
	97 or older	97	
	Not relevant.	98	
	Missing	99	
209	Estimated Age	_ _	19-20
	97 or older.	97	
	Not relevant	98	
	Missing.	99	
210	Race		21
	White.	0	
	Black.	1	
	Latino	2	
	Other.	3	
	Not relevant	8	
	Missing.	9	
211	Is complainant a Champaign-Urbana resident?		22
	Yes.	0	
	No, but in surrounding area.	1	
	No, but in state	2	
	No, out of state	3	
	Don't know	9	

Complainant #2

212	Sex		23
	Male	0	
	Female	1	
	Not relevant	8	
	Missing.	9	
213	Age	_ _	24-25
	97 or older.	97	

	Not relevant 98	
	Missing. 99	

214   Estimated Age   26-27
        97 or older. . . . . $-\overline{}$ 97
        Not relevant 98
        Missing. 99

215   Race   28
        White. 0
        Black. 1
        Latino 2
        Other. 3
        Not relevant 8
        Missing. 9

216   Is complainant a Champaign -Urbana resident?   29
        Yes. 0
        No, but in surrounding area. 1
        No, but in state 2
        No, out of state 3
        Not relevant 8
        Don't know 9

217   Did the incident giving rise to the call occur: 30

        Over a period of days. 1
        Over a period of hours 2
        At a point or brief interval of time 3
        Not relevant 8
        Not known. 9

218   If over a period of days:
                                                               31-33
        Day began (approximate when possible if unclear)   _ _ _
          Use Julian calendar
              Not relevant 888
              Not known. 999

219   Day ended   _ _ _   34-36
        Use Julian calendar
              Not relevant 888
              Not known. 999

      If over a period of hours:

220   Day   _ _ _   37-39
        Use Julian calendar
              Not relevant 888
              Not known. 999

221   Approximate time began   _ _ _ _   40-43
              Not relevant 8888
              Missing. 9999

222   Day or night   44
              A.M. 0
              P.M. 1
              Not relevant 8
              Not known. 9

223   Approximate time ended   _ _ _ _   45-48
              Not relevant 8888
              Missing. 9999

224   Day or night   49
              A.M. 0
              P.M. 1

                        Not relevant   8
                        Not known.   9

225   If over an unspecified number of hours, does it appear that
         incident occurred:
                                                                                   50
                  Between 12:00 a.m. and 8:00 a.m.   1
                  Between 8:00 a.m. and 4:00 p.m.   2
                  Between 4:00 p.m. and 12:00 a.m.   3
                  Not relevant   8
                  Don't know   9

         If at a point in time:

226   Time of incident (Code direct)   _ _ _ _   51-54
                       Not relevant.   8888
                       Don't know.   9999

227   Approximate time of incident (Code direct)   _ _ _ _   55-58
                       Not relevant.   8888
                       Missing.   9999

228   Night or Day   59
                       A.M.   0
                       P.M.   1
                       Not relevant.   8
                       Don't know.   9
229   Day   _ _ _   60-62
                  Code from Julian calendar
                       Not relevant.   888
                       Don't know.   999
230   Time incident reported (Code direct)   _ _ _ _   63-66
                       Don't know.   9999

231   Night or Day   67
                       A.M.   0
                       P.M.   1

232   Day   _ _ _   68-70
                  Code from Julian calendar
                       Don't know   999

233   How was call reported?
                                                                                      71
                  Telephone.   1
                  At desk.   2
                  To officer on street   3
                  Don't know   9

234   If call was reported at station, was it reported directly
         to a detective?
                                                                                      72
                  Yes   0
                  No.   1
                  Not relevant.   8
                  Don't know.   9

235   Was call reported from scene of incident?
                                                                                      73
                  Yes   0
                  No.   1
                  Don't know.   9,

236   Was call made by complainant or representative (if an entity)
                                                                                      74
                  Yes   1
                  No.   2

                                           178

```
                     Unclear . . . . . . . . . . . . . . . . . . . . . .      3
                     Not relevant. . . . . . . . . . . . . . . . . . . .      8
                     Missing . . . . . . . . . . . . . . . . . . . . . .      9
```

237   If call not made by complainant, who was it made by?

75

```
                     Relative or friend. . . . . . . . . . . . . . . . .      1
                     Unrelated bystander . . . . . . . . . . . . . . . .      2
                     Policeman . . . . . . . . . . . . . . . . . . . . .      3
                     Other (specify _____) . . . . .      4
                     Not relevant. . . . . . . . . . . . . . . . . . . .      8
                     Missing . . . . . . . . . . . . . . . . . . . . . .      9
```

Deck 2

238   Dispatch Ticket Number   _ _ _ _ _   1-5

239   Number of officers assigned   6
       Don't know. . . . .   9̄

240   1st Officer assigned   _ _ _   7-9

```
       _____
                     Not relevant. . . . . . . . . . . . . . . . . . . .    888
                     Missing . . . . . . . . . . . . . . . . . . . . . .    999
```

241   2nd Officer assigned   _ _ _   10-12

```
       _____
                     Not relevant. . . . . . . . . . . . . . . . . . . .    888
                     Missing . . . . . . . . . . . . . . . . . . . . . .    999
```

242   Officer preparing report   _ _ _   13-15

```
       _____
                     Not relevant . . . . . . . . . . . . . . . . . . .     888
                     Missing. . . . . . . . . . . . . . . . . . . . . . .   999
```

243   How many offenses were involved? (7 = 7 or more)   _   16
       Not relevant . . . .   8̄
       Missing.   9

244   What was 1st offense involved as initially listed   _ _ _ _   17-20
       (Use crime code)
       Not relevant   8888
       Missing. 9999

245   Was this reported as a crime? (See lower right hand corner of
       incident report - a check mark indicates it was not counted.)   21
       Yes.   1
       No   2
       Unclear.   3
       Not relevant   8
       Don't know   9

246   What was the final crime code?   _ _ _ _   22-25
       Same as above. 0000
       Not relevant 8888
       Missing. 9999

247   What was 2nd offense involved as initially listed   _ _ _ _   26-29
       (Use crime code)
```
```

```
                    Not relevant . . . . . . . . . . . . . . . . . . . .   8888
                    Missing. . . . . . . . . . . . . . . . . . . . . . .   9999

  248       Was victim a:
                                                                                    30-31
                    Individual . . . . . . . . . . . . . . . . . . . . .    1
                    Individual, police officer (on duty) . . . . . . . . .  2
                    Restaurant . . . . . . . . . . . . . . . . . . . . .    3
                    Tavern . . . . . . . . . . . . . . . . . . . . . . .    4
                    Theatre. . . . . . . . . . . . . . . . . . . . . . .    5
                    Loan or finance office . . . . . . . . . . . . . . .    6
                    Laundromat . . . . . . . . . . . . . . . . . . . . .    7
                    Filling station. . . . . . . . . . . . . . . . . . .    8
                    Chain store (grocery or convenience store) . . . . . .  9
                    State, federal, or municipal property (nonschool). . . . 10
                    Liquor store . . . . . . . . . . . . . . . . . . . .   11
                    Elementary or high school. . . . . . . . . . . . . .   12
                    College. . . . . . . . . . . . . . . . . . . . . . .   13
                    Bank . . . . . . . . . . . . . . . . . . . . . . . .   14
                    Retail store . . . . . . . . . . . . . . . . . . . .   15
                    General commercial business. . . . . . . . . . . . .   16
                    Industrial establishment . . . . . . . . . . . . . .   17
                    Noncommercial entity . . . . . . . . . . . . . . . .   18
                    Other (Specify _____). . . . . . .  19
                    Not relevant . . . . . . . . . . . . . . . . . . . .   88
                    Missing. . . . . . . . . . . . . . . . . . . . . . .   99



          INFORMATION ON NATURE AND EXTENT OF DAMAGE TO PERSON OR PROPERTY

          ASSAULT AND RELATED OFFENSES
                (Not relevant in this sequence means no one was injured
                or personally attacked.)
  249       Number of individuals personally attacked:           _                32

                Code direct (7 = 7 or more)
                    Not relevant. . . . . . . . . . . . . . . . . . .    8
                    Don't know. . . . . . . . . . . . . . . . . . . .    9


250,251     Means of attack (record 2 most serious only)
                                                                                    33,34
                    Rifle, shotgun,  pistol . . . . . . . . . . . . . . .   1  1
                    Knife. . . . . . . . . . . . . . . . . . . . . . . .    2  2
                    Sharp instrument . . . . . . . . . . . . . . . . . .    3  3
                    Blunt instrument . . . . . . . . . . . . . . . . . .    4  4
                    Arms, legs, feet, fists. . . . . . . . . . . . . . .    5  5
                    Voice. . . . . . . . . . . . . . . . . . . . . . . .    6  6
                    Other (Specify _____). . . . . . .  7  7
                    Not relevant . . . . . . . . . . . . . . . . . . . .    8  8
                    Missing. . . . . . . . . . . . . . . . . . . . . . .    9  9


  252       Was any weapon (including arms, etc.) actually used on anyone?
                                                                                    35
                    Yes, 1st . . . . . . . . . . . . . . . . . . . . . . .     1
                    Yes, 2nd . . . . . . . . . . . . . . . . . . . . . . .     2
                    Yes, 1st and 2nd . . . . . . . . . . . . . . . . . . .     3
                    No . . . . . . . . . . . . . . . . . . . . . . . . . .     4
                    Not relevant . . . . . . . . . . . . . . . . . . . . .     8
                    Missing. . . . . . . . . . . . . . . . . . . . . . . .     9


253,254     Extent of injury to Victim #1
                                                                                    36-37,
                                                                                    38-39
                    Intimidated. . . . . . . . . . . . . . . . . . . .    2  2
                    Cuts and bruises (not serious) . . . . . . . . . .    3  3
                    Cuts and bruises (serious, required medical
                        treatment). . . . . . . . . . . . . . . . . . .   4  4
```

180

Cuts and bruises (very serious, required
    hospitalization).   5   5
Knife wound.   6   6
Shot wound   7   7
Raped.   8   8
Murdered   9   9
Not relevant 88 88
Missing. 99 99

255,256   Extent of injury to Victim #2

                                                                    40-41,
Intimidated.   2   2   42-43
Cuts and bruises (not serious)   3   3
Cuts and bruises (serious, required medical
    treatment).   4   4
Cuts and bruises (very serious, required
    hospitalization).   5   5
Knife wound.   6   6
Shot wound   7   7
Raped.   8   8
Murdered   9   9
Not relevant 88 88
Missing. 99 99

BURGLARY, THEFT, AND RELATED CRIMES
(Not relevant in this sequence means no property theft
was involved.)

257   How many pieces of property were stolen?   —   44
           (Count attempts as 0)
           Code direct
               7 or more   7
               Not relevant.   8
               Missing   9

258,259,   Type of property stolen:
260
                                                                    45-46,
Radio.   1   1   1   47-48,
Television   2   2   2   49-50
Stereo   3   3   3
Money and/or checks.   4   4   4
Jewelry.   5   5   5
Watches, clocks.   6   6   6
Cameras.   7   7   7
Tools.   8   8   8
Clothing   9   9   9
Office equipment 10 10 10
Furniture. 11 11 11
Firearms or other type of weapons. 12 12 12
Auto or truck CB or tape deck. 13 13 13
Other auto or truck parts. 14 14 14
Bicycle and/or parts 15 15 15
Purse or wallet. 16 16 16
Food or grocery items. 17 17 17
Drugs. 18 18 18
Luggage. 19 19 19
General store merchandise. 20 20 20
Services 21 21 21
Other (Specify _____). . .   22 22 22
Not relevant 88 88 88
Missing. 99 99 99

261   Total value of property stolen (in dollars)   _ _ _ _ _   51-55

More than $99,996.   99997
Not relevant   99998
Missing.   99999

181

262

If there is no figure on the amount of property stolen
would you estimate it to be

56

```
Less than $50. . . . . . . . . . . . . . . . . . . .    1
$50 - $100 . . . . . . . . . . . . . . . . . . . . .    2
$100 - $150. . . . . . . . . . . . . . . . . . . . .    3
$150 - $250. . . . . . . . . . . . . . . . . . . . .    4
$250 - $500. . . . . . . . . . . . . . . . . . . . .    5
$500 - $1000 . . . . . . . . . . . . . . . . . . . .    6
$1000 and up . . . . . . . . . . . . . . . . . . . .    7
Not relevant . . . . . . . . . . . . . . . . . . . .    8
Don't know . . . . . . . . . . . . . . . . . . . . .    9
```

VANDALISM, AND RELATED OFFENSES (Not relevant in this sequence
means no property damage was involved.)

263   How many pieces of property were damaged?(Attempts = 0)   __   57
Code direct
```
       7 or more . . . . . . . . . . . . . . . . . . .    7
       Not relevant. . . . . . . . . . . . . . . . . .    8
       Missing . . . . . . . . . . . . . . . . . . . .    9
```

264   Type of property damaged:

58

```
Personal property (not car). . . . . . . . . . . . .    1
Car. . . . . . . . . . . . . . . . . . . . . . . . .    2
Home . . . . . . . . . . . . . . . . . . . . . . . .    3
Real property surrounding home . . . . . . . . . . .    4
Building . . . . . . . . . . . . . . . . . . . . . .    5
Real property surrounding building . . . . . . . . .    6
Other (Specify _____ ) . . .         7
Not relevant . . . . . . . . . . . . . . . . . . . .    8
Missing. . . . . . . . . . . . . . . . . . . . . . .    9
```

265   If a car, was damage done to:

59

```
Windows. . . . . . . . . . . . . . . . . . . . . . .    1
Top (slit, for example). . . . . . . . . . . . . . .    2
Body . . . . . . . . . . . . . . . . . . . . . . . .    3
Mechanical parts . . . . . . . . . . . . . . . . . .    4
Not relevant . . . . . . . . . . . . . . . . . . . .    8
Don't know . . . . . . . . . . . . . . . . . . . . .    9
```

266   If a home or building, were just windows broken?

60

```
Yes. . . . . . . . . . . . . . . . . . . . . . . . .    1
No, windows and other minor damage . . . . . . . . .    2
No, windows and other major damage . . . . . . . . .    3
No . . . . . . . . . . . . . . . . . . . . . . . . .    4
Not relevant . . . . . . . . . . . . . . . . . . . .    8
Don't know . . . . . . . . . . . . . . . . . . . . .    9
```

267   What was used to cause the property damage?

61-62

```
Firearm (gun or pistol). . . . . . . . . . . . . . .    1
Firearm (B.B. gun, pellet gun) . . . . . . . . . . .    2
Hands, arms, legs, etc.. . . . . . . . . . . . . . .    3
Fire . . . . . . . . . . . . . . . . . . . . . . . .    4
Chemical substance . . . . . . . . . . . . . . . . .    5
Projectile (rock, etc.). . . . . . . . . . . . . . .    6
Paint. . . . . . . . . . . . . . . . . . . . . . . .    7
Blunt instrument . . . . . . . . . . . . . . . . . .    8
Sharp instrument . . . . . . . . . . . . . . . . . .    9
Car. . . . . . . . . . . . . . . . . . . . . . . . .   10
Other (Specify _____ ) . . .        11
Not relevant . . . . . . . . . . . . . . . . . . . .   88
Missing. . . . . . . . . . . . . . . . . . . . . . .   99
```

268   Total value of property damaged: _ _ _ _ _   63-67

                More than $99,996   99997
                Not relevant.   99998
                Missing   99999

269   If there is no figure on the amount of property damage
         done would you estimate it to be

                                                                     68

                Less than $50   1
                $50 - $100.   2
                $100 - $150   3
                $150 - $250   4
                $250 - $500   5
                $500 - $1000.   6
                $1000 and up.   7
                Not relevant.   8
                Don't know.   9

         INFORMATION ON SUSPECT, LINKAGES TO INCIDENT, RELATION TO VICTIM

270   How many perpetrators appear to be involved?   _   69
         Code direct (Code 1 unless evidence of more)
                7 or more.   7
                Not relevant   8
                Missing.   9

271   Were any perpetrators actually viewed on the scene?
         Specify number   70
                8 or more. . . . .   8̄
                Don't know   9

272   Was anyone able to give a description of the perpetrator(s)?
                                                                    71

                Yes   0
                No.   1
                Not relevant (no perpetrator was viewed).   8
                Missing   9

273   Characteristics of Perpetrator #1

         Sex   72
                Male   0
                Female   1
                Not relevant   8
                Missing.   9

274   Age   _ _   73-74
         Code direct
                   97 or older   97
                   Not relevant.   98
                   Missing   99

275   Estimated Age   _ _   75-76
         Code direct
                   97 or older   97
                   Not relevant.   98
                   Missing   99

276   Race   77
                White.   0
                Black.   1
                Latino   2
                Other.   3

```
                        Not relevant . . . . . . . . . . . . . . . . . . . . . .    8
                        Missing. . . . . . . . . . . . . . . . . . . . . . . .      9       Deck 3

277       Dispatch Ticket Number                                _ _ _ _ _           1-5

          Characteristics of Perpetrator #2

278           Sex                                                                   6
                        Male . . . . . . . . . . . . . . . . . . . . . . . . .      0
                        Female . . . . . . . . . . . . . . . . . . . . . . . .      1
                        Not relevant . . . . . . . . . . . . . . . . . . . . .      8
                        Missing. . . . . . . . . . . . . . . . . . . . . . . .      9

279           Age                                                   _ _            7-8
              Code direct
                        97 or older . . . . . . . . . . . . . . . . . .            97
                        Not relevant. . . . . . . . . . . . . . . . . .            98
                        Missing . . . . . . . . . . . . . . . . . . . .            99

280           Estimated Age                                         _ _            9-10
              Code direct
                        97 or older . . . . . . . . . . . . . . . . . .            97
                        Not relevant. . . . . . . . . . . . . . . . . .            98
                        Missing . . . . . . . . . . . . . . . . . . . .            99

281           Race                                                                  11
                        White. . . . . . . . . . . . . . . . . . . . . . . .        0
                        Black. . . . . . . . . . . . . . . . . . . . . . . .        1
                        Latino . . . . . . . . . . . . . . . . . . . . . . .        2
                        Other. . . . . . . . . . . . . . . . . . . . . . . .        3
                        Not relevant . . . . . . . . . . . . . . . . . . . .        8
                        Missing. . . . . . . . . . . . . . . . . . . . . . .        9

282       Are there any specific suspects (i.e., not just a description
          of someone)?
                                                                                    12
                        Yes . . . . . . . . . . . . . . . . . . . . . . . . .       0
                        No. . . . . . . . . . . . . . . . . . . . . . . . . .       1
                        Unclear . . . . . . . . . . . . . . . . . . . . . . .       2
                        Not relevant. . . . . . . . . . . . . . . . . . . . .       8
                        Missing . . . . . . . . . . . . . . . . . . . . . . .       9

283       How was the suspect's identity determined?                              13-14

                        Suspect was apprehended on the spot . . . . . . . . .       1
                        Suspect was seen and later identified by witnesses. . .     2
                        An eyewitness observed suspect and knew him . . . . . .      3
                        Circumstantial evidence . . . . . . . . . . . . . .         4
                        A reasoned supposition, but no initial evidence . . . .     5
                        A hunch (no specific reason). . . . . . . . . . . . .       6
                        A tip . . . . . . . . . . . . . . . . . . . . . . . .       7
                        Unclear . . . . . . . . . . . . . . . . . . . . . . .       8
                        Other (Specify _____). . .              9
                        Not relevant. . . . . . . . . . . . . . . . . . . . .      88
                        Don't know. . . . . . . . . . . . . . . . . . . . . .      99

284       If the suspect was not immediately apprehended is there
          evidence of a suspect's name?
                                                                                    15
                        Yes . . . . . . . . . . . . . . . . . . . . . . . . .       0
                        No. . . . . . . . . . . . . . . . . . . . . . . . . .       1
                        Unclear . . . . . . . . . . . . . . . . . . . . . . .       2
                        Not relevant (no suspect or apprehended on scene) . . .     8
                        Missing . . . . . . . . . . . . . . . . . . . . . . .       9

285       If the suspect was not immediately apprehended, is there
          evidence of a suspect's address?
```

Yes   0
No.   1
Unclear   2
Not relevant (no suspect or apprehended on scene) . . .   8
Missing   9

286   If there is an address, does narrative or supplement
          indicate that the address is:

Local   1
Out of town   2
Out of state.   3
Unclear   4
Not relevant (no suspect or apprehended on scene) . . .   8
Don't know.   9

287   Does it appear that the police have apprehended, located,
          or made some contact with a suspect(s)?

Yes   1
No.   2
It appears so, but somewhat unclear   3
Not relevant.   8
Don't know.   9

288   Is there evidence of a prior relationship between at least
          one victim and at least one perpetrator?

Yes   0
No.   1
Not relevant (no suspect)   8
Missing   9

289   From the narrative does it appear that the prior relationship
          was:

Casual.   1
Close   2
Personal.   3
Not relevant (no prior relationship).   8
Missing (no suspect).   9

290   Type of prior relationship:

Spouse.   1
Ex-spouse   2
Lovers (boyfriend - girlfriend)   3
Parent - child.   4
Brother - sister.   5
Friends   6
Neighbor.   7
Fellow employees.   8
Recurrent business associate.   9
Casual business associate 10
Casual acquaintance 11
Employer - employee 12
Landlord - tenant 13
Other (Specify) _____). . . . 14

Not relevant (no relationship). 88
Missing (no suspect). 99

A fraud or theft (or other property offenses) among strangers
is often very different from one among acquaintances. Often,

in the latter case, the purported victim is only marginally concerned with the criminal offense; he is primarily concerned with the restoration of a prior condition (return of property, having the offender leave him alone, etc.)

291   Does it appear that the primary concern in this case is for
        a restoration of some sort?   23

            Yes, definitely.   1
            Yes, it appears so   2
            No   3
            Not relevant   8
            Missing.   9

Often assault cases, and to a lesser extent rape cases, arise out of a personal dispute among people who know each other quite well. A call is made to the police to effect some type of settlement, to cool things down, or to seek revenge.

292   Does it appear that this case primarily arises out of a personal
        dispute?
                                                                            24
            Yes, definitely.   1
            Yes, it appears so   2
            No   3
            Not relevant   8
            Missing.   9

293   Many incidents of vandalism or related crimes result from
        retaliation for a prior incident or series of incidents. Is
        there an indication that this is the case here?
                                                                            25
            Yes.   1
            Yes, it appears so   2
            No   3
            Not relevant   8
            Don't know   9

294   Is there evidence in the official record that
        some kind of a private resolution was effectuated (restitu-
        tion, apologies, promises not to bother again, etc.)?
                                                                            26
            Yes   1
            No.   2
            Unclear   3
            Not relevant.   8
            Missing   9

        EVIDENCE

295   Is it explicitly stated in the report that someone can identify
        perpetrators if they saw them again?
                                                                            27
            Yes   0
            No.   1
            State maybe they can identify   2
            Not mentioned   3
            Not relevant (no one viewed).   8
            Missing   9

296   How many people state they can identify the perpetrator(s)?   —   28

Code direct
7 or more. 7
Not relevant (no explicit statement) 8
Missing. 9

297   Does it appear from the report that someone viewed the
perpetrators and could identify them even though this is
not explicitly stated?

                                                           29

Yes 0
No. 1
It appears that they might be able to identify. 2
Not relevant (explicit i.d., no one viewed) 8
Missing 9

298   How many people does it appear can identify the perpetrator?   ——   30

Code direct
7 or more. 7
Not relevant 8
Missing 9

299,300   Who were these witnesses?
301   31,32,33

The victim.	1	1	1
Friends or relatives or employees of victim	2	2	2
Unacquainted bystander	3	3	3
Police.	4	4	4
Other . . . . . , ...	5	5	5
Not relevant (no eye witnesses)	8	8	8
Don't know. . . . . . , ...	9	9	9

302,303   Does it appear that one or more of the witnesses <u>have</u>
identified <u>a suspect</u>?

                                                           34,35

Yes, on scene	1	1
Yes, in mugshots. . . . . ＼	2	2
Yes, in lineup.	3	3
Yes, some other means	4	4
No.	5	5
Not relevant (no witnesses and/or no suspects).	8	8
Missing	9	9

304   How many witnesses actually made positive I.D.'s?   —   36

7 or more 7
Not relevant (no witnesses and/or no suspects). 8
Missing 9

305,306,   What physical evidence was available?
307   37,38,39

Fingerprints.	1	1	1
Proceeds from theft,etc., or damaged property	2	2	2
Materials used to defraud or deceive.	3	3	3
Incriminating polygraph results	4	4	4
Weapon used to commit crime	5	5	5
Tools used to commit crime.	6	6	6

```
                 Other (Specify _____ ) . . . .  7  7  7
                 Not relevant (none) . . . . . . . . . . . . . . . .  8  8  8
                 Don't know. . . . . . . . . . . . . . . . . . . . .  9  9  9
```

308   Were there more than three independent pieces of physical
        evidence?

                                                                          40
            Yes 0
            No. 1
            Not relevant (none) 8
            Don't know. 9

309,310 Was the 1st (2nd, 3rd) piece of evidence
  311
                                                                    41,42,43
            Directly tied to a suspect 1 1 1
            Indirectly tied to a suspect 2 2 2
            Not tied to a suspect. 3 3 3
            Not relevant (no evidence or no suspect) 8 8 8
            Don't know 9 9 9

312   Can stolen goods be identified by a serial number
        or some other I.D.?
                                                                          44
            Yes, all 1
            Yes, some. 2
            No 3
            Not relevant (no stolen goods) 8
            Don't know 9

313   Was an incriminating statement made by the suspect?
                                                                          45
            Yes, admitted crime. 1
            Yes, but only damaging statement 2
            No 3
            Not relevant (no suspect). 8
            Don't know 9

314   Did a suspect offer any alibis?
                                                                          46
            Yes. 0
            No 1
            Not relevant (no suspect). 8
            Don't know 9

315   Is there an indication that these alibis were
                                                                          47
            Checked into and verified. 1
            Checked into and found groundless. 2
            Not checked into 3
            Not verifiable 4
            Not relevant (no alibi or no suspect). 8
            Don't know 9

316   Was there incriminating evidence other than that captured
        in earlier questions?
                                                                          48
            Yes, strong and direct 1
            Yes, mediocore and direct. 2
            Yes, strong and circumstantial 3
            Yes, mediocore and circumstantial. 4
            No 5
            Don't know, unclear. 9

ACTIONS TAKEN (POLICE RESPONSES)

An investigation is reflected in a routine report which merely
lists what happens, names of individuals involved, lists injuries suffered or property damaged or stolen, etc. It is usually
completed on day of incident. A nonroutine report goes beyond recording what has happened and applies police technology, expertise,
or resources to the situation in an effort to do something (follows
up leads, uncovers new evidence, checks with pawn shops, etc.).
It usually is spread over a period of time.

317   Is there evidence that the report on file is

                                                               49

          Routine   1
          Nonroutine.   2
          Extensive   3

318   Is there an indication that the report was posted?

                                                               50

          Yes   0
          No.   1
          Missing, unclear.   9

319   Is there an indication that fingerprints were checked for?

                                                               51

          Yes   0
          No.   1
          Missing, unclear.   9

320   Is there evidence that a detective was assigned to the case?

                                                               52

          Yes, 1.   1
          Yes, 2.   2
          Yes, 3 or more.   3
          No.   4
          Unclear, perhaps.   5
          Missing, don't know   9

321   Principal Detective Involved   __   53-54

          Not relevant (none assigned)   88
          Don't know   99

322   Is there evidence that anything was sent to the crime lab for
      further analysis?

                                                                55

          Yes   0
          No.   1
          Not relevant (no evidence).   8
          Don't know.   9

323   Is there evidence that a polygraph test was suggested by
      the police?

                                                                56

          Yes   0

```
                            No. . . . . . . . . . . . . . . . . . . . . . . . . . . . . .    1
                            Irrelevant (no suspects). . . . . . . . . . . . . . . . .       8
                            Don't know. . . . . . . . . . . . . . . . . . . . . . . .        9


324        Is there an indication that polygraph tests were administered?
                                                                                                        57
                            Yes . . . . . . . . . . . . . . . . . . . . . . . . . . . .     0
                            No. . . . . . . . . . . . . . . . . . . . . . . . . . . . .     1
                            No, suspect refused . . . . . . . . . . . . . . . . . . .       2
                            Irrelevant (no suspect or no suggestion). . . . . . . .          8
                            Don't know. . . . . . . . . . . . . . . . . . . . . . . .        9


325        Is there evidence that mug shots were examined?
                                                                                                        58
                            Yes . . . . . . . . . . . . . . . . . . . . . . . . . . . .     0
                            No. . . . . . . . . . . . . . . . . . . . . . . . . . . . .     1
                            Irrelevant (No witnesses or D was known to V or D was
                               apprehended on scene). . . . . . . . . . . . . . . .         8
                            Don't know. . . . . . . . . . . . . . . . . . . . . . . .        9


326        Is there an indication that a line-up was held?
                                                                                                        59
                            Yes . . . . . . . . . . . . . . . . . . . . . . . . . . . .     0
                            No. . . . . . . . . . . . . . . . . . . . . . . . . . . . .     1
                            Irrelevant (no witnesses, no suspects, D was known to V
                               or D was apprehended on scene) . . . . . . . . . . .         8
                            Don't know. . . . . . . . . . . . . . . . . . . . . . . .        9


327        Is there an indication that the police cruised the immediate
           vicinity in search of a suspect?
                                                                                                        60
                            Yes . . . . . . . . . . . . . . . . . . . . . . . . . . . .     0
                            No. . . . . . . . . . . . . . . . . . . . . . . . . . . . .     1
                            Don't know, unclear . . . . . . . . . . . . . . . . . . .       9


328        Is there evidence of a complainant-initiated supplemental
           report?  (Specify number)                                            __           61

                            None . . . . . . . . . . . . . . . . . . . . . . . . . . .      0
                            7 or more. . . . . . . . . . . . . . . . . . . . . . . . .      7
                            Don't know, unclear. . . . . . . . . . . . . . . . . . .        9


329        Nature:
                                                                                                        62
                            Inquisitory. . . . . . . . . . . . . . . . . . . . . . . .      1
                            Changed mind about pursuing. . . . . . . . . . . . . . .        2
                            Wanted to press the investigation. . . . . . . . . . . .        3
                            Provided new leads or information. . . . . . . . . . . .        4
                            Provided property identification (serial numbers). . . .        5
                            Other (Specify _____).  . . .         6
                            Not relevant . . . . . . . . . . . . . . . . . . . . . .        8
                            Don't know, unclear. . . . . . . . . . . . . . . . . . .        9

330        Date (Use Julian Calendar)                                         _ _ _        63-65
                            Not relevant. . . . . . . . . . . . . . . . . . . . . . .      888
                            Missing . . . . . . . . . . . . . . . . . . . . . . . . .      999

331        Is there evidence of police initiated supplemental reports?
           (specify number)                                                     _            66

                            None . . . . . . . . . . . . . . . . . . . . . . . . . . .      0
                            7 or more. . . . . . . . . . . . . . . . . . . . . . . . .      7
                            Don't know . . . . . . . . . . . . . . . . . . . . . . . .      9
```

332 Number submitted by detectives   ___   67

     None   0
     7 or more.   7
     Not relevant   8
     Don't know   9

333 Date of first   _ _ _   68-70

     Not relevant   888
     Don't know   999

334 Date of last   _ _ _   71-73

     Not relevant   888
     Don't know   999

335 Did the subsequent investigation turn up a suspect whose
     identify was not known at the time of the call?
                                                                         74
     Yes   1
     No.   2
     Unclear whether or not identity was previously known. .   3
     Not relevant (suspect's identity was known)   8
     Don't know.   9

336 How?
                                                                         75
     Mug shot I.D.   1
     Cruising the area   2
     Follow-up of a tip.   3
     Suspect was apprehended for something else and was
        somehow connected to this incident   4
     Other (Specify _____)   5
     Not relevant (didn't turn up anyone new).   8
     Don't know.   9

     OUTCOMES

337 Is there any indication of a referral to some type of social
     agency (not juvenile court)?
                                                                         76
     Yes   1
     No.   2
     Unclear   3
     Not relevant.   8
     Don't know.   9

338 Is the code in the lower right hand corner of the incident report
                                                                         77
     3   (not cleared)   1
     3-4   (unfounded)   2
     3-5   (unfounded - wrong jurisdiction).   3
     3-6   (exceptionally cleared - refusal to prosecute). .   4
     3-7   (exceptionally cleared - juvenile - refused to
               prosecute).   5
     3-8   (exceptionally cleared)   6
     3-9   (exceptionally cleared - juvenile).   7
     3-10   (cleared by arrest)   8
     3-11   (cleared by arrest - juvenile).   9

                                    191

339   Does a reading of the narrative indicate that there is
something unique or interesting about the case which might
make good anecdotal material and should be referred back to?

                      78

                     Yes   0
                     No.   1

340   Does anything in the record indicate that the suspect
in this incident was involved in other <u>unsolved</u> crimes?

                     Yes   0   79
                     No.   1
                     Not relevant (no suspect)   8
                     Don't know.   9

341   Were there multiple clearances involved in this case?
(Specify #)   —   80

                     7 or more   7
                     Not relevant (no clearance here).   8
                     Don't know.   9

CHAMPAIGN DELIVERY OF POLICE SERVICES PROJECT
ACCIDENT CASES
GENERAL INFORMATION

Variable	General Information	Columns

401   Dispatch Ticket Number   _ _ _ _ _   1-5

402   Day of Accident

       (Use Julian calendar)   _ _ _   6-8
       Not relevant. 888
       Not known 999

403   Time of Accident   _ _ _ _   9-12

       Not relevant. 8888
       Missing 9999

404   Day or night   13

       A.M. 0
       P.M. 1
       Not known 9

405   Day of week   14

       Monday. 1
       Tuesday 2
       Wednesday 3
       Thursday. 4
       Friday. 5
       Saturday. 6
       Sunday. 7
       Don't know. 9

406   Time incident reported (code direct)   _ _ _ _   15-18

       Don't know. 9999

407   Night or Day   19

       A.M. 0
       P.M. 1

408   Day incident reported

       (Use Julian calendar)   _ _ _   20-22
       Same as day of accident 000
       Don't know. 999

409   Date report completed

           (Use Julian calendar)   23-25
           Same as day of accident . . . . $\overline{0}\,\overline{0}\,\overline{0}$
           Don't know.   999

410   Number of units involved   _   26

           Code direct
           More than seven   8
           Don't know.   9

                    INFORMATION ON UNIT #1

411   Year of Driver's Birth   _ _   27-28

           Code direct
           Don't know.   99

412   Sex   29

           Male.   0
           Female.   1
           Missing   9

413   Injury Code   30

           O   1
           C   2
           B   3
           A   4
           k   5
           Not relevant.   8
           Don't know.   9

414   Taken to hospital?   31

           Yes   1
           No.   2
           Not relevant.   8
           Don't know.   9

415   Street address of driver

           Code direct   _ _ _ _   32-35
           Local resident but
           Not a Champaign resident.   9996
           Not a local resident.   9997
           Champaign resident, Don't
           know address.   9998
           Don't know residency.   9999

                              194

416	Street direction		36

North 1
South 2
East. 3
West. 4
Not relevant. 8
Don't know. 9

417   Street   _ _ _   37-39

(Use street code)
Not a Champaign resident. 997
Champaign resident, Don't know address. 998
Don't know. 999

418   Is driver the owner?   _   40

Yes 1
No, but member of immediate family. 2
No, but his employer is 3
No. 4
Uncertain, but appears to 5
Not relevant. 8
Don't know. 9

419   Vehicle type   _ _   41-42

(Use vehicle type code)

420   Vehicle make . . . . _ _   43-44

(Use vehicle make code)

421   Year of make . . . . _ _   45-46

(Last two digits only)
Don't know. 99

422   Size of car   47

subcompact. 1
compact 2
mid sized 3
large 4
sportscar 5
not relevant. 8
don't know. 9

423   Damage to vehicle   48

195

```
                    None. . . . . . . . . . . . . . . . . . .  0
                    Minor damage. . . . . . . . . . . . . . .  1
                    Substantial damage. . . . . . . . . . . .  2
                    Very substantial damage . . . . . . . . .  3
                    Totaled . . . . . . . . . . . . . . . . .  4
                    Don't know. . . . . . . . . . . . . . . .  9


424      Was vehicle                                                    49

                    Driven away . . . . . . . . . . . . . . .  1
                    Towed away. . . . . . . . . . . . . . . .  2
                    Not relevant. . . . . . . . . . . . . . .  8
                    Don't know. . . . . . . . . . . . . . . .  9


425      Total number of occupants                                      50

                    (code direct   don't include driver)
                    7 or more . . . . . . . . . . . . . . . .  7
                    Not relevant. . . . . . . . . . . . . . .  8
                    Don't know. . . . . . . . . . . . . . . .  9


426, 427  Was unit #1 hit
                    (regardless of damage)                 _ _   51-52

                    in rear . . . . . . . . . . . . . . . .  1 1
                    in front. . . . . . . . . . . . . . . .  2 2
                    on left side. . . . . . . . . . . . . .  3 3
                    on right side . . . . . . . . . . . . .  4 4
                    not relevant (not hit, bicycle, etc). .  8 8
                    don't know. . . . . . . . . . . . . . .  9 9


                         INFORMATION ON UNIT #2


428      Is this unit?                                                  53

                    a motor vehicle . . . . . . . . . . . . .  1
                    a pedestrian. . . . . . . . . . . . . . .  2
                    a bicyclist . . . . . . . . . . . . . . .  3
                    other . . . . . . . . . . . . . . . . . .  8
                    don't know. . . . . . . . . . . . . . . .  9


429      Year of driver's birth                          _ _   54-55

                    Code direct
                    Don't know. . . . . . . . . . . . . . . . 99


430      Sex                                                            56

                    Male. . . . . . . . . . . . . . . . . . .  0
                    Female. . . . . . . . . . . . . . . . . .  1
                    Missing . . . . . . . . . . . . . . . . .  9
```

431   Injury code   57

       0   1
       C   2
       B   3
       A   4
       K   5
       Not relevant.   8
       Don't know.   9

432   Taken to hospital?   58

       Yes   1
       No.   2
       Not relevant.   8
       Don't know.   9

433   Street address of Driver   _ _ _ _   59-62

       Code direct
       local resident but
       Not a Champaign resident.   9996
       Not a local resident.   9997
       Champaign resident, don't know address. . .   9998
       Don't know residency.   9999

434   Street direction   63

       North   1
       South   2
       East.   3
       West.   4
       Not relevant.   8
       Don't know.   9

435   Street   _ _ _   64-66

       (Use street code)
       Not a Champaign resident.   997
       Champaign resident, don't know address. . . .   998
       Don't know.   999

436   Is driver the owner?   67

       Yes   1
       No, but member of immediate family.   2
       No, but his employer is   3
       No.   4
       Uncertain, but appears so   5
       Not relevant.   8
       Don't know.   9

                              197

437   Vehicle type   _ _   68-69
              (Use vehicle type code)

438   Vehicle make   _ _   70-71
              (Use vehicle make code)

439   Year of Make   _ _   72-73
              (Last two digits only)

440   Size of Car   74

              Subcompact. 1
              Compact 2
              Mid sized 3
              Large 4
              Sportscar 5
              Not relevant. 8
              Don't know. 9

441   Damage to Vehicle   75

              None. 0
              Minor damage. 1
              Substantial damage. 2
              Very substantial damage 3
              Totaled 4
              Don't know. 9

442   Was Vehicle   76

              Driven away 1
              Towed away. 2
              Not relevant. 8
              Don't know. 9

443   Total Number of Occupants   _   77

              (code direct, don't include driver)
              7 or more 7
              Not relevant. 8
              Don't know. 9

444, 445   Was unit #2 hit   78-79
              (regardless of damage)

              in rear 1 1
              in front. 2 2
              on left side. 3 3

on right side 4 4
not relevant (not hit, bicycle, etc). 8 8
don't know. 9 9

446 Type of Report   80

Conventional. 1
Desk. 2
Animal. 3
Private Property. 4
Hit and Run 5
Supplementary 8
Not marked. 9

447 Dispatch Ticket Number   _ _ _ _ _ 1-5

Occupants of Unit #1

Occupant #1

448 Sex   6

Male. 0
Female. 1
Not relevant. 8
Missing 9

449 Age   _ _ 7-8

97 or older 97
Not relevant. 98
Missing 99

450 Injury Code   9

O 1
C 2
B 3
A 4
K 5
Not relevant. 8
Don't know. 9

451 Occupant #2

Sex   10

Male. 0
Female. 1
Not relevant. 8
Missing 9

452   Age   _ _   11-12

             97 or older 97
             Not relevant. 98
             Missing 99

453   Injury Code   13

             0 1
             C 2
             B 3
             A 4
             K 5
             Not relevant. 8
             Don't know. 9

Occupants of Unit #2

Occupant #1

454   Sex   14

             Male. 0
             Female. 1
             Not relevant. 8
             Missing 9

455   Age   _ _   15-16

             97 or older 97
             Not relevant. 98
             Missing 99

456   Injury Code   17

             0 1
             C 2
             B 3
             A 4
             K 5
             Not relevant. 8
             Don't know. 9

Occupant #2

457   Sex   18

             Male. 0
             Female. 1
             Not relevant. 8
             Missing 9

458   Age   _ _   19-20

           97 or older 97
           Not relevant. 98
           Missing 99

459   Injury Code   21

           0 1
           C 2
           B 3
           A 4
           K 5
           Not relevant. 8
           Don't know. 9

460   Number of Witnesses Listed   _   22

           Code direct (indicated by "W" in unit box)
           None. 0
           7 or more 7
           Not relevant. 8
           Don't know. 9

461   Was There Damage to Property other than Vehicles?   23

           Yes 0
           No. 1
           Don't know. 9

462   Investigating Officer (Use Officer Code)   _ _ _   24-26

           Missing 999

463   Number of Tickets Given to Unit #1   _   27

           None. 0
           7 or more 7
           Not relevant. 8
           Don't know. 9

464   Section Violation (code direct)   _ _ _ _   28-32

           Not relevant (None) 88888
           Missing 99999

465   Subsection?   _   33
           (a=1, b=2, c=3, etc.)

           Not relevant. 8
           Missing 9

466   Number of Tickets Given to Unit #2   _   34

            None. 0
            7 or more 7
            Not relevant. 8
            Don't know. 9

467   Section Violation (code direct)   _ _ _ _ _   35-39

            Not relevant (None) 88888
            Missing 99999

468   Subsection?   _   40
        (a=1, b=2, c=3, etc.)

            Not relevant. 8
            Missing 9

469   Block 8   _ _   41-42

            Code direct
            Not marked. 99

            Block 10

470   Unit #1   _ _   43-44

            Code direct
             Not marked. 99

471   Unit #2   _ _   45-46

            Code direct
             Not marked. 99

            Block 12

472   Unit #1   _   47

            Code direct
             Not marked. 9

473   Unit #2   _   48

            Code direct
             Not marked. 9

            Block 14

474   Alcohol Test Offered to driver #1   _   49

```
         Yes . . . . . . . . . . . . . . . . . . . . .  1
         No. . . . . . . . . . . . . . . . . . . . . .  2
         Not marked. . . . . . . . . . . . . . . . . .  9

475      Alcohol Test Refused by driver #1              _          50

         Yes . . . . . . . . . . . . . . . . . . . . .  1
         No. . . . . . . . . . . . . . . . . . . . . .  2
         Not marked. . . . . . . . . . . . . . . . . .  9

476      Results for driver #1                        _ _ _       51-53

         Not relevant. . . . . . . . . . . . . . . .  888
         Not marked. . . . . . . . . . . . . . . . .  999

477      Alcohol Test Offered to driver #2              _          54

         Yes . . . . . . . . . . . . . . . . . . . . .  1
         No. . . . . . . . . . . . . . . . . . . . . .  2
         Not marked. . . . . . . . . . . . . . . . . .  9

478      Alcohol Test Refused by driver #2              _          55

         Yes . . . . . . . . . . . . . . . . . . . . .  1
         No. . . . . . . . . . . . . . . . . . . . . .  2
         Not marked. . . . . . . . . . . . . . . . . .  9

479      Results for driver #2                        _ _ _       56-58

         Not relevant. . . . . . . . . . . . . . . .  888
         Not marked. . . . . . . . . . . . . . . . .  999


         Block 13

480      Unit #1                                       _ _        59-60

         Code direct
         Not marked. . . . . . . . . . . . . . . . .  99

481      Unit #2                                       _ _        61-62

         Code direct
         Not marked. . . . . . . . . . . . . . . . .  99

482      Block 16                                       _          63

         Code direct
         Not marked. . . . . . . . . . . . . . . . . .  9

483      Block 17                                       _          64
```

```
                    Code direct
                    Not marked. . . . . . . . . . . . . . . . . . 9


484                 Block 18                                  _        65

                    Code direct
                    Not marked. . . . . . . . . . . . . . . . . . 9


485                 Block 19                                  _        66

                    Code direct
                    Not marked. . . . . . . . . . . . . . . . . . 9


                    Block 21

486                 Unit #1                                 _ _      67-68

                    Code direct
                    Not marked. . . . . . . . . . . . . . . . . 99


487                 Unit #2                                 _ _      69-70

                    Code direct
                    Not marked. . . . . . . . . . . . . . . . . 99


                    Block 24

488                 Unit #1                                   _        71

                    Code direct
                    Not marked. . . . . . . . . . . . . . . . . . 9


489                 Unit #2                                 _ _      72-73

                    Code direct
                    Not marked. . . . . . . . . . . . . . . . . 99
```

Index

Accidents: characteristics of, 152–154; effort in response to, 155–159; and locational variables, 88–91; number of cars responding to, 155–156; number of cases, 103; outcomes of, 159–164; speed in response to, 154–155; time spent on, 156–159

Administration, early focus of police studies on, 4

Aldrich, John 133

Antunes, George E., 14, 28, 29

Arrest, and common crimes; 148–150

Assault cases: detective and, 117, 121–123; effort as indicator of police response, 117–123; and locational variables, 88–91; number of, 103; number of cars responding to, 117, 119–120; outcomes of, 123–131; and response speed, 112–116; time spent on call, 117, 120–121; types of, 110–112

Banfield, Edward C., 15, 29

Beat, size of and response speed, 114–116

Bittner, Egon, 68, 69, 79

Black, Gordon, 28, 30

Blacks, in Champaign, 36

Bloch, Peter B., 4, 8, 99, 106

Boland, Barbara, 4, 9

Boydstud, John E., 4, 8

Brody, Richard A., 73, 79

Brown, Charles E., 8

Bureaucracies: influence from, 13, 15–20; procedures and community preferences of, 26–28

Bureaucratic decision rules, 2

Bureaucratic hierarchies, and sociopolitical influence, 24–25

Callow, Alexander B., 29

Campustown, 43, 83, 84. *See also* Students

Champaign: commercial-industrial area of, 43–44; political system of, 32–35; subcommunities of, 35–44

Champaign Human Relations Commission, 59

Champaign Police Department: citizen response to questionnaire about, 62–64; history of, 49–57; image of, 58–59; and Northend, 59–60, 63–64; organizational structure of, 45–49; professionalization in, 52–57; and students, 60–62, 63–64

Chang, Samson K., 4, 8

Chanute Air Force Base, 83

Clarren, Summer N., 4, 9

Clawson, Calvin, 4, 8

Cnudde, Charles, 133

Cohen, Jacob, 98, 106

Cohen, Patricia, 98, 106

Commercial-industrial area, of Champaign, 43–44

Common crimes: and arrest, 148–150; characteristics of, 136–138; detectives and, 144–146; effort in response to, 141–146; and locational variables, 88–91; number of cars sent to, 141–143; number of cases of, 103, outcomes of, 146–150; speed in response to, 138–140; and time spent on calls, 143–144

Decision rules: influences on, 99, nature of, 16–19; role of, 19–20; and service delivery, 11–12; as source of influence, 101

Decisions, criteria for, 17–19

Dieckman, Duane, 8

Demand: analysis of total number of calls, 82–88; analysis by types of calls, 88–93; contrasted with response analysis, 167; model, 68–74

Disbursement, issue of in urban service delivery, 5

Effort: indicators of, 104; and police response to assault cases, 117–123; in response to accidents, 155–159; in response to common crimes, 141–146

Resource constraints, measures of, 100, 104–105
Response, contrasted with demand analysis, 167. *See also* Police response
Rich, Richard C., 30
Rogers, David, 9, 27, 30
Rothman, Rozanne, 32, 34, 35, 44

Salisbury, Robert H., 28, 30
Schiesl, Martin J., 14, 30
Schwartz, Alfred, 4, 9
Selective Traffic Enforcement Patrol, 46, 56
Service delivery: early research on, 2–3; need for first-hand observational research on, 170–171; new focus for research on, 165
Sherry, Michael E., 4, 8
Shoup, Carl, 11, 30
Situation, decisions and, 100, 101
Sniderman, Paul M., 73, 79
Southwest Champaign, 39, 41; demand level of, 86–87; service-delivery indicators for, 96, 97, and time spent on call in assault cases, 121; type of service demand in, 91, 93
Speed: indicators of, 104; in response to accidents, 154–155; of response in assault cases, 112–116; in response to common crimes, 138–140
STEP. *See* Selective Traffic Enforcement Patrol
Stonecash, Jeffrey M., 30
Students: in Champaign, 36, 42–43; and Champaign Police Department,

60–62, 63–64; demand for services for, 83–84, 87, 89; on police beat, 46, 48, 49; service-delivery indicators for, 96, 97; and type of service demand, 90, 91, 93

Team-policing programs, 56
Ticketing, in accident cases, 159–164

University of Illinois, 36, 42, 44, 60–62; police, 61–62, 81; Psychology Department, 74
Urbana Police Department, 58
Urban High Crime Program, 56, 74

Verba, Sidney, 74, 79

Wildavsky, Aaron, 14, 29, 99, 107
Wilson, James Q., 4, 9, 15, 29, 52, 65
Wingo, Lowden, 29
Work groups, and sociopolitical influence, 23–24
Working-class district: and attitudes toward police department, 63–64; demand level of, 87–88; location of, 43; police beat in, 49; service-delivery indicators for, 97

Yates, Douglas, 1, 9, 14, 30

Ziegler, L. Harmon, 29
Zisk, Betty, 28, 29

Peter F. Nardulli is an associate professor of political science in the Institute of Government and Public Affairs and the Department of Political Science at the University of Illinois. He is the author of *The Courtroom Elite: An Organizational Perspective on Criminal Justice* and the editor of *The Study of Criminal Courts: Political Perspectives.* He is currently collaborating on a three–state, nine–county study of criminal courts with James Eisenstein and Roy B. Flemming.

Jeffrey M. Stonecash is an assistant professor of political science in the Maxwell School of Public Affairs at Syracuse University. His areas of concern are urban and state politics and intergovernmental relations. He is the author of articles that have appeared in *American Politics Quarterly; Publius; Western Political Quarterly;* and *Political Methodology.*